Person-Centered
Graduate Education

Person-Centered
Graduate
Education

Roy P. Fairfield

PB *Prometheus Books*

Buffalo, N.Y. 14215

Published by Prometheus Books
1203 Kensington Avenue, Buffalo, New York 14215

Library of Congress Catalog Card Number 77-77206
ISBN 0-87975-072-3

Printed in the United States of America

to

my
UGS learning colleagues
&
my tribe
&
my family
world & time
around . . .

Foreword

Much has been written about the vision of what innovative, self-directed education might be. There have been criticisms aplenty of graduate education as it now exists in our universities. There have been some accounts of what it means to put a person-centered approach to learning into practice in small or limited ways. But there has been no attempt to spell out what it means to implement this newer way of education in a whole school, over a period of years.

Now Roy Fairfield has filled this gap. He speaks from eight years of intimate daily experience working with Union Graduate School (UGS), probably the first major graduate school without walls. He is a literate, witty innovator in education, with the mind of a humanist, the feelings of a warmly caring person, and the soul of a poet. He gives us a skillfully written and splendidly detailed picture of the agonies and ecstasies of the pioneering venture which is UGS. He evidences a broad perspective and a sense of the humor and irony of the human situation as he recounts the vicissitudes and growth pains of this adventurous institution.

Outsiders frequently think that schools offering programs of independent study do not have "standards," do not make sufficient demands on their students, that it is all too easy. The examples in this book make it abundantly evident that the pathway of independent, self-directed learning is far more difficult for, and makes many more demands on the student than the traditional way. Some simply cannot stand the responsibility of continually making significant choices, and opt out to take the easier path of being told what to study. But for those who can follow this pathway the creative fruitfulness is rich indeed. Independence is a difficult burden, but it pays off in learning and in personal growth.

But the book does much more than present the positive side of self-directed learning. It is clear that the pathway is as new and difficult for the faculty and administration as it is for the students. Is a rigidifying bureaucracy inevitable as the years go by, even in an innovative institution? The question is faced honestly. What losses of vision occur over a decade? Are they balanced by gains in experience? And what about accreditation, that difficult interface between all this newness and the traditions of society? One of the charming things about the author is his openness in dealing with such issues, presenting the failures, the compromises, the unresolved problems in as much clarity and detail as the more immediately satisfying elements of progress.

This book gives to the person who is innovating in education a splendid map of the paths and the pitfalls, the peaks and the valleys which have been encountered by one who has been there.

It gives to the student who is considering a program of self-directed study an aerial view of the terrain—the personal issues he or she will face, the problem of choosing a committee of faculty *and* peers, the involved procedures, the loneliness and the always present possibilities of failure or true creativity.

It gives us a perception of the author as a person, an intriguing and multifaceted individual, who can encourage a troubled student with a haiku, or can be, if necessary, a "son of a bitch" when quality work is not evident. He is serious, yet he doesn't take himself too seriously—a refreshing characteristic. It seems obvious that he had fun writing this book.

A sentence like this challenges my imagination with its implications: "The learning blob which self-destructs . . . may be the most stable element assuring UGS continuity." The impact of that sentence is not particularly diminished by knowing that a group of students, faculty and administration formed to discuss, decide, and implement a policy about learning is a "learning blob," which, when no longer needed, goes out of existence. This makes the sentence clearer. But the view that continuity comes best through continually changing groups which eliminate themselves when they have served their function stays with me as a germinal thought. There are numerous gems like this in these pages.

This is not only the story of Union Graduate School; it is not only the story of one perceptive and facilitative educator; it is a description and analysis of the problems and the potentialities of an alternative mode of education. As such I see it as a most valuable contribution.

Carl R. Rogers
Resident Fellow
Center for Studies of the Person
La Jolla, California

Preface

Graduate education in the United States is a gigantic enterprise. It involves hundreds of thousands of students, thousands of professors and other personnel, millions of dollars worth of books, equipment, and materials, and capital investment for buildings and laboratories running into the billions. If one includes postbaccalaureate education of all kinds, the sums are even more astounding.

But I will not try to document expenditures of money and energy in any definitive way or attempt to justify the total thrust of graduate education. The history of graduate education in this country is the story of pushing back the frontiers of knowledge, perpetuating Western heritage, and serving community and national needs. In short, graduate schools have been instrumental in the evolution of both material and nonmaterial qualities of life. Such evolution, however, has not been an unmixed blessing, as critics of the "academy" repeatedly remark.[1]

This book focuses on some of the experimentation with different modes of learning related to both the evolution and the criticism of graduate programs. Although I do not think that graduate schools should be eliminated from the American landscape, I do feel that alternatives should be increased in ways that make learning modes more humanistic. I discuss some of the critical issues related to learning, issues that have implications and applications for every manner of human situation in a graduate context. I am concerned with forward-looking processes that make wider, even visionary, use of experience. And from many angles I shall deal with such questions as:

- Why do we give so little formal credence to experiential learning? Isn't this paradoxical in so pragmatic a society as ours?

- How long does it take for credible learning experiences to become accreditable, and what does it mean to be "accredited" in a credentials-oriented society?
- What does it require to move a student from the language of his or her rhetoric to the first steps toward risk?
- Can professors (facilitators, teachers, learning resources, consultants or whatever) be of real use to students without absorbing a certain amount of abuse from them?
- Can students of any occupation, culture, sex, geography, race, creed, or clan become lifelong learners without gaining an appreciation of paradox, irony, and humor?
- If learning is central to living, why bother with degrees?
- Are students really ever finished, even at commencement?
- Must "residency" in *any* program require that a student be *in residence* at a particular place and time?
- Must graduate learning be entirely cognitive and/or skill oriented? Where does the affective domain fit into that perspective?
- How does one distinguish between the experiential and the experimental?
- What constitutes "excellence"? "accountability"? "competency-based" anything?
- What kinds of interpersonal or intercommunicational relationships optimize learning? or inhibit it?
- What is person-centered or self-directed learning?

In more institutional or social terms, I also want to address the following questions:

- Is it inevitable that experimental programs become increasingly like those from which they revolt? Must institutions inevitably move from "charisma to bureaucracy" and hence become increasingly routinized, abstract, and dehumanizing?[2]
- Why has graduate education been, for the most part, a manifestation of philosophical idealism? Where do other methodologies, such as the pragmatic, phenomenological, and existential, "fit in" or serve as models to guide the learner?
- Are there more imaginative and less dehumanizing means to underwrite graduate learners than those of fellowships,

grants, teaching assistantships, and the accompanying apparatus required for sustaining those means?

● What implications are there in the newer pathways for such groups as Blacks, Chicanos, Puerto Ricans, Native Americans, and consciousness-raised women who systematically have been cut off from education beyond the baccalaureate degree?

Such questions, naturally, cannot be "answered" definitively. In fact, such questions may be little more than shaped and sharpened through the asking and discussing. But I believe that we need more general public dialogue about graduate education. It is too important a part of our national life to be entrusted to professors and deans alone.

This is hardly an objective book. In fact, traditionalists may even regard it as a polemic designed to capture the imagination of graduate students or would-be students searching for an extension of the alternative paths that they discovered in university without walls undergraduate programs. It also might be an "answer" for those persons looking for graduate programs to extend their careers in a particular direction but who have lost all courage to swallow those graduate programs perceived (rightly or wrongly) as unresponsive to their needs. It also may be regarded as a controversial document, raising more questions than it pretends to "answer."

For more than a decade I have been coordinator/director of two graduate programs, a masters' developed at Antioch College, and doctoral sequences evolving a thirty-three institution consortium, The Union for Experimenting Colleges and Universities (UECU).[3] While others have been talking about ways and means of "reforming" or "revising" graduate programs, Antioch and UECU have taken steps to make them more humanistic and responsive. Hence, my biases are both apparent and transparent. In my more facetious moments I quote the moral from a fable I wrote in the James Thurber mode to illustrate the social scientist's fatuous claim of objectivity; namely, "Objectivity is what I *say* it is!" This is not to disclaim responsibility for such remarks; it is to claim joy in making them! So I feel reasonably certain that persons who finish reading this book will have some sense of me as a person, how (with my students) I have mixed my life with the institutions I have helped to evolve. Also, I hope the honesty comes through, for we have made more than our share of mistakes in following a kind of "plan as you go" mode of development. Our efforts have backfired, misfired, short-cir-cuited—pick your metaphor. But we know that we have been *alive*, and not beating on some ancient drum covered with heads of shriveled skins, even if at times we have been warned by skull and crossbones!

One of our graduates, Walt Kleeman, a man in his early fifties who sold his family furniture business to become a professor, consul-tant, and specialist in designing more humane living spaces, once re-marked, "It took me twenty years to move from economics to ergonomics, but I got there through the Union Graduate School." His comment characterizes my hopes. In my judgment such pro-grams as those considered here are the wave of the future even if our economy sputters and world energy shortages increase. Fortunately, such programs focus upon *people's* needs, upon the *processes* of learning, rather than buildings and other material artifacts even as they use infrastructures of knowledge, libraries, and many worlds of work.

This wave will grow in size and impact as the perception of life-long learning expands, as we become a more leisured society, and as the vision of improving the quality of life and work becomes more widely adopted. Furthermore, the wave will mount in power and force as many populations previously excluded from college insist upon new learning modes that accommodate a wider range of life-styles. There are many Walts "out there" who know they can't re-sume their schooling again under the currently available programs.

Contents

Person-Centered Graduate Education

1 Some New Designs: To Bury the Albatross?[1]

Since William James wrote "The Ph.D. Octopus" early in this century, the route to a doctorate in the United States has been under attack. Graduate students have grumbled about it, many agreeing that it often takes ten years to acquire the degree and ten years—if ever—to recover! One of my former master's degree students, writing to his family and friends at Christmas, remarked:

> We have passed the year in good health and without any major crisis or trauma. I am into the third (and hopefully final) year of my doctoral program. To those who have forgone the pleasure of such an educational adventure I should explain the question of duration of such a program. Unlike undergraduate or Master's degree programs where the degree is obtained upon completing a fixed number of credit or semester hours, a doctorate is more like the production of vintage wine. Having crushed the grape during the first year, you are then boarded into a stout oaken cask and left to mature. Two years later (three from the first picking of the grape) the cask is tapped and a committee after ceremonial sniffing and sipping declares you of worthy vintage and entitled to the privileges of new rank. You can imagine the risks inherent in such a process and those who have worked among many who hold the sacred title have probably noticed the faint odor of vinegar in one labeled V.S.O. (Ph.D.).[2]

Actually, if this man "made it" in three or four years, he was fortunate; in 1970–71 the national average was about five years in the natural sciences, seven years in the social sciences, and nine in the humanities.[3]

Meanwhile, since World War II, graduate deans have grouped,

regrouped, and regrouped again to discuss the degree. Between 1967 and 1972 the Ford Foundation awarded ten of the prestigious graduate schools in the country $41,500,000 for programs "designed to cut the time for study and dissertation to four, or at most five, years instead of the more common seven-to-nine years" by means of more continuous, full-time study, elimination of excessive requirements, and restructuring of curriculums.[4] Yet, to the radical critic, these decades of effort seem little more than tinkering with the machinery.

Bolder efforts also have been made. Alternative degrees, such as the Doctor of Education, Doctor of Psychology, and more recently the Doctor of Arts, have been invented as routes around or direct challenges to the Germanic form of Ph.D. All such efforts are commendable; yet, it is a rare campus where recipients of these alternative degrees are not perceived by their Ph.D. colleagues as something slightly less than first-class citizens. For all the money that the Carnegie Foundation and others have poured into such programs as the Doctor of Arts, where the focus is on teaching and not research, the Ph.D. still is perceived as the highest academic degree both in status and marketability. Also, for all the difficulty of obtaining the Ph.D. degree and despite every manner of criticism, the annual number of Ph.D. recipients increased from four thousand in 1948 to twenty-five thousand in 1969 to about thirty-five thousand in the mid-seventies; meanwhile, the total number of holders is pushing toward the half-million mark.[5]

Several commissions in the early seventies attempted to define nontraditional study and to ascertain ways of reforming graduate education in the context of these new definitions. Perhaps one of the best statements in Samuel B. Gould's report for the Commission on Non-Traditional Study appeared in the preface:

> ... non-traditional study is more an *attitude* than a system and thus can never be defined except tangentially. This attitude *puts the student first* and the institution second, concentrates more on the *former's need* than the latter's convenience, encourages diversity of individual opportunity rather than uniform prescription, and deemphasizes time, space, and even course requirements in favor of competence and, where applicable, performance. It has *concern for the learner* of any age and circumstance, for the degree aspirant as well as the person who finds sufficient reward in enriching life through constant,

periodic, or occasional study. This attitude is not new; it is simply more prevalent than it used to be.[6]

Although Gould's commission was concerned with learning at many levels, three other task forces dealt specifically with graduate education. Frank Newman's report damned the graduate schools for having "shirked their resonsibilities," for having failed to create "new programs that match expected national needs for highly trained manpower of the next few decades—for example the social demand for skilled researchers and practitioners to tackle the problem of population control, environmental problems, city management, the delivery of health services, and so on." Newman also criticized graduate schools for being "hostile to relevance" and claimed that the root of that hostility lay in "an instinct of self-aggrandizement."[7] Not so, said David D. Henry in the report of the National Board on Graduate Education: "Enrollment trends in various fields suggest that, in fact, first-time graduate enrollments in many traditional academic disciplines are declining while substantial, often spectacular growth is occurring in disciplines that are 'externally oriented' and relevant to social problem-solving needs."[8]

More important, perhaps, was the work of the Panel on Alternate Approaches to Graduate Education, a group of sixteen persons drawn from diverse segments of the academic community that actually reached unanimity in making twenty-six concrete proposals for change. Among the more important recommendations from an innovative viewpoint were that "a deliberate and significant component of discipline-related work" should be carried on "outside university walls"; panels of "nonuniversity-based doers" should "meet regularly with the instructional staffs"; universities should create and fund "permanent long-range planning groups to develop, through research, consultation, and other broad-based inquiry, means of insuring successful institutional adaptation to environmental change"; and significantly, "course sequences, residence regulations, and other institutional requirements should be adapted to meet the needs of students with family responsibilities, adult learners, professionals, those forced to pursue their studies intermittently, and others whose admission to graduate education and preferred patterns of study differ from those regarded as standard."[9]

Of course, it is one thing for commissions to deliberate, quite another for universities to legislate and promulgate. The long-range impact of these commission analyses and recommendations remains to be seen.

A NEW ECONOMICS?

Meanwhile, many of the current attacks have resulted in other kinds of action; for instance, Commissioner Ewald B. Nyquist of the New York State Department of Education not only curbed the expansion of Ph.D. programs but also eliminated those deemed weaker.[10] Expansion of graduate education, a status symbol for many universities following World War II, seems to have come to a halt. The reasons are primarily economic. Also, markets for Ph.D. recipients, seemingly infinite a few years ago, seem to have dried up. The academic worlds and the worlds of business and government simply do not need the number of Ph.D.'s that have been produced. Regional and national associations of graduate schools are very concerned with retrenchment, regrouping, and territoriality.

But my concern is not to focus so much upon quantity of degree holders as to analyze the process the student goes through in obtaining the degree. Attacks have been bountiful; self-studies have been legion; yet, for the most part the learning steps expected from the student have changed little: complete course work; take prelims and/or orals and/or comprehensives; design thesis proposal; conduct research; write dissertation. Graduate work usually has been specialized, frustrating, and dehumanizing. Often a person obtains his degree approximately at the moment that he realizes a paradox; namely, that he has come to "know more and more about less and less until he knows practically everything about nothing."[11] Also, he may wake up some morning to realize that his specialization, say in Southeast Asian studies, for which he has gained federal funds, no longer has national security relevance. Hence, he may ask, "Why have I devoted five years of my life to gain knowledge that has little value for anybody?" He may wonder why and how he ever got led into such elegant masochism, especially if it leaves him essentially incapable of earning a living or living in a world where feeling does matter. Further, many doctoral candidates in every field—the liberal arts, medicine, law, and science—complete their work at precisely the moment of life when they feel the need to pursue a Doctorate of Imagination or Doctorate of Learning. And no doubt every graduate or professional student at one time or another has felt that seeking any kind of higher degree has all the qualities of living in a monastery without the accompanying spiritual benefits. Increasingly, some Ph.D.'s have felt like many holders of bachelor's degrees: "prepared to do what?"

A HISTORICAL INTERLUDE

In February 1975, the Illinois Wesleyan University *Library News Letter* carried an interesting, even refreshing, note that not only provides perspective but has a tinge of quaint nostalgia:

> The Archives now has 238 theses accepted for Ph-D [*sic*] degrees by the non-Resident School associated with Illinois Wesleyan University from 1874 to 1910. These dissertations were the final requirement of a course of study which consisted primarily of directed reading and periodic examination. The program, which was the first of its kind in the United States, was a forerunner of the correspondence and extension services developed by larger institutions around the turn of the century. For over three decades, the program had importance for those individuals, mostly teachers and ministers, who desired more education, but found it impossible to attend a university full-time. Students enrolled from all over the United States and there was even a Canadian Branch with headquarters in downtown Toronto.
>
> The theses are curiosities by today's standards. Almost all are handwritten and most are under 75 pages in length. Only a handful can be considered as examples of original research (the modern standard for doctoral dissertations); most are simply position papers. Nearly half are written on topics relating to religion and ethics, about one quarter on history and government with the remainder dealing with topics in fields such as physics, chemistry, elocution, sociology, and education. They reflect the moral and social concerns of their day. Several writers investigated man's relation to his God, others debated the liquor problem, or Southern racism, economic policy, crime, or the restrictions on immigration.

Foreshadowings of universities without walls!

AN OVERVIEW OF HAPPENINGS

Fortunately, things are changing. Master's degree programs have not increased in number as rapidly as doctoral programs in the past quarter-century, but many of them are more flexible. Language and thesis requirements have been modified substantially and functionally; also, a few, such as those that Goddard College, Lone Mountain, the Fielding Institute, and the College of Liberal Studies at the University of Oklahoma have developed, are beginning to encompass the vision of undergraduate programs known by such diverse descriptions as "university without walls," "external" or "extended degrees," and "open universities." M.D. programs are undergoing radical "surgery," and I have little doubt that somewhere in the United States there is on the drafting boards a Medical School Without Walls, one not only utilizing many untapped resources of medical knowledge but one benefiting two major minority groups: ethnic people short of medical services who only now are seeing their members moving farther up the academic ladder and married women who historically have been locked into their husband's locations—or denied acceptance for medical degree training by arbitrary quota systems. In short, ethnic movements and feminism should benefit many individual minority persons and groups in the years and decades ahead.

Likewise, legal education is also under attack and modification. The Antioch Law Institute, launched in Washington, D.C., in 1972, was a direct response to the need for more practicums, more up-to-the-elbows-in-life experiences (as well as cases). A Law School Without Walls is inevitable. Hopefully such a program would focus on the "oughts" of American life, since both youth and practicing lawyers—to say nothing of laypersons affected by Watergate—are well aware that lawyers normally aim to win cases, not necessarily to effect justice. For too long, legal professors and the legal profession have neglected the great ethical questions; legal education has been long on contracts, torts, and property, short on jurisprudence and values. The greatest long-range contribution of the Nixon administration might well be a heightened awareness of the need for legal education that approaches justice from ethical angles and not merely opportunistic advocacy. Ironically enough, Thomas Jefferson might feel more comfortable in the Antioch Institute or in some new Law School Without Walls than at Harvard, Yale, or the university he founded in Virginia!

In the arts and sciences the period since the war has seen some important formal changes in graduate work, both at the master's and doctoral levels. Broad-based interdisciplinary programs in American Civilization, Black and Afro-American Studies, Feminist Studies, Urban Studies, Southeast Asian Studies, and some branches of education encourage students, on paper at least, to develop wider perspectives intellectually, geographically, and conceptually; they also encourage implementing a broader tactic and strategy for approaching problems in those given areas. Action-study master's programs such as those developed by Goddard and Antioch reflect the desire to teach students skills in the logistics of social change.

Nevertheless, many interdisciplinary programs are run by traditionalists who believe in the "purity" and superiority of their own specialties, whether in physics, economics, or English literature. Unfortunately though understandably enough, they are still *inter*disciplinary and not *trans*disciplinary, for the payoff in university teaching has been in the disciplines and departmental loyalty, in research, and in maintaining the "publish or perish" posture to insure mobility of the teacher from one university to another. Also unfortunately, the departments in most universities have the quality of medieval fiefdoms, with their lords, vassals, and serfs; such arrangements merely perpetuate specialization and territoriality. Whether one analyzes such factors and forces from a Marxist viewpoint or from the viewpoint of the several humanisms, specialization and territoriality (protecting one's turf) erode human values of both those effecting and those affected.

Students in most graduate programs, even when they are permitted or encouraged to depart from their specialty or read across fields, *may* do so at their peril, for they also must read their advisor's cues. The truth is, as I shall indicate at greater length in discussing ways to move students from rhetoric to risk, that most students and professors do not dare test the limits of their freedom. They cannot "let go." Most students are convinced, brainwashed, or even obsessed with the view that a person with a master's degree (especially if he or she is a teacher) is a Master of Sorts, or that a Ph.D. or holder of other doctorates (especially a teacher) is a kind of perambulating encyclopedia in his or her field. Hence, people frequently forget that the knowledge explosion makes a mockery of the traditional views of knowledge and that breakthroughs in the behavioral

sciences and phenomenological approaches to understanding bring
into serious doubt most traditional learning methods. Surely the lecture, library, and book as the predominant pedagogical tools are
anachronistic if not downright archaic.

Yet it appears that nearly every foundation supporting graduate
education, the university departmental structure, the credential-
granting associations, the generals of grantsmanship, and so on ad
nauseum continue to support traditional research, or "abstracted
empiricism," as C. Wright Mills so aptly described the process.[12]
Also, the major users of such knowledge, those in the military-indus-
trial-governmental-educational complex, seem to perpetuate those
methods. And they seem to sanction these processes with little
awareness of, or concern for, fundamental criticisms. The fact, for
instance, that few have accepted the offer of the U.S. Office of Education to support interdisciplinary doctoral programs illustrates how
firm establishmentarian forces are.[13] Anyone who has dared to do a
joint program with faculty members from fields other than his or her
own can attest to the blinding frustrations, petty jealousies, pecking-
order rituals and idiocies, and enervating results. We may not know
until the eighties or nineties whether or not the widespread retrenchment growing out of economic recession will lead to lasting cooperative structures that alleviate such dehumanizing processes. Whether
or not some of the institutions that have appeared on the landscape
as fundamental efforts to meet some of these criticisms will endure
also remains to be seen. In evaluating them, however, we may want
to judge them by assessing the impact and intensity of the learning
experience upon participants rather than by assessing their success
or failure by their longevity.

After personally spending at least two decades struggling to
gain insights across fields and having been put tight up against walls
of my own guilt and expectations upon being asked, "What's your
field?" I woke up free one morning and solemnly resolved on the al-
tar of Socrates to respond, "My field is humans!"

SOME VARIATIONS ON A THEME

Since the mid-sixties, a number of important baccalaureate, master's, and doctoral programs have challenged more traditional approaches to higher education in this country. Detailed descriptions
may be found elsewhere.[14] While we are mainly concerned with mas-

ter's and doctoral programs, perhaps a word should be said about the special bachelor's degree programs, known by the variety of names mentioned above: external or extended degree, open university, continuing education, and university without walls. Both public and private agencies are involved in this movement. Empire State College in New York, which has the most thoroughly developed program in the public sector, has devised both centers and processes to help a large number of persons work out self-directed learning programs. Other states, such as Florida, California, Pennsylvania, and Wisconsin, are actively engaged in catching up. Unfortunately, the motivation for devising such programs more often is economy than student self-actualization. Yet, perhaps we should judge such programs by their fruits rather than their roots.

In the private domain any list of colleges stressing experimental and experiential learning and student self-direction must include Antioch and Goddard. Antioch has a far-flung network in the country that includes a variety of work-study configurations—work and study in alternate rhythms, work and study concurrently, work *as* study, etc. Nor can Goddard's pioneering efforts be overlooked in any definitive study of such patterns; in their adult degree programs, students spend two or three weeks on the campus in Vermont, contract with a faculty member to perform a particular learning task, then return to their homes, jobs, and families to complete that task. Antioch has recently adopted this scheme as a means of assisting adults whose formal education has been interrupted at some point to complete requirements for the bachelor's degree. The University of Oklahoma's program is similar, recognizing the fact that life experience often leads to more solid educational foundations than courses themselves. No survey of a definitive nature would neglect the efforts of such older institutions as Bennington or Sarah Lawrence to encourage creativity and student self-direction or newer colleges, such as Metro, Shimer, and Evergreen, to evolve and perpetuate similar processes.

Deserving special mention is the Union for Experimenting Colleges and Universities, a thirty-plus institution consortium (including Antioch, Goddard, Bard, and Skidmore but also larger universities such as Minnesota, Wisconsin at Green Bay, Pacific, and Florida International). It is the only consortium in the country offering degree-granting programs at both bachelor's and doctoral levels.

Under the aegis of some of the country's outstanding educators, the Union has pioneered in the effort to involve a wide range of geographically dispersed institutions, both public and private, both experimental and nominally traditional, in experimenting with a variety of forms. Some of the schools with university without walls programs offer the Union degree as an alternate to their own degree. Some of the institutions, as their names suggest, focus primarily upon the needs of ethnic minorities (Universidad Boricua, Universidad de Campesinos Libres, Flaming Rainbow [Native Americans], Morgan State, and Shaw Universities).

Most such programs encourage students to be their own chairpersons, feature a student working with learning facilitators, and encourage the student to become more aware of personal life experience (whether work or play) and to translate that into intense learning or human development. The learning set is also characterized by the student's evolution of a learning contract and development of a portfolio as evidence to support what eventually is translated into a narrative transcript. Hopefully, the total learning experience is one of close interaction between students and those from whom and with whom they are learning. Perhaps the most dramatic of the undergraduate programs is the Life Lab sequence developed by McGregor Smith and his associates at Miami-Dade Community College in Florida. Working within a context of traditional requirements and standard introductory courses in a host of fields, students are encouraged to listen to cassette lectures and meetings, watch a great variety of films, learn from their work experience, and attend rap sessions; in short, they integrate their lives and their learning *outside* the usual context of attending classes, lectures, and accumulating course credits toward the Associate in Arts degree. In an era in which "competency" has become a shibboleth if not a panacea, one cannot overlook the competency-based approach of Alverno College, Milwaukee, where forty competency-level units have replaced grades and credits. Any institution doing that, of course, can conduct educational and testing activity both on and off campus!

Fortunately, for those wanting to experiment, there is currently no commonly accepted definition of a bachelor's degree. In fact, the degree approximates whatever any local faculty *says* it is! Hence experimentation becomes a function of faculty politics and power;

also, much of the impetus for freer learning forms has been top-down. A powerful professor or administrator, locating both idea and money, could start an external degree program. The next major task would be to lend continuity and integrate it into ongoing programs without having it emasculated by traditional-minded faculty or other pressures.

SOME "FOR INSTANCES"

In recent years there certainly has not been as much activity at the master's and doctoral levels as in earlier times, but the *quality* and challenges of that effort are what this book is about. Since World War II steps toward the master's degree in many fields, but especially education, generally have been less restrictive. As most university catalogues reveal, some departments still require thirty to forty semester hours, a thesis, and oral and/or written exams to ascertain the candidate's knowledge base. Yet, there are many institutions, including some in teacher education, where the master's degree is merely an accumulation of thirty or so hours with few requirements as to knowledge, sequence of courses, or quality checks. In fact, a glut of such programs, often added as concessions to community pressures from without and political pressures from within the university, makes the master's degree in some institutions extraordinarily suspect.

Any definitive history of the liberalizing of master's programs in this country would have to include the Putney Graduate School of Education in Putney, Vermont, which operated from 1950 to 1964. Founded by Morris Mitchell, a man of great energy and vision, the master's program incorporated most features we have come to associate with experiential education, namely, personal journals as learning instruments, field trips, informal seminars, work on ecology projects, growing organic foods, and many other activities. It was this school that Antioch College absorbed in 1964 to evolve a program stressing student-evolved curriculums, independent study, and practical experience, all integrated into more meaningful and more relevant preparation for teaching. Beginning with only ten students and two campus sites (Yellow Springs, Ohio, and Putney), the program was designed to reform social studies teaching at the secondary level. The program now enrolls students by the hundreds in a half-dozen urban and rural patterns across the country. Also, the program has moved from a narrow focus on social studies to elementary education, educational administration, and counseling. A fascinating program graduating many women and persons of ethnic minority background, it has made a major difference in the lives of many teachers. Also, it has made a social difference in communities which have felt the pressure to change schools in a time of urban decay (see Appendix A).

The Goddard College master's programs, one in Cambridge, Massachusetts, and the other national in scope, also give students an opportunity to utilize the work-study pattern. The former uses both the collective and individual approaches as organizational patterns for studying and effecting change in the Boston area. The latter requires minimal residency in Vermont for gaining familiarity with the program's requirements and personnel; then the student studies wherever he or she lives and holds periodic seminars with field faculty members, who serve as facilitators to the student's learning in groups, at work—wherever, whatever, however. Again, the learning mode is self-direction, even when a student works with groups.

Other more established programs, such as that at The Bank Street College of Education, are extending new learning frontiers for their master's degree students. In humanistic psychology, Sonoma State and West Georgia College have exciting programs. Few institutions can neglect the demand for such programs, which are long on flexibility, short on hard-and-fast requirements. The task: To adapt formal needs to individual human need!

A LAST BASTION?

In the late sixties the University of Massachusetts, under the leadership of Dwight Allen, dean of the School of Education, called a year-long moratorium on all courses in order to develop a new curriculum, a new divisional structure, and new tactics and strategies for questioning old educational forms. In fact, students and faculty at the university participated in the reorientation. Despite both internal and external stresses, the new doctoral program has since achieved much more flexibility. Students may do much of their work away from the campus, for there is a clear recognition of the value of life experience. Both faculty and students are connected with the everyday world of classroom learning in every conceivable context through internships, consultancies, outreach programs, and in-service projects extending far beyond the state's borders. The fact that openings for students in this program fill rapidly, leaving students waiting at the campus gate, illustrates the demand for such a program. In addition, Dean Allen and his associates introduced week-long marathons, featuring every nameable educational philosophy, reports on on-going programs, etc., a veritable smorgasbord of offerings for whoever wished to participate—and thousands have attended. Because administrators were alert to the advantages of contracting the services of controversial educators such as Rhoady McCoy, who gained national prominence when the Ocean-Hill Brownsville Project in New York tested key assumptions about community education, those educators have become part of the University of Massachusetts staff for varying lengths of time.

Other doctoral programs are growing in size and number. One successful example is The Humanistic Psychology Institute (HPI) of San Francisco, sponsored by some of the most influential members of the Association of Humanist Psychology. HPI offers an interdisciplinary program that is national in scope and proposes "to institute high quality humanistic research" while also including "the behavioral and social sciences, arts, humanistic philosophy, humanistic uses of technology" toward "the humanization of contemporary society and . . . the enhancement of individual human capacities."[15] Riding the crest of a need in the field of psychology to go beyond the usual doctorate in experimental psychology, HPI quickly filled its billets, encountered the usual pitfalls of a successful enterprise, and continues to experience pressure to bring its program into line with normative practices in the field.

Nova University may be the most ambitious of all graduate programs without walls. Clusters of about twenty-five school administrators in each of various parts of the United States pursue specialization in educational administration leading to the Doctor of Education degree. Distinguished authorities circuit ride among the clusters, giving lectures, discussing their specialties, and evaluating papers in eight fields of administration: curriculum development, education policy systems, evaluation, finance, management, resources, supervision, and technology. Each student is expected to participate in four practicums, a "Mini," which is "intended to help a participant learn how to do a practicum and write a report," a "Midi" which is "intended to achieve an improvement . . . feasible within a six-month span," and two "Maxis," one group and the other individual in which the student considers major problems "of considerable scope and depth."[16] Nova has expanded so rapidly that its students number in the hundreds.

Walden University, based in Naples, Florida, brings advanced graduate students together each summer to consider the problems and special concerns of American education, to strengthen or acquire skills in research design and methodology, and to develop a thesis proposal. Students then return to their respective homes, jobs, and academic advisors to fulfill their proposals or learning contracts. A recent catalogue carries a statement by President Bernard L. Turner that describes Walden as "a far-flung community, . . . not a brick and mortar university, . . . a community of researchers: who "direct [their] energies toward personally meaningful objectives."[17] Doctoral theses written in this context have the external appearance of and read like theses from traditional institutions; it is the method by which they are derived that sets Walden apart.

The Fielding Institute in Santa Barbara, California, offers several doctoral programs encouraging students to develop projects evolving from the course of their professional tasks. Programs are individualized, feature school-community cooperation, and the learning contract as a focus for quality control.

In addition to these, East Coast University of Dade City, Florida, runs open-learning doctoral programs "for in-service professionals"; beginning in 1974, Open University, in a St. Louis suburb, offered a Ph.D. and an Ed.D. for professional educators and strives for "positive change in education" and a "forum where experienced educators can share ideas and seek solutions to common and unique problems." The cover for their brochure features a seagull with the caption, "dedicated to individual growth." The University of the Southern Highlands in Maryville, Tennessee, is another short-residence program aimed at professional educators. The International Community College of Los Angeles places a student with a tutor; it is a mentor-apprenticeship model with persons as distinguished as the late Anais Nin and Lawrence Durrell assuming responsibility for several students, both individually and in groups. Another school on the West Coast, Wright Institute at Berkeley, stresses multidisciplinary and study-field experience approaches leading to the Ph.D. in social-clinical psychology, preparing persons "for careers of re-

search and action on human problems." While the residency requirements are relatively traditional, the contract system for self-
evolution of a program involving seminars, tutorials, and clinical experience puts Wright in the category of innovative institutions.

Even as this is being written there no doubt are other programs
on the drawing boards that eventually will be included in the definitive history of this period of burgeoning institutions, inevitably leading to another problem.

WHAT PRICE LAISSEZ-FAIRE?

Before launching into a more lengthy description of the Union
Graduate School and fundamental problems and processes of
graduate education, a word is necessary about the societal promises
and pitfalls of such new efforts.

On the positive side, of course, the burgeoning of such institutions and their considerable number of configurations continues the
age-old American propensity to create and invent, to promote self-
reliance, and to provide for a rich range of alternatives. Without
question most established graduate schools have not responded to
the bitter criticisms of both students and reasonable professionals.
And they have not been flexible enough to meet a wide variety of
human needs. Hence, many institutions have been created to fill intellectual, emotional, and social vacuums.

But in every occupation charlatans emerge if there is money to
be made or prestige to be sold. And this field may be no different
than any other. Indeed, as the press has discovered, it has been possible to buy degrees. For instance, one report indicated that 808
Americans bought honorary degrees on their Diner's Club cards
from the London Institute of Applied Research.[18] Some schools were
closed, others sued, when they were exposed as proverbial "diploma
mills." Occasionally one runs into an advertisement as follows:
"HONORARY DEGREE Doctor of Divinity. $15 donation, free in-
formation, Church of Universal Brotherhood, 6311 Yucca, Holly-
wood, California 90028. Satisfaction Guaranteed."[19]

The accrediting associations and the U.S. Office of Education
ostensibly serve as consumer protective agencies in such situations.
With 300 nonaccredited colleges and universities granting degrees
and some states often quite lax in chartering schools, it's not always
easy to protect potential consumers. But more of that when we dis-

cuss excellence and accreditation matters.

THE UNION PROGRAM: PROCESS AND PROSPECT

As suggested above, more than a decade of experience with Antioch's master's program and the Union Graduate School (UGS) has made me a true believer. Comparing the outcomes for more than a thousand students in universities without walls with several thousand I have taught in five other colleges and universities convinces me that the experimental-experiential approach leads to more durable and life-relevant learning, greater rates and magnitudes of personal growth, and unpredictable explosions of creativity. Yet, as many UGS students have observed, taking this road is *not* easy. These programs are *not* for persons wanting "business as usual." They are *not* for the traditional scholar. They *are* for those with a self-perception of being person- or self-directed or on the leading edges of seeking personal change; they *are* for late bloomers or those seeking a new means to effect personal change. They *are* for persons concerned with linking knowledge to action and social change.

In order to set a backdrop for the remaining chapters in this book, it seems most relevant at this point to discuss many of the problems related to the doctoral world by considering, in broad outline, the specifics of the Union Graduate School. This is not to downgrade, by omission or neglect, other efforts. Rather, I know UGS best.

The Union program had a long period of gestation, but it evolved from a specific, felt need. Members of the Union, a consortium that began with twelve experimental institutions in 1964 and now numbers more than thirty, found it increasingly difficult to locate faculty members who could transcend the limitations of their graduate specialization. Hence, Harold Hodgkinson, then dean at Bard, asked, "Why don't we start our own program and train our own Ph.D.'s?" During the next few years, Judson Jerome of Antioch, Goodwin Watson of the Columbia University faculty, Samuel Baskin, president of the Union, myself, and a score of others contributed to the development of a proposal to found a Ph.D. program with both theoretical and action components; in fact, this program has many founding fathers but rests pretty solidly on the philosophical foundations laid by men like Jean Jacques Rousseau, Friedrich Froebel, John Dewey, and the phenomenologists.[20]

Founded in 1969, the Union Graduate School became operational in January 1970, when we admitted our first students. Our students have fulfilled their residential requirements at colloquia held in Colorado, Ohio, Florida, New York, Illinois, Maine, Massachusetts, California, Switzerland, and Kenya and are literally pursuing independent work from Honolulu to Nairobi, Saskatoon to St. Thomas. They average thirty-six years of age; in occupation they cover a universe. In fact, every time ten UGS students assemble, fifty occupational experiences are probably represented. Students and graduates include many college professors, one former and two current college presidents, corporation presidents, practitioners from the fields of psychotherapy, organizational development, art, social work, community change, a police captain, and a fire chief. A colloquium assembling thirty such persons at one location becomes a "mind-blowing" experience for students, consultants, and faculty members for one major reason: the key resource persons are peers.

But let us look briefly at the conceptual framework (key concepts), some operational aspects, and some problems related to the evolution of such a venture. In a shorthand way these may be fairly simply stated:

- Application is encouraged by those who cannot get the advanced training they require in more conventional programs.
- Admission depends upon high intelligence and the demonstrated capacity for self-direction and disciplined effort toward self-chosen objectives.
- Students are encouraged to use the world as their classroom, developing workable plans, implementing them by drawing upon resources both within and outside academic institutions, and fitting means to need; each program is a tailor-made one, with students participating with faculty in selection of advisors, evolving a learning contract jointly with a committee comprised of a minimum of two adjunct professors (specialists in their fields), two UGS peers, and a UGS core faculty member.
- Each student's program consists of a study component ("What do you want to learn?"), an experiential component (an internship or practicum, broadly defined), and a Project Demonstrating Excellence (PDE).

- Since a student either passes or drops out, there are no credits, grades, or points; a cumulative record, consisting of log materials, papers, anything he or she and the committee deem relevant, becomes the basis of evaluation.
- A Project Demonstrating Excellence or PDE (we eschew the terms *thesis* and *dissertation*) may acquire any number of forms and is limited only by the imagination and daring of the student and his committee. He may publish a book or a number of scholarly articles, design and implement a project of significant social change, create poetry, painting, sculpture, musical composition, dances, films, or other art forms that win recognition.[21]

In short, we perceive our program as synthesizing thought and action, the affective and cognitive, the conceptual and perceptual. We aim to transcend abstracted empiricism while recognizing the value of pragmatic method. We believe that a fact is a function of the method used to derive it and hence must be judged by the internal logic and criticism of that methodology. Ours is a praxis approach to learning. Our thrust is both transdisciplinary and interdisciplinary. Insofar as one may draw upon the achievements, postulates, and methodology of any given discipline, fine. But if those disciplines would cripple imagination or preclude exploring in an effort to develop insights that might go beyond them, our program is, indeed, transdisciplinary. Better to use as models the Newtons, Freuds, Joyces, and other seminal figures than to be satisfied with the model of the lab worker or carrel dweller trying to count the feathers in the wings of that angel standing on the point of a pin—or is it an eight-penny nail?

INITIATION

Normally the UGS student starts with a colloquium, though in some extenuating circumstances he or she may begin with independent study following an extended conference with a UGS faculty member. The colloquium is designed not only to broaden personal awareness as the student meets a wide array of other highly-motivated and experienced people but also to challenge fundamental assumptions. It tests his ability to do independent work and his tolerance for ambiguity and incredible anxieties, since he will not be supported by the usual warm arms of alma mater (as in theory, at least, he is so supported). The colloquium also gives him an opportunity to expose his prospective program to his peers and become accustomed to the idea that peer feedback, especially from those outside what he perceives as his field, may be as valuable as faculty feedback. Through such interaction he may experience the tension of humanly supporting peers who dare to criticize him and later recognize the creative value in a comparable tension when he is evaluating. Further, it is the student's first genuine involvement in building a program and a human network, the learning "community" if you will, which is the Union Graduate School.

At the colloquium, too, the student is introduced to the unique processes that comprise our thrust. This is no Sears-Roebuck model! Rather, the colloquium is an event comprising a billion events, all of which have a reality. Hence, experience at a colloquium is a reality testing. A student learns how to construct a functional committee, and as he becomes acquainted with the material and human resources at his command, he is encouraged to take risks he may never have thought about before.

FROM CERTIFICATION TO THE SESSION

As in every other program of higher learning, there are moments of truth. In the Union Graduate School, with its emphasis on process over formality, one such moment occurs during certification, which is comparable to entering into candidacy in a traditional program. This is the time when a student has assembled his committee to consider three major motifs: Where have you been? Where are you now? Where are you going? No two certifications are alike either in process or in substance. Since months and months have gone into developing intercommunication with a committee, certification is not merely an oral exam to test what a person knows. It also is an opportunity for the diverse elements of a committee to meet (usually for the first time), summarize, assess, and prospect. From this session comes a written learning agreement or contract, one in which the members of the committee make a personal and an institutional commitment to see the student through to closure. Such contracts usually contain a flexibility clause indicating that any serious programmatic changes are subject to criticism by any member of the committee. If a student takes an about-face in his work, he may have to start all over again.

Sometime between the certification session and a terminar (terminating seminar) a student must obtain his committee's approval to hold the final session. This approval is possible only after all members have reviewed and commented on a manuscript, a film, a poetry reading, or some other evidence of achievement. At this point, all difficulties and disagreements are resolved. Thus the final session, which may take the form of a committee meeting, a concert, a public lecture, a soirée, a conference ad infinitum, becomes a joyful humanistic event, a celebration rather than a castration.

SOME QUERIES, THEORIES, AND PARADOXES

As John Dewey reminded us in *Democracy and Education,* that amazingly current book published in 1916, it's all right to reinvent the steamboat. It's only appropriate to observe that some parts of our program were new when Socrates was busy "corrupting" Athenian youth or when medieval scholars were leading their students from one university to another. Nevertheless, there are a great many questions that such a program raises and on which one can speculate with a spirit of joy, bewilderment, and weltschmerz:[22]

1. Why do we give so little formal credence to experiential learning?

   Though we laughed at the thought of graduating from a College of the Workaday World or University of Hard Knocks (as, during the Great Depression, many were the jokes about graduating into CCC Tech), we know that Tom Sawyer and Huckleberry Finn learned at breakneck speed while floating on those Mississippi River rafts and that cooperative education introduced at the University of Cincinnati and Antioch more than a half-century ago has become a vital part of a landscape that Huck and Tom would not recognize. We know that the field trip experience, despite recurrent quips in "Peanuts," can be an integral part of some credit courses. The record also indicates that many colleges and universities grant credit for military experience, but it seems to be more in the spirit of patriotism than out of convictions about learning. And such institutions as Goddard in their adult degree program continue to struggle with the evaluation of life experience. It's very difficult to measure such experience except in terms of conventional courses, though perhaps in time Goddard, the Open University in London, Empire State, the University Without Walls, Educational Testing Service, and other American institutions will evolve ways to quantify such nonquantifiable experiences and to solve the problem in phenomenological terms. The Union Graduate School is dedicated to the proposition that getting students to mix the sweat of their life experience with the gray matter in their brains will give new credibility to all forms of human endeavor. But to quantify experience is a contradiction if not an abomination.

2. How long does it take for the credible to become accreditable? Is accreditation necessary?

A corollary to question number 1 concerns student interaction. Every schoolboy and schoolgirl knows that he or she learns from peers; they learn about sex, sports, people, criticism, and learning itself. Undeniably, one's peers constitute a sourcebook of plenitude. For centuries teachers have used this knowledge in conducting classes, either encouraging Hazel to learn from Harry or playing them off against one another in sanction games. Yet even many Union graduate students enter our program not quite convinced that the learning they get from their peers has the same authenticity as that gained from consultants and faculty. The explanation may be relatively simple. Who ever got credit for Bull Sessioning 302 or Saloon Rapping 401? It's the *crediting* that counts in American society! We have a transcript, the demand for a transcript, and the promise of that kind of lifelong credentialing syndrome to prove it. In short, it's credible enough to learn from peers, but it's not accreditable.

So the challenge to Union Graduate School is to make the credible accreditable, not so much in terms of externals like transcripts, degrees, and other such searchings for a sign, but psychologically. Sometimes when UGS students ask me about assembling their committees, I ask "Who are the students on your committee?" And if the response is, "Oh, I forget!" I rejoin, "You know, students are also people." (See chapter on accreditation.)

3. How does a student move beyond rhetoric to risk?
    It's not too difficult to master the rhetoric of experimental
    and experiential education (and the experimental is not
    necessarily the experiential). Educational literature is full of
    it; youth culture is full of it; inner colleges, free schools, and
    other such forms are full of it. In fact, it often seems to per-
    vade the air. But what is the distance from word to act? Can
    the author of a recipe for learning stand the heat in the
    kitchen? What happens when persons leave the protective
    custody of a familiar process and walk into new spaces? Can
    they tolerate the question, "Who am I?" Can they face an-
    swers ranging from "I don't know" to "I once thought I
    knew"? Can they ask in all genuineness, "What is the
    meaning of a life or a process which I must make for my-
    self?"
         Since the day in 1964 that my Antioch colleague Ben
    Thompson remarked that the Antioch-Putney program
    would test whether or not freedom would work, I have
    wrestled with a host of implications related to rhetoric and
    risking. Threaten a student by driving him back to his cen-
    ter, and there may be serious consequences. Find a means
    for helping him do it, and there are consequences. These
    two sets of consequences may not be the same, but as Ben
    has remarked, education is a dangerous game.[23] Nor does
    one solve the matter of risking by referring to the provoca-
    tive writings of Norman Brown or E. M. Cioran or by dis-
    missing it as the "snake pit," a "can of worms," or
    "Pandora's box."
         There's another dimension to experiencing the student
    confronting his own anxieties. I've watched husbands and
    wives separate over the tensions growing out of such
    matrices; I've watched the descent of schizophrenic curtains
    over mouths too frozen to emit a primal scream; and I've
    watched a student become literally insane. This is not to say
    that traditional programs do not generate tensions and that
    students do not crack up in a variety of ways. But encourag-
    ing students to move beyond rhetoric to daring to do what
    they say they want to do is playing educational chicken.
    Similarly, at the institutional level, it's threatening to facul-

ty members to do what they *say* they want to do. Institutional hypocrisy and game playing are safe compared with daring students to dare—and meaning it. Furthermore, it's not professional; for professionalism is simply another way of spelling out the mediocrity that most of us can enjoy as comfortably as an old shoe. No, there are not many of us who can face the dying of our self-concepts or speak as easily from the grave of self as some of Edgar Lee Master's *Spoon River* characters. But occasionally we can raise these issues with those who dare to dare by asking at a colloquium that they write their obituary and share it with a couple of other people! And occasionally we can face such sticky questions as "How much learning is therapy?" or "Am I morally responsible for her life?"

One conclusion I've drawn from my experience in working with more than a thousand master's and doctoral candidates in free-form matrices is that once a student crosses the threshold of risking and internalizes a new sense of being and self-verification, a whole new universe opens. He feels a sense of power in self-programming. She dares to try other styles of life and expression, to think the unthinkable, and to defy (often with a vengeance) parents, school counselors, or other brainwashers who have attempted to define her life for her. He gains a sense of release and joy. Then he's in danger of becoming a true believer! If he also works on compensation and return, he can master the dynamics of such élan.

4. If learning is central to living, why bother with a degree?
Paradoxically enough, both students and faculty of the Union Graduate School may be most successful where they seem to have failed cum laude; namely, when students drop out after realizing that our processes may be more important than the product. It's a rare colloquium in which several do not exclaim, "I don't need the degree!" A cynic might say that this is merely sour grapes; after all, the disclaimant knew he couldn't succeed anyway, so he shouted in the dark to keep himself company. However, it may also be observed that such a conclusion most often results when a student is turned around by an experience that reveals him

and his culture as more phony than he thought. But it puts the Union Graduate School in a double bind: if we know that credential giving is so irrelevant to the central issues of living as vital beings, why do we grant the degree? Why do we lead students into potentially dehumanizing processes in the name of humanistic approaches?

Obviously it's easy to beg these questions, which are anything but straw men, in the day-to-day patterns of living and learning in UGS. We can simply point out that one needs credentials to live in the world. We can readily fall back on the paradoxes with which the literature of humanism is replete; or consult Abraham Maslow, Sidney Jourard, and Carl Rogers, to name a few, as well as the pages of *The Humanist*. But the questions raised here are not designed to be begged. Rather, they are questions being studied. To state them is at least a start on that famous problem which Archimedes posited, "Give me a place to stand and I'll move the world."

5. "How do you know," I am frequently asked, "when a student has finished?"

Not an easy question! In fact, it may not even be a good question because it is an accumulation of a whole culture full of questionable assumptions. It assumes that students finish learning. It points to the abomination of commencement which, for decade upon decade, has been metamorphosed into a terminal achievement. The girl gets a credit card when she completes junior high school. Youths of all ages don caps and gowns and get a new Mustang upon graduating from high school or college. We measure out our lives with both coffee spoons and degrees.[24] And yet we know that learning does not necessarily stop until death. The real question is, how soon and in what form the dying?

In the Union Graduate School we have established a process with normative "gos" and "stops." A student and his committee can develop a mushy approach to interrelating and to evaluating, or they can establish ground rules that are as exacting as in any other doctoral program. There are obvious checks and balances. As I attempted to indicate in a working paper for UGS students called "Quality Control and/or Health in UGS," there are both "preventative-positive-reinforcing" methods, as well as "corrective-negative-restraining" ones to help us with the problem. The former are perhaps more obvious and evident in the above discussion and would include careful admissions processes, colloquia design, and the encouragement of an individual's verification of self through both process and product. Also, it's important to have faculty who are "more cosmopolitan than provincial, more open than closed, more learned than ignorant, more sensitive than indifferent to human need, more sympathetic and attuned to interdisciplinary approaches than highly specialized in a narrow field, and more, rather than less, familiar with group processes. . . ." Also, accessibility for human support—without creating dependency relationships—is a sine qua non of faculty involvement.

The negative sanctions, however, may need more explication, since they seem to contradict the goals of the program, a point discussed in more detail later (see Chapter 6). How do we know when a student is finished? Probably never! But having established a process, we develop trust in that process, remembering that even a moving picture film is merely a series of frozen moments captured by an eye, brain, and hand employing a variety of criteria—a kind of idealized realism.

6. Will the Union Graduate School and similar innovative programs survive?
I don't know! There is certainly enough opposition, ranging from our own internal inertia, to marginal financial operation, to hostile threats by establishment types. Such opposition usually guarantees inner coherence and strength, as group and cultural analysts (to say nothing about such philosophers of history as Arnold Toynbee) have observed. I'm inclined to perceive such questions in a context of irony, paradox, and humor, much as M. C. Escher, the provocative Dutch etcher, perceives the world. But as in any Escher drawing, it's vital to know whether one is observing the real from the vantage point of inner space or outer space; also, just as it's important to know on what side of Escher's line

one is perceiving the world, it's important to know which side of a paradox is closest to one's inner being.

The Union Graduate School, like its companion graduate schools without walls, runs a real risk of being destroyed by its own success. We're so deluged by inquiries that it is *theoretically* possible for us to spend all of our income on the postage and labor needed to respond to them. Also, it's theoretically possible that we could use all of our energy handling applications in humanistic ways. Or, ironically enough, with some of our students recommending open admissions, we could convert a humanistic concern for the frontiers of student learning into a wasteland of bureaucratic indifference. Where there's a seller's market, buyer beware! As a result, those of us working close to the evolution of the program and its several evolving variations are made sharply aware of several of my own pet paradoxes, namely:

- The closer one is to the center of power, the less he has.
- The more publicity, the less freedom to do what one wishes to do.
- The closer one gets to the mainstream, the less identifiable the eddy.

And of course the outsider, attacking the program from any and all angles, can always yell that currently popular pejorative, "Why be so defensive!" No amount of being offensive is perceived as empirical analysis; it seems, rather, to be perceived as more defensiveness. This is part of the problem of even thinking about accreditation, let alone doing anything about it. Perceptive students ask, "Why start a revolution, or even a quasi revolution, then expect the establishment to supply you with the guns?"

Then, too, why collectivize an individual learning process?

A VISION AND RE-VISION

The Union Graduate School is very much alive and lively, since it is a human network, a complex of interlocking human processes. It is *not* a place; it has little to do with ivy, stadiums, and other such traditional accoutrements of higher learning. It *is* a student starting a free school in San Francisco, or another studying women in Mexico or Haiti, or a man writing poetry in a Xenia, Ohio, hotel, or a woman working with Native American education in British Columbia. It *is* a faculty member (core or adjunct) conversing with students in a New York hotel, traveling on a jet from Miami to Dayton or from San Francisco to San Diego, or meeting thirty people in a colloquium.

Discussion of survival may be as fruitless as asking "Is life worth living?" when the very joy of a sunset or scribbling a haiku about that sunset seems answer enough. If those of us in innovative education perceive the process as an art form, then a single flash of insight becomes as valuable as a volume about survival. Perhaps we can make up in intensity what we may lack in longevity.

One day while dreaming, "Why the Union Graduate School?" I speculated:[25]

- Men and women will hypothesize mountains to conquer even where there are none.
- The urge toward monolithic certainty will always be counteracted by men who love danger (masochists?) or challenge their peers to love it (sadists?).
- Some men and women get bored by routine (bored nonrelating?).
- Frontiers lurk behind the forehead, even when they do not exist physically.
- Many men do have faith in the continuing rebirth of freedom.
- Process *can* be perceived as reality.
- Some men have faith in the continuity of dreams, even where the evidence suggests fractionization.
- Some people believe in Aristotle's dream of "actualizing" human potentiality or in Maslow's empirical vision that "peak experiences" may be creative rather than pathological.
- Human will, intelligence, and love are more precious than real estate. The sweat of reading a book may mix with the sweat of working in a mental hospital or a congressman's office to create a learning admixture more value-producing than study alone.
- The search for relevance, the search for alternative strate-

gies for living creatively, the search for tactics to develop tactile and other sense awarenesses, the search for better ways of searching—all are higher on lists of priorities than the end result, whether it is book, plan, or vision as static entity; rather, each end is a new beginning.

More recently I've suggested that our vision must be not to lose our vision.[26]

Perhaps there is no danger of doing that, either institutionally or individually, since the human spirit *will prevail* if it has an opportunity. And if no opportunity is provided, it will find one! And the Union seems to be just such a freedom catalyzer. Whereas we had only one program until 1974, we now have several. Possibly others will be born between the time these words go to press and publication. Building on the same essential patterns as outlined above, our program, Leadership in Education, attracts those who wish to turn some of our learning patterns around, to counteract the message in such books as *Our Children Are Dying* and *Death at an Early Age*, or meet the criticisms of Ivan Illich's *Deschooling Society*.[27] Although the doctoral feature of the Goodwin Watson Institute for Research and Program Development, in conception at least, is as modern as medieval France, in application it enables contemporaries to concentrate on empirical research and/or social change in collaboration with renowned mentors in any field or fields. Our Urban Center for Minority Studies, located in Baltimore, is a five-dimensional program. Concentrating on urban problems, it enables a student to enter at any point in or between secondary education, then leave at the completion of GED (administered by the Baltimore Public School system), Associate of Arts (granted by Morgan State University), bachelor's (granted by the Union), master's (granted by Antioch), or Ph.D. (granted by the Union Graduate School). Discussing any of these programs is a book in itself, and no doubt within the next several years, assuming no world catastrophe, there will be regional variations designed in relatively small units to maximize human interaction and human networking. UGS/West in San Francisco, founded in 1975, is one such regional variation.

IN SUM, . . . TENTATIVELY!

All Union programs, like their counterparts throughout the country, stress self-direction. They are short on formal residency, long on us-

ing committees consisting of specialists and peers, the learning contract, and somewhat rigid *procedural* requirements. But we eschew
rigid *substantive* requirements, such as formal courses, points, and
credits, though we do take all previous study into consideration in
helping a student design a program. We expect high degrees of performance and personal integrity. Faculty in UGS and other innovative programs must be committed to such processes and develop
"the courage to *let* be";[28] students must learn that the weight of success or failure falls squarely on their shoulders; hence, prospects for
risk and growth are far higher than in traditional programs where
faculty normally design and evaluate courses, exams, and projects.

2   Rhetoric to Risk

Any educator or layperson familiar with the history of student dissent since the Free Speech movement began at Berkeley in the fall of 1966 is poignantly aware of fundamental criticisms of American higher education; both undergraduate and graduate students label it irrelevant, impersonal, bureaucratic, dehumanizing, abstract, and so on.

These complaints are not new. The work of Thorstein Veblen, John Dewey, Abraham Maslow, Carl Rogers, Sidney Jourard, and Arthur Jersild represents the legions of critics who have wrestled with educational problems throughout the twentieth century.[1] We are all familiar with the concept of learning by doing manifest in the variety of work-study programs pioneered by Antioch and the University of Cincinnati and now numbering in the hundreds. Most people have at least heard of such educational devices as the field trip, the learning contract, audiovisual aids, seminars—each has had its day in the limelight and gradually has been integrated into a multiplicity of programs. And one cannot forget the good old-fashioned American virtue of rugged individualism or the Emersonian dictum of self-reliance.

Add to these factors the myth that we live in an open-class society where hard work and education spell success; add a dash of belief in the liberal arts as a liberalizing process; mix it with a growing notion that equal educational opportunity should be available to persons of every creed, race, class, and sex as a kind of human right in these United States; stir into the pot a general opposition to bureaucracy and authoritarianism of most kinds, and a mixture emerges from which the rhetoric of free-form education steams, though I would be cautious in ascribing causality to any educational movement. Naturally, such generalizations, including this one, are probably untrue, yet it may provide us with a start. Why would anyone want the freedom to design his own program? The answer lies in the individual's socialization and individuation.

One thing is certain: of the several thousand applications that I have read for the Antioch and Union Graduate School programs, many, surely more than 50 percent, of the persons applying believe they want a freer form for their work than the ones they have experienced or have heard about. And the rhetoric is usually the same; for instance:

- My knowledge has been broadened through my work as assistant principal and coordinator of adult classes. It has enabled me to understand education from every point of view—that of the teacher, the student, the parent, and the administrator.
- I would like to be a part of Union Graduate School because it provides just the type of help from selected people plus self-directed study which I feel is what I need to enable me to explore in depth all of the areas connected with adult education.
- I just found out about you a few weeks ago, read the brochure, and became so enthused that I began to take action on it almost immediately. The idea of directing my own course of intellectual and professional growth and of being able to coordinate my degree work so closely with my clinical and research work in family therapy is exciting indeed.[2]

Conversations with graduate students at the University of Massachusetts, Nova, Walden, and Humanist Psychology Institute reveal similar motivations and expressions. I do not claim that students can or should necessarily articulate their desires, intentions, and plans in any other form. Persons who have completed at least sixteen years of schooling in this country almost inevitably articulate their thoughts in similar phrases—words commonly understood by peers, professors, and parents. Most Americans who have made it through college have had to rely on rhetorical formulas. Both teachers' and students' individualities are assaulted by class loads of

25 to 30 students in grade school, 125 to 180 students in high school, and 75 to 3,000 in college. In short, it is little wonder that verbal stylization is the outcome of *most* education.

And it is little wonder that students can run the K–12 gauntlet without developing skills in written expression when the electronics revolution (TV, radio, cinema) and easy access to the telephone have made writing almost anachronistic.[3] And where is the sensitive art or language teacher who can appreciate an individual creation that is different! I sometimes wonder if a graduate student I had in a class on Long Island, one who insisted on my signing her exit waiver for a class she entered by "mistake," is still saying that there is only one way to teach art to children; namely "Sky is up and ground is down; sky is up and ground is down!" That is what she repeated ten times when I asked her why she should drop out of a course where we were considering alternative methods of looking at a great variety of books, disciplines, and experiences. And I wonder, too, why many fifth graders can write beautiful haiku but lose that touch, that inspiration, within a grade or two. Quite apart from forces that tend to downgrade the expression of feeling in American schools, beware the young dissenter (unless he develops debating skills that allow him to dissent on either side of any given issue with equal *lack* of conviction), especially if he espouses an unpopular ideology or tactic such as Marxism, pacificism, or outspokenism! Individual manifestos aren't very popular in the United States, rhetoric to the contrary.[4]

So, American education promotes and feeds on cognitive learning. It is easier to pass along, generation to generation. It is easier to grade, especially if one is dealing with large numbers of students. It is easier for both professor and student to know that one knows how much one knows; it can be measured by SAT, IQ, and a variety of other metersticks; furthermore, such measurements can be pointed off two or three decimal places for the college or graduate admissions officer who then can know who can "make it" and who cannot. And, of course, the self-fulfilling prophecy invariably works!

Hence, it is no surprise that most persons seeking experiential and experimental graduate programs (and they are not necessarily the same) *know* what they *think* they want. They also may know how they feel. But until they are sure that a program is genuine or that what people say about their programs is genuine, it is easy to stick with the knowing and to avoid the feeling. I've held hundreds of interviews with prospective students (and read as many more applications) in which it was clear that applicants were not leveling with themselves *or* us. Usually the dissonance between feeling and knowing or even cognitive dissonance itself is apparent to the experienced interviewer or reader. At the extreme, of course, is the prospective student who uses the rhetoric of innovative education, whatever happens to be in vogue at the moment, and then includes a vita or three times as many letters of recommendation as required by the application; he thereby hangs himself on his own anxiety. He has read neither our application form nor our brochure, where it is clear that we are interested in where the prospective student has been, where he is now, and where he wants to go; namely,

1. How would you describe your background (e.g., your work history, intellectual development, schooling, personal growth, achievements and products, etc.)?
2. What are your current interests and activities (nature of your work and/or studies, type of reading you have been doing lately, areas of special interest, career plans, etc.)?
3. What do you plan to *do* in the Union Graduate School program (areas of study, internship plans, projects you would like to undertake, people or kinds of people you would like to work with, etc.)?[5]

There are other telltale signs when a person is retaining one foot in tradition while attempting a half step toward self-direction. Interviews often are filled with deferential minuets in which the prospective student will dance in neat 3/4 time rhythms to any questions asked, not questioning a deliberately vague question or not responding to straightforward questions, such as "What do *you* want to do? What do you *really* want to do?" And, of course, in such situations, in both interviews and applications, one hears and reads buckets of nonsense, such as "I want to help people save them from their worst selves. . . ."[6] Also, one easily detects confusion over what self-direction is when one listens to or reads ambiguous plans or plans that couldn't be consummated in fifty-seven lifetimes; to wit:[7]

- I want to develop skill in every kind of psychotherapy.

- My book will "blow the minds" of everybody in the field.
- I want to synthesize all the theory in that field.
- My book would necessarily use approximately six to eight models.
- Nobody has before put it altogether, but through your inter-disciplinary program I intend to. . . .
- I intend to read or read again every piece of literature that has ever been written on the topic.

Yet, on the positive side of dealing with the student's state of mind and heart at entry, the first two questions often elicit some of the most insightful autobiographical statements imaginable. In fact, I often am overwhelmed by such openness and self-disclosure. And when prospective students dare to take off their public masks at the point of admission, they often gain a running start toward developing their UGS programs and processes. Most indicate that our request for autobiographical information makes it difficult to apply for the program since they are thrown back on their own devices. Ironically, we have had to develop some guidelines for applying that not only include a few words about length but also the notion that we are interested in some kind of preliminary plan (it may be changed upon entry), even though we do not expect a blueprint. It is regrettable that most graduate programs gain so little sense of applicants *as persons* before they enter. This combination of autobiography and self-verification often helps a student take that first tentative step toward risk. The person's confrontation of self in this context also serves him as an important referent. Many students return to their initial statement toward the end of their graduate work to see how far they have traveled. In short, it's a first half step.

Some of the applications have been so moving that I have often found myself writing poetry about the persons and their experiences, poetry later shared with the persons admitted as preface to a dialogue. An illustration may open up this vista a little more clearly. We frequently receive applications from women in their middle years concerned about returning to study to complete a doctorate. Also frequently, these people agonize rather publicly over being a single parent. After reading applications and discovering three of these in a group of twenty-five, I wrote:

Singular!

I'm
overwhelmed
as single parent
the pressure
always rising:
  ("Mommy,"
    nineteen times an hour
  "I'm hungry!"
    six times three times a day
  "Where's my sox?"
  "He hit me!"
  "She started it!"
    and so it comes. . .)
and I wonder
if or even when
that nightmare
will stop neighing
thru
my silence?

Surely, communicating this poem to a new student, suggesting that one has empathy for a life situation, helps the student to risk, just as in a traditional program being able to converse intelligently about a potential political scientist's interest in the philosophy of Plato or Walter Lippmann might effect a common starting point.

Nor was it difficult to use the following as a touchstone for assisting a student from rhetoric to risk; I called it "Whose Routing?"

  "Actually," he wrote,
  "I'm more sure
  of direction
  than destination,"
  thus laid on a line
  my own
    estimation. . .

Actually, in evaluating the possibility of a graduate student's movement from rhetoric to risk, at least in the preliminary stages when I am listening or reading an application, I find so often that the student hoists himself with his own petard. Having been conditioned by parents and teachers to seek perfection during sixteen to twenty years of education, he continues to expect that graduate school will demand it. He often casts himself in the role of underdog, while at the same time declaring his belief in his power to do successful graduate work. After running into several cases of this kind one evening, I couldn't resist two grooks which I captioned "Touches":

To aim for perfection	He tackled Russell
a tragic flaw	iconoclastic
search for a weakness	discovered a self
accept it raw.	so dully plastic.

AT ENTRY

So the student embarks upon an open-ended, university without walls–type of graduate program, what then?

While it is impossible to describe every situation without writing a kind of *Ulysses* for each student, a few generalizations can be made:

- It's a long step from those learning situations or matrices in which a faculty determines the curriculum to those in which the student shapes the substance of his or her own program, albeit in the context of institutional process requirements.
- It's perceived as a calculated risk to believe that one does have the power to shape that program as well as to participate in the shaping of a committee on which he or she will serve as a chairperson and use as a cooperative and coordinating group to further his or her own learning.
- At a UGS colloquium (and it is no doubt true of the starting moments in other programs), students find it mind-blowing to realize that persons from outside their perceived field of interest can often contribute more to their learning than persons inside their field (student or professor) may have contributed in the past.
- Also, it is a shock to realize that student peers are credible teachers.

- Furthermore, anxiety over these new learning *sets* is a block to hearing and seeing.
- However, feelings do count; learning is not exclusively cognitive, as most higher education has come to be expected.

Varieties and Vagaries

I am unaware of any certain formula for guaranteeing movements through and past any of these problems of credibility, anxiety, hang-ups—call them what one may. While there is a fantastic variety of educational philosophies, psychologies, and methodologies, programs that emphasize self-direction must, it seems, recognize a nearly infinite number of approaches. Furthermore, it would be a paradox if not a downright hoax to entice a person into a program on the ground that the person must be self-directed only to prescribe a precise course of action. We come dangerously close to the paradox, though not the hoax, in the Union Graduate School when we set out a process route; however, we do allow an almost infinite latitude of substantive variation. This is an important question when we discuss issues pivoting around concepts of excellence (see Chapter 6).

Since the founding of UGS, we have used a great variety of beginnings to help students *past* the rhetoric *into* the risking (and notice the paradox of "helping"). In some of our earlier colloquia we broke the thirty students into three groups by using an alphabetical or birthday system of sectioning (random) groups working on a process called Understanding Self and Others (USO). Since some members of our core faculty were veterans of National Training Laboratory (NTL) experiences, they were aware of the variety of encounter, sensitivity, and learning-living methods for enhancing self-disclosure, interpersonal communication, and sharing designed to help students across the thresholds of their concerns. But the very division of the group in this manner only increased the anxiety of some members of the colloquium and reduced the credibility of our catalogue statements about self-direction. Furthermore, although faculty conveners of the groups assured persons that attendance was not compulsory, social pressure and individual guilt often complicated matters. Since I did not possess my colleagues' experience in NTL techniques, I often was the ear for those students who preferred not to participate in USO activities but needed some place to go. Hence a new group evolved!

Over the years we have modified these opening moments (hours, days, weeks) of a colloquium in the direction of more open-ended group sessions where rapping is more normative than encounter—though encounter often occurs over racial, sexual, international, ideological, and social change issues, to name but a few. We have learned, too, that as faculty we must be patient in repeatedly outlining the nature of our expectations that *they*, the students, are in charge of their learning. Although we will make presentations (seminars, lectures) on various topics at their request, *they* must request them after they understand some of our specialties and interests. We feel that our only major obligation is to be open in presenting who we are so that students can utilize or reject our assistance as they see fit. Likewise, since we are in the process of weaving them into a network that includes adjunct professors and peers, we feel that all adjuncts or peers present are obliged to say who they are so that others may decide whether or not to use their services.

After a week or so of autobiography, students then know whether or not they wish to join others of similar views or concerns about certain issues. Hence they may form special interest groups. Sometimes it happens, sometimes it doesn't. Students often find it easier to risk their ideas and their feelings around topics such as Marxist theory or change in higher education than to join a yoga group, a meditation group, or a session on advanced group dynamics.

In many ways a UGS colloquium is a four-week marathon. Fatigue both increases and decreases anxiety, both slows and speeds a student's willingness to risk. By the end of the first week a student realizes that many high-powered people, who have had worlds of experience and might—and certainly could—chop them down, are present. But the conveners of the colloquia usually make it clear that any student can include or exclude people from any given session. In fact, if a student wants a warmup or trial session before the "main event," that's fine, too. After all, if a student is going to be chairperson of his learning, he should set his own parameters. Yet, even old-timers will admit that this step is easier to affirm than to take. After all, risk is risky. And every student knows that every program has the proper rites of passage that must be observed. It is not easy to accept the notion that the student himself *is* that passage. It is not easy to accept the simple *is*.

UGS PROCESSES AND CURRICULUM PROCEDURES

There is more to any self-directed program than facing one's own public transparency or testing one's views against the backdrop of friendly peers and faculty. We in UGS, for instance, can say, "You, the student, *are* the institution" or "Here we are, gathered together in a colloquium; hence the UGS is now in session." Nevertheless, in a society where institutions usually mean mortar, libraries, and stadiums, it is not easy to accept this "floating crap game" as an institution. So, we accept this reality. Legally, we are a division of a corporation; spatially, we have an office headquarters; operationally, we do have some process requirements. Hence, it ill behooves any student to leave a colloquium without assurances that those givens relate to his or her life. And, as discussed in more detail at a later point (see Chapter 11), we must learn to deal together with the paradoxes in and around those seemingly conflicting realities.

A student must pass through various steps within a time framework (see Chapter 1 and Figure 2.1). The student is admitted, attends a colloquium, builds a six-person committee with himself as chairperson, spends no less than six months evolving a program in

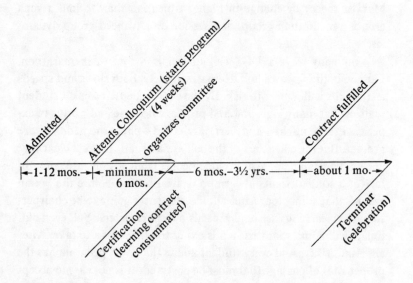

Figure 2.1.

conjunction with the committee, holds a certification session (entering into candidacy) to hammer out a learning contract, fulfills the learning contract in no more than three and one-half years (though extensions may be granted), and holds a terminar or celebration that constitutes graduation. Easy to understand? Yes. Easy to accept and implement? Maybe yes, maybe no.

SO THERE ARE QUESTIONS, RISKY ONES

"How do I find the right peers for my committee?"

The answer is simple: look around you at a colloquium. Becoming acquainted with persons in some depth should tell you who you want. You need two.

"And what if I don't find them here?"
"The core faculty should be able to help you. They know other UGS students who are doing what, where, when."

The shaping begins as students begin to gain a sense of trust in other peers and in their own competence to choose persons who will help them with their own learning. We recommend that their committee consist of persons who will provide constructive criticism, persons who may not reflect too much sameness—no wives, uncles, husbands, mothers, fathers, etc., unless they want to serve as consultants; after all, the politics of institutional survival precludes nepotism.

So the questions continue.

"And what if I choose somebody who turns out to be destructive or unsupportive of my program?"
"Easy. You always have the right to fire anybody, including the core faculty, from your committee."
"Isn't firing committee members risky?"
"Yes, but there are rules of thumb for doing it."

Does it seem too good to be true? credible? incredible? Frowns and scowls and reiteration of the questions suggest that it is not easy to select peers.

And it is not all that easy to choose adjunct professors.

Every external degree program employs specialists. They serve as a kind of intellectual anchor, giving a student's program both integrity and credibility. A student may test his or her knowledge, wisdom, skill, hunches, artistic achievements, whatever, via the knowledge, wisdom, and skill of such specialists. One such resource in UGS is the adjunct professor.

So, how does a student obtain the two adjuncts and engage them in the process? We have evolved two or three ways. He may:

- Choose adjuncts from a basic public list of persons who have agreed to serve in this role to enhance a person's learning; in this instance, we as an institution have seen the adjuncts' vitae or talked with them or recognize the persons in their respective fields or disciplines; by now, of course, we have worked with a large number of such persons and know there is mutual trust in the process.

- Or by utilizing those persons who have agreed to serve as adjuncts but who do not wish to appear on a public list for fear of being overwhelmed by requests. (In fact, some were, until we made the distinction as a matter of convenience to those persons.)

- Or by nominating a person or persons with whom the student wishes to work, a person who normally holds a doctoral degree or has achieved distinction in his or her field.[8]

Naturally, this phenomenon raises in the student's mind a host of questions that often require long explanations: How can I be sure that a new adjunct will adapt to this free-form process, quite beyond the confines of classroom, courses, points, credits, and hours? Can I be sure of competence, despite external credentials? Who pays the adjuncts? How do I communicate what their role will be? How much time should they be prepared to spend? Won't they be threatened by the fact that the student is chairperson of her own committee? Do they feel a conflict of interest, especially if they are members of a graduate faculty with a doctoral program? What access is there to the Union institutions?

These and many more questions become the central concerns of students who must approach the involvement of specialists on somewhat equitable terms rather than choosing them as authority figures or because the specialists are offering a course in which the student enrolls through some impersonal registration process. Hence, there's lots of risk here! The tone and number of the questions are frequently more important than their content.

In brief, naturally it is *safer* to approach somebody on the established adjunct list because the basic spade work has been done. Naturally it is safer to choose a person who has already had experience in external degree programs rather than those who may be serving for the first time. And, of course, the recommendation of a core faculty member or a graduate of an adjunct's previous performance is often treated as hard data on which to base a decision. We indicate that students do not have an automatic "open sesame" to Union institutions because any approach to a faculty member must be a negotiated one. Also, during the colloquia we indicate what roles an adjunct might serve. We also suggest some "no-no's"; to wit, don't ask

- your therapist
- your boss
- your relatives
- your colleagues, beyond *one* at the very most
- members of your institution, beyond *one* at the very most

Some other guidelines or criteria also are designed to ease student anxiety yet enable them to consider what they have done after they leave the colloquium. We recommend that they ask these questions:

- How do you feel about the people on your committee? Did you pick the persons because you liked them? Can you accept them intellectually?
- Can you be involved with them in open give-and-take?
- Can you, as negotiator, involve yourself and them in the mutual decision making that is necessary if one is to optimize their use?
- Can you give your committee members the freedom to learn with you and vice versa? let them *be* who they are?[9]

The issue of money can be sticky if students don't face up to it. We have developed guidelines galore to assist the student in determining a fair honorarium for service, yet students have had so little experience in coping with this issue that in some instances they complete a program without ever facing it *as an issue* integrally related to determining a total learning matrix. Naturally, it also deals with the ethics of paying a man or woman who is to serve as their collaborator, evaluator, and degree-grantor. Yet, with the tuition money available for such payment and with the normal honorarium of $200 to $300 per total program for persons serving on such committees, it is difficult to see why any person willing to serve would perceive payment as a bribe! Some of the persons who serve on external degree committees in UGS and similar programs make more from one public lecture or appearance than the student's total tuition per year! Furthermore, you can't even pay some persons to serve if they really want to!

Thus we've thrashed this issue through in a dozen ways. In recent times we've given students the option of choosing a fixed amount to offer an adjunct, then working out the arrangement in a contractual mode. As I perceive it, only time will tell whether or not this is a "cop out." But it is a way, nevertheless, of reducing both anxiety and risking.[10]

THE CONTROVERSIAL ISSUE OF CORE FACULTY

Regardless of the university without walls program, undergraduate or graduate, students usually perceive faculty members as the key people in the institution; after all, tuition pays them. And in some instances, of course, they do have exclusive power or considerably more power than others in the degree-granting process. Elsewhere I have described in some detail what a core faculty member *does* (see Chapters 3 and 8). It is true that in many ways the core does have more power than other members of a student's committee; after all, a core member participates in admissions, convenes colloquia, links new students and adjuncts with old, and is a conveyor of the institution's life history wherever necessary. This member also serves as a kind of checkpoint for approving or rejecting prospective adjuncts. The core member also participates in a variety of policy and administrative decisions.

Therefore a student may rightly ask, "Aren't you caught in a contradiction by saying that I am chairperson of my committee, yet putting a lot of power in the hands of the core?" The answer, like the answers to most complex questions, is both yes and no. If the system works, that is, if it helps the student adapt to the process, then the core's major task may be that of staying out of the student's way. However, if the student runs into trouble by failing to follow institutionally prescribed procedures, encounters personality or academic difficulty with particular members of a committee, or does not live up to expectations of any or all members of his committee, then the core as "keeper of the process" must step into such sticky situations to cut the Gordian knot. The recommendation of the core is important if the student asks for waivers on some procedures (for instance, wanting three adjuncts and one peer in the event of difficult geographical logistics or asking to extend tenure beyond the four-year limitation). In addition, our Student Progress Assessment, discussed in the context of excellence (see Chapter 6), assumes that the core is in a better position than any member of a student's committee to question the student's progress, the kind of issue that could lead to dismissal from the program.

But the risk questions, however importantly related to power, also relate to a variety of other learning questions. Students rightly ask, Will the core really respond to my letters or phone calls? Is the core flexible, open to my changing self-concept? Can the core move beyond personal ideology to let me learn and grow? Is the core, closer to UGS procedures than other members of my committee, likely to give with one hand and take away with the other if "push comes to shove"? Is the core concerned enough with *my* learning to have time for me, if I ask for it, or am I competing with other interests and activities for attention?

Furthermore, as I point out in Chapter 5 (organizational development), UGS, like most evolving institutions, has suffered a shortage of personnel. Hemmed in by the need to aim for a thirty-to-one ratio of students to core faculty and thwarted by student demands for more minority persons and women on the faculty, we have not always had core available at colloquia where the student supposedly has the opportunity to choose among a variety of people who might meet individual needs. In a couple of instances such shortages have not only intensified anxiety and increased the perception of risk for individuals but also have come close to creating group paralysis. When we are able to extend a student's vision past the limited time frame of a colloquium, then the more precise nature of the risk can be faced. If that becomes impossible, as it has in a few instances, those students sometimes drop out for lack of certainty.

As ideological identifications among faculty toward feminism and minority empathy became more clearly defined, one important vision of the program was modified somewhat; namely, any core might serve any student, regardless of the student's field, race, creed, sex, or clan. While we may not have reinvented Behemoth University, with all its organizational paraphernalia, we have taken a giant step in that direction in succumbing to the pressure to find people who represent ideological and minority positions. As a humanist and a critic of doctrinaire notions of representation, I hope that it is only a matter of time before there is a willingness to discuss openly the pros and cons of this issue. Naturally, a difference of opinion among the core is often cued publicly. In other words, the attempt is made *to increase* the sense of risk, and some students do all they can to stay out of harm's way. On the other hand, those students who feel more comfortable with a person of their own race, creed, or sex may both gain and lose learning opportunities and growing potential by choosing only these kinds of people.

LEARNING IN MID-FLOW

Risking, of course, does not begin and end at the initial session of any external degree program. Learning in any university without walls context is fraught with both adventure and danger. In short, the variables are infinitely larger in number and complexity than in traditional higher education with classes to attend, hours to fulfill, professors' lectures to digest, library methods to master, and exams to take. I am not attempting to make an invidious distinction between the two processes but simply to say that they are different. They may work equally well for two different persons, if such a comparison can ever be made.

Following the UGS colloquium, students often have considerable difficulty selecting a committee and establishing an acceptable system for communications frequent enough to make all members of the committee comfortable with progress. And there are some new shoals to navigate, shoals suggested by specific illustrations:

- A man, an educational administrator, discovers that he so much enjoys writing the history of his own learning experiences that his original purposes, as outlined in the colloquium, are altered in midcourse; so he asks, "What will my committee think? And if they do go along with my revised contract, will I continue to feel bad about feeling good? Is it really learning at the graduate level to tie my own growth over twenty years to the problems which I face as an administrator?"

- Another man, in charge of Black Studies at a major university, comes to a certification session somewhat anxious because he thinks that his committee has a particular expectation about the form of his Project Demonstrating Excellence; he is relieved when we encourage him to share the insights of his research and life experience in poetic rather than prose form—if that's what he wishes to do.
- A woman therapist brings to a certification session a friendly male colleague who explains his presence by claiming, "I came to protect Maryllyn from those on this committee who would not support her program!"
- Another woman, deeply embroiled in complex family separation and divorce hassles, digs herself a deep hole of guilt and proceeds to hide in it for all too many months during her tenure.

These are only tiny peepholes into the landscape of human changing as students attempt to move from one learning style to another. And persons in UGS often have difficulty believing that the institution supports that personal movement, frequently referring to their own disbelief in conventional terms:

- "I keep waiting for the other shoe to drop."
- "I kept feeling guilty because I was not studying every day."
- "I had to live through the experience to believe it, no matter what was said at the colloquium."

It is difficult to deal with the anxiety, the credibility syndrome, the self-verifying process itself. Although students in UGS and other external degree programs are more mature by chronological and work experience standards, nevertheless, in a society that conditions us to follow others' rules, it is *not* easy to accept and internalize new tricks even if one understands them. Since our university without walls students more often than not continue their jobs and their lifestyles, the context in which they live those lives normally is similar both before and after they enter such a program. Hence, as UGS students frequently remark, the social gestalt in which they are immersed is often diametrically opposed to that which we encourage.

Some real examples:

- A university system requiring the Ph.D. for academic tenure downgrades that instructor enrolled in UGS who would question the tenure system as a viable route to human creativity.
- A therapist enrolled in UGS embarks on a new therapy system and encounters opposition from colleagues and every professional force imaginable.
- A man developing a new discipline confronts countless obstructions whether he needs human resources (adjuncts) or access to information (diverse library materials).

While it is true that many dissenters and rugged individualists find joy in confronting opponents—in fact, may gain sustenance from such opposition—this is far from universal.

I am not speaking as a clinician when I discuss anxiety, depression, elation, and other similar emotions. While I have done an enormous amount of thinking about relationships between a variety of therapies and learning processes, I do not presume to say that learning is *necessarily* therapeutic or that therapy is educational. I know of specific instances, however, where individual students have claimed emphatically that working through a particular learning pattern, objective, or set of problems, was more therapeutic than therapy itself. There is an enormous amount of evidence in the UGS files dealing with the relationships between these two phenomena. Psychological literature is filled with data relating this phenomenon to self-acceptance.[11] An interesting research project that some enterprising person may wish to undertake in a variety of external degree contexts is the application of concepts of self-acceptance to what I have called moving from rhetoric to risk.

CLIMATE FOR PRACTICUM

The question of student anticipation, expectation, and risking, the question of learning and therapy, and the matter of social matrix in which a given student carries out an external degree program also relates to UGS goals. For instance, we require each student to develop an internship or practicum as an integral part of a total learning program (which also includes a learning strategy and a Project Demonstrating Excellence). We set wide parameters for determining just what an internship might be; namely,

- use of the medical model of residency or interning
- the mentor and/or apprentice model (a poet working with a poet, a clinician with a clinician, etc.)
- working in two or more fields to test one's capacities, interests, and expectancies
- redefinition of current profession/occupation

Our greatest task is encouraging some students to reevaluate their jobs or even convert some fantasy into reality in light of their learning objectives and long-range professional goals. The temptation to conduct "business as usual" is ever-present. Yet, the fact that work-study programs have evolved in an almost bewildering variety during the past couple of decades does make it much easier to integrate the practicum with a total learning program at the graduate level for *all* occupations, not merely medicine and education. Hence, it is more credible to *expect* a student to wade into deeper water to test her ability to swim under entirely new circumstances. Here, however, a student's committee, at UGS at least, must often probe repeatedly to get that student who uses her job as an internship to find new ground from which to see that job or encourage the student to put enough pressure on her supervisors to give her the space to see that job from a new angle. Naturally, this sometimes means that the student may jeopardize job security, unless her boss is empathetic to these changes. By starting with the expectancy of evolving new job perspectives, the student may change her tasks so that she may either enhance her organization or see that she should get out!

But no matter how the internship is organized, it may also provide a sturdy bridge across which to travel from one occupation to another. Quite apart from the fact that a degree at any level may be the sine qua non for entering a new occupation, the internship provides the student with an opportunity to risk with a measure of psychological safety! For instance, it gave Walt Kleeman an opportunity to shift from business and economics to education and ergonomics. It enabled Eleanor Smith to move from elementary teaching to university history. It has enabled a large number of persons with a self-image as housewife to enter various occupations. In short, the risk may be translated into adventure. With a larger number of persons seeking means to change careers in midlife and the changing nature of the world almost demanding it, perhaps it is safe to

predict that anxiety overcoming anxiety throug UGS is constructive.[12]

MAKING AND FULFILLING THE CONTRACT

Whatever the external degree program is, a learning contract usually
spells out what the student will do, what the possible consequences
are if he doesn't do it, and what he must do if he later has a change
of mind and wishes to modify it. So much has been written about
this educational tool that it seems unnecessary to describe it in detail. It is an unquestionably excellent device for enabling a student to
develop with peers and faculty a viable route to the achievement of
learning objectives that are both personally relevant and sufficiently
verifiable to fulfill the requirements for institutional survival in a
credentials-oriented society.

Actually, formulating a contract has an anxiety-reducing impact—once it is consummated. It indicates that the student's committee, hence the institution, agrees to see the student through to the
completion of his work. While it does not guarantee success, it does
reduce the prospective hassling. My own advice to students whom I
serve as core in UGS is to share as many steps as possible in the
shaping of plans. I advise them to share both orally and in writing,
so that the certification session (entering candidacy) becomes an opportunity to discuss a tentative contract around the three major
components of a program; namely, Learning Strategy, Internship,
and Project Demonstrating Excellence (PDE). With adequate preparation of one or two tentative learning contracts, the certification
session, which might last from one to five hours, becomes an exploration of ways and means by which a student can achieve proposed goals. We then can discover whether or not the student needs
to do any more reading or take additional courses or has devised
adequate methodological means for reaching stated ends (for each of
the three components).

Of course there may be some hassling in and around the negotiating. But certification usually is perceived as a working session for
that human interaction (often members of the committee are meeting for the first time) rather than a court of law to evaluate knowledge and competence alone before passing on to the next stage. Certainly, not all students pass this stage of their work without anxiety
or risky feelings; for that matter, students do not pass automatically.

But it ill behooves any committee to encourage a student to attempt certification without adequate preparation. Hence, when the certification is worked out with skill by both student and committee, it is a most exciting and insightful meeting. Frequently, the committee finds it impossible to sign the contract without amending it, but this is usually done quickly, easily, and painlessly. And it does provide the student with a certain stabilizing guarantee: a stage is passed *formally*. In view of the fact that the student is not, as in traditional programs, taking courses that are recorded in a registrar's office term after term, she needs and deserves such a guarantee. It also illustrates my contention that these kinds of programs are *derivative*, whereas more traditional ones are *arrivative*. In a more traditional program, the student eventually *arrives* at the point where she has fulfilled somebody else's statement of substantive requirements, but universities without walls ask that the student *derive* her own program.

SOME STICKY PROBLEMS

But all is not necessarily settled after the contract is approved. If a student is slow to execute his program, he may have a sharp turn of mind requiring a new contract and perhaps a new committee to help him write and execute it. Sometimes committees fall apart because of death, geographical relocation, or change of heart. Sometimes perceptions of excellence among the committee differ so dramatically that a student, as in traditional programs, finds it difficult to hammer out consensus among peers, adjuncts, and core. Sometimes, at the very end there is a split vote. Sometimes a student simply cannot learn to feel good about what he has done, no matter how excellent, and converts the terminar from the celebration it ought to be into a masochistic rite. So much depends upon the evolution of a student's self-concept. Some persons, of course, especially those with an exaggerated expectation of self-perfection, may never bury their hangups. For others, the psychology of inertia becomes the momentum of guilt, and their procrastination almost precludes finishing (and some never do). Also, if it becomes difficult for a student to develop "a willing suspension of disbelief" about the credibility of his work, then he may continue to wait for the impending disaster rather than act to fulfill the contract.

FRIEND AS PARAMETER

Another interesting problem in free-form education sometimes evolves often enough to warrant thorough study; namely perfect strangers, adjuncts, peers, core (called field faculty and the like in programs other than UGS) often do become friends! And this, of course, raises some exquisitely imaginative horrors: a student may ask, "Will my friends really tell me what they are thinking about my work? Will they level? Should I keep them on my committee if they become my friends? Is that consistent with the objective evaluation supposedly characterizing graduate work? Or, if my friend criticizes my work, does he like me anymore?" An adjunct may ask, "Since this situation is not like that in which I normally work, is it OK? Am I tough-minded enough (usually a male question)? Is it alright to assume three or four roles rather than the usual one of teacher? Should I be affected by the student's affective life?" And a core may rightly ask, especially as she is becoming accustomed to these processes, "How much should I lead, and how much should I follow? Am I creating unhealthy dependency relationships? Does the student really want me to know her family or is she merely being polite?"

Such questions only begin to suggest the dimension of interaction between student and committee which is a new and perhaps somewhat uncomfortable situation. At the close of at least three students' programs in which I've been involved, one adjunct has remarked, "I began as a teacher and became a friend, and I wasn't sure that I should!" The implication of this remark is profound: imagine a society in which it is uncomfortable or downright dangerous for a teacher to be a student's friend!

While I do not condone back-scratching, nepotism, bribery, and the thousand other frailties to which humans are heir, I do contend that programs such as UGS offer a unique opportunity for persons to test the proposition that friends may be both horizons and walls, for even in universities without walls there are many walls. If learning is to be humanized, then one must work with *persons*—and we certainly know enough about routinized, bureaucratized, and indifferent learning situations to know what it is we do *not* want.

A CRITICAL PRIVACY FACTOR

The trust in self and trust in committee that facilitates a personal exploration of new fields of knowledge, new relationships between feeling and understanding and new skills, a willingness perhaps even to surrender, depends heavily upon self-exploration. Hence, evolution of that private self, as I suggest in Chapter 4, becomes critical. Whether one chooses to develop a methodology that includes a log, therapy, or group discussion to effect self-verification will, of course, depend upon the individual and what works for him. But somehow or other a student must convey to a committee, which does have to affirm him in a practical sense, that it is permissible to be private about some aspects of learning. That is why, perhaps, one of the key tasks of committee members is that of developing "the courage to [let] be."[13] This does not mean an "anything goes" syndrome. Rather, the trust relationship must include a viewpoint fostering rather than discouraging a student's wish to maintain privacy about some aspects of his degree work. No easy paradox to resolve!

One technique that helps is encouraging a student to develop a log or journal and then to share all or part of it with some one member of the committee as a kind of evidence-verifier. A log often affords the student the courage to be himself and enables him to deal with questions of self-acceptance and coping. It may also give him the opportunity to deal with concepts he has never heard of before, paradoxes previously unthought of, and similar new experiences. For instance, most persons need what I call "basic assumptions therapy," a sophisticated concept encountered early in a UGS program. Or a student accustomed to attending highly competitive institutions, as most American schools are, may wish to consider in his log his problem of dealing with a Zen contention that striving is the root of human problems. In short, the authentic committee is that in which members, including the student, are free to respond *as* themselves. No cat-and-mouse games here.

Hence, the committee may not live up to one student's fantasy that it should be a family surrogate; but if loyalties and processes are shaped with some feeling, there ought to be at least one or two members who respect and promote the student's privacy. Privacy is important in the maintenance of official records; students need to know that private areas are indeed private. Or relating the question to the power of committee members, we might assume, as an editor of *Harper's* once observed, that "Power that flows from the bottom up is the most fluid, most responsive and most effective. . . . Our assumption is that the power rippling outward from concerned and active individuals is the power to watch and encourage."[14]

SUMMARY

It is only realistic for any student in any external degree program to calculate his threat index and for all persons involved in these learning arrangements to recognize the ethics of consequences of action or interaction that occurs. Holding as we do that lifetime learning is lifeline learning, we cannot deny the relationship between perception of risk and the real risks involved. And if we would agree with Alan Watts that "we are all the Universe exploring itself," we must encourage that exploration.

Those of us centrally involved in such programs have a special responsibility to recognize that we may succeed most when we afford persons the opportunity to fail by all normal standards—and we may fail cum laude with many persons who successfully complete their work *if* those persons graduate with unchanged self-concepts. In many ways, of course, this is a battle between birth and death if one recognizes the constant process of evolving personality. Also, if we aid forces moving us toward an increasingly predictable institutional structure, especially if we do it deliberately to reduce anxiety, risk, paranoia—call it what you will—we may be undermining the very objectives we wish to achieve. Finally, even if we persist in our vision to achieve alternate routes to A.B., A.M., or Ph.D., in a society where such degrees are not only expected but respected, we must continually question all of those assumptions. Or, as one UGS graduate queried, "Should these be secure places in which to peddle risk?"[15]

May Sarton in her beautiful and insightful *Journal of a Solitude* remarks of her life in a small New Hampshire town, "So much of my life here is precarious," to which I responded in my own log, "But, May, isn't so much of life 'precarious,' period?"[16]

3

The Uses and
Abuses of Faculty

Although it is tempting at this point to discuss the evolution of the Antioch-Putney program and the Union Graduate School, since their organizational development is intrinsically related to fundamental questions about this kind of education, it may be important to resist that logical temptation and move to the function of core faculty. After all, the core, (facilitator, field faculty, etc.) serves a pivotal role, regardless of the university without walls program. He serves more vitally as a "connector" to the institution than any other person, even in a committee of equals where the student serves as his own chairperson. There is at once a promise and a danger in that vitality. The promise lies in finding faculty who share the vision of innovative education, are committed to it in some holistic way, and are willing to learn and grow concurrently with their students' learning and growing. The danger lies in being perceived in a one-dimensional role, as authority figure, keeper of the clout, or teacher working in a traditional mode. Regardless of the specifics of UGS, clearly any facilitator of learning must possess unique characteristics or be willing to develop them.

In many ways the roles for such centrally positioned faculty evolve in light of particular institutional needs. In the Nova program, for instance, where specialists carry their knowledge from cluster to cluster, the coordinator of a local group may be little more than a scheduler, leaving much of the decision making on broader issues to the central office. In the Walden program the regional coordinators or deans, working in collaboration with students and academic advisors, serve a unique double role of keeper of process *and* standards. The Goddard field faculty in the master's programs, having to deal with both substance and process of their students' programs, more closely approximate the roles of the UGS core.

Having been one of the parents of the Union Graduate School and having assumed more responsibility for the nurturing and care of program and students during its infancy than any other individual, I have naturally given much attention and thought to the role of the core faculty. After all, I assumed responsibility for serving as coordinator/director as well as core faculty. When we began UGS, we surely were not too clear about the precise role of the faculty. Goodwin Watson and I, serving jointly as core at the first admissions meetings and at the first colloquia, knew we were in charge for evolving processes. We were *there*, our roles were not defined. By the end of the first year of operation, however, there was an enormous amount of pressure to define the core faculty role, a task I attempted during the Fifth Colloquium. Although the role may have changed somewhat, becoming a bit more specialized, my 1971 statement still has much currency. Furthermore, by including it here in its near-original form, we give those interested in institution building an opportunity to make comparisons and contrasts. I called the working paper "The Uses and Abuses of Core Faculty: One Man's View."[1]

As I've heard various people discuss the role of core faculty at various times since UGS started in January 1970, I've suggested, "If you want to know what a core faculty's role is, why not ask one what his/her perception is." Hence it seems appropriate to address that question, clearly realizing, however, that any effort is clearly reductionist and open to amendment or modification in light of subsequent needs, deeds and creeds.

From a meeting at the Sarasota I Colloquium (January 1971) and a core faculty meeting at Yellow Springs in mid-April 1971, evolved a list of possible requirements for core faculty, a list circulated widely among all students for the purpose of determining how students perceived the priorities:

Some Criteria for Core Faculty (not all necessarily applicable to any one person):
- have access to facilities
- be a facilitator of students' programs and plans
- be a member of a minority
- be approachable—ease of establishing relationships with students

- have breadth of experience
- have experience in guidance of doctoral candidates
- complement present core faculty
- be stable personally
- have a Ph.D.
- be tough-minded (have capacity to "inflict pain" if necessary)
- be able to function within our cooperative or ad hoc forms of organization

After moonlighting as a core faculty member during the six-month set-up period, (January–June, 1970), working 8/9 time during 1970–71, and full time since July 1, 1971, I've seen the task evolve into various meaningful patterns including the pattern of patternlessness activity.

Discussed in terms of tasks: we've implemented most of the ideas in the original conceptualization, meaning: writing and modifying admissions processes, developing programmatic processes (study, internships, certification, terminating), evolving colloquia designs and implementation, working on ongoing programmatic support, revising brochures, designing and executing governing processes, etc. In other words, we started with a plan and have been evolving workable blueprints.

Translated into specific activity: carrying on the *admissions process* has meant interviewing students both personally and on the phone, reading more than a thousand applications, meeting every two to four weeks to talk through each person's qualifications in a consensus setting, following up with letters of acceptance and rejection, putting potential students into contact with other UGS students or inviting them to colloquia for interviewing purposes, reviewing frequently our learning processes to help revise application forms, brochures and other "literature" sent to the public, participating in compilation and review of statistics to gain a sense of where we are at any given moment.

Colloquium design has become easier with experience and with the recommendations from each colloquia that as much latitude as possible be given to each new group of colloquists to govern the design. Yet we have given much prethought to each colloquium, first Goodwin, then Goodwin and I, then Goodwin, Betty Pool, and I, then additional core faculty joining the process and assuming responsibility after appropriate brainstorming months ahead of any given session.

Colloquium attending has been both fun and agony. The fun has been the early meeting of the persons behind the names, working with individuals in evolving learning strategies, participating in group sessions to discuss every nameable topic and to consider a vast variety of psychological needs. Each colloquium has become a major mind-blowing experience for me personally; I feel great personal growth; also, great satisfaction in watching individuals verify themselves or give both selves and program credibility by actually living it. Although I've never felt pushed intellectually as hard as one might expect with a group of graduate students, I have felt myself drawing upon my own broad study-reading-thinking experiences (thirty years in process and seven years in crisis). Fortunately blessed with a fairly good Endurance Index, I've enjoyed the round-the-clock kinds of pressures which have made it possible to work with the wide range of human needs.

The agony has been related to being locked into pressures, such as the push for accreditation. The agony has also related to being slugged over the head repeatedly with demands on which I knew there was a particular origin, on which I've known things were happening if only we had time to evolve processes set loose by students in other parts of the system. While at Antioch-Putney, I developed a whimsical motto, "To be of use, you must take abuse," which alongside Jung's observation that 95 percent of perception is projection, has helped me get through some of the stormier periods. I believe so much in humanistic processes and objectives that I've learned some of the patience necessary to cope with my own raw nerves; yet, I've also kept in close touch with my anger; indignation often *does* keep me warm (with apologies to Irving Stone and Michelangelo).[2]

UGS Processes Beyond the Colloquium—Early in our history, all students entering UGS prior to a colloquium were required to have an in-depth discussion (by phone or in person) with a core faculty member. We've occasionally done this recently although our policy is now to start students at a colloquium. At this point in our development, whether during or following a colloquium, a core faculty must be "keeper of the process." Meaning: he or she *must* press students to evolve a committee and keep that committee informed, *must* participate in developing a learning contract between student and committee to outline the salient features of a self-developed program, *must* insure that certification and termination events will be creative, *must* follow up on those events using whatever media are most appropriate for the occasion. Hence Goodwin's perception that a core faculty person must be "tough-minded" and if necessary "inflict pain." (I personally hope [naively?] that rapport between core faculty and individual student will be sufficiently open to preclude inflicting pain.)

As keeper of the processes I perceive the core faculty person as master of a particular discipline, field or interdisciplinary area where he can be of help to a student. But above all he must have a damn good crap detector.[3] He's well advised to have skills with the major analytical methodologies as well as more contemporary process philosophies. I cannot see him as an admirer of ignorance; rather, he'd better know something but not feel the urge to "lay it" on another unless that other wants to explore what he knows. He'd also best know the major learning theories and applications. He'd best know how to listen with fifth and sixth ears.

Consistent with the UGS credo developed during the Saratoga Springs colloquium (June 1971):[4] he'd best have a sense of the major life-death issues besetting the modern world, a sense of the tragic, pathetic and comic. And on the issues of race and sex, surely *major* ones but not the *only* ones: we have moved to gain "representation" of women and ethnic minorities. But I'm not sure that we can leave unquestioned the comfortable generalization and/or assumption that representatives represent, nor that representatives of any given militant minority will *necessarily* recognize the underdog psychology which motivates most men and women . . . the underdog psychology which he may not wish to display in any public way but which may be as painful from his viewpoint as the pain for the visible minority. The perception of being oppressed is hardly the monopoly of any race, creed, sex or clan. Hence, a basic question: can any core faculty member *not* identify with the frontier of any UGS student's pain, need, concern, perception, identify with it as a precondition of establishing rapport, understanding, the evolving of processes, the collaboration which is a prerequisite for learning in such a context as UGS?

Which leads to my own views regarding human need: that one must be sensitive to those on whose committee he or she is serving, as well as ready, willing and able to use whatever means of communication (phone, letter, cassette, dictaphone, etc.) to meet those needs without developing unhealthy dependency-independency relationships. Such an outlook must be more than rhetoric and requires putting one's body where her or his words are; it requires flexibility of viewpoint about *where* UGS is (cf. my three position papers, "Where is Antioch?" "What is Antioch?" and "Why UGS?" and substitute UGS for Antioch in most places).[5]

Being a core faculty person also requires enough personal security to expect and to take criticism, though not *necessarily* insult!

In my judgment it helps rather than hurts if: a core faculty is involved in educational and/or learning and/or community outreaches beyond UGS or his particular environs . . . for, isn't life lived on many frontiers? That is why I'm constantly writing, working on editing of *The Humanist*, lecturing around the country, and promoting various kinds of nonprofit community enterprises quite beyond visibility and merit-badging. Also, it is my own experience, without laying it on any colleague, that I gain energy by "designing" a life of alternating patterns (with degrees of periodicity ranging from seconds to weeks) of activity including haiku, grooks, fables, trail blazing, carpentering, sports score reading, siestas, planned blue-skying and vacationing, laughing, crying (yes, literally), touching, seeking solitude, etc. and some of that "designing" has increasingly been of the order of letting happen what happens and *not* pushing the river.[6]

There's lots more to say and it will eventually come. . . . But until it does, a couple of things, grooks and haiku flashed-off at this colloquium:

Crap detecting
five ought six
god, we need it!
in our mix.

How cope with paradox
in these our years
mix all the irony
with bitter tears?

If you think of energy
in terms of pie
you'll not do enuf
to struggle with why.

Afternoon shadows
light thru green leaves
    and brown stems
delicate rhythms.

Bright sun on grey wood
weatherworthy redwood tree
a bench for joying.

A MODIFIED VIEW

Although we persistently and systematically shared this statement on the "uses and abuses of core faculty" with every student entering UGS, new students still asked, "What does a core faculty really do?" So, almost two years later, while in the middle of another colloquium, I tried again. This time it seemed more appropriate to be more impressionistic, even existential, than analytical.

What a Core Faculty Does

He/she. . .

spends half a lifetime getting to the point where he/she dares take on such a formidable task . . . participates in admissions processes . . . interviews prospective students . . . listens carefully, at many levels, to detect the differences between anxiety and meaning, rhetoric and risk (even in his/her own life) . . . remains accessible to assist in as many ways as possible, that is, assist, facilitate, teach, learn, support . . . and distinguishes between supporting and nonsupporting, dependency and independency . . . goes to colloquia . . . consults in spare time, lectures in spare time, or whatever . . . takes recommendations of books to read, TV programs to watch, issues to consider, takes them from students (colearners) seriously . . . writes letters, makes cassettes and video, places phone calls on behalf of UGS students . . . reads stacks of letters, listens to tapes, watches movies and video with students to compare perceptions . . . is sometimes father/mother confessor even while being called "motherfucker" (a sexless term) . . . reads a book to retain some semblance of academic sharpness, reads lots of books and other materials to assist a particular student . . . reads a specific book as a result of a specific request of a student in order to gain a vantage point from which to talk about a point or assist in a paper . . . writes more letters of recommendation, now knowing and working with fewer students, than when working with hundreds in large lecture classes . . . learns how to use the jet bible of plane schedules in order to optimize use of time on the road where it is more costly than at home . . . meets students and adjuncts in planes, at airports, in hotels-motels-inns, at schools, in parks, at zoos, in homes, on wharves, in prisons, in fact: wherever . . . becomes a specialist in third-class hotels in order to optimize use of the UGS dollar.

. . . also resigns self to a certain amount of family separation in order to roam the jetways to support students . . . takes family members to colloquia and learns to set up shop quickly (give me a card table and a typewriter and I'm in business) . . . sits under maple trees, in odd corners, cross-legged on floors, under wild oaks, in swimming pools and oceans, relating . . . participates in the decision-making process, at colloquia, in committees, at governance meetings, in core faculty meetings; in fact, wherever . . . scouts for colloquia sites . . . agonizes when called names, striving to remember Jung's observations about perception being 95 percent projection (Ben Thompson says the percentage is often too small!) . . . agonizes when new colloquists disregard the fact that there have been many UGS students who have worked on similar problems before . . . ecstasizes when new colloquists *face* issues which have been faced before . . . writes poetry or suggests that one "carry an unfinished poem in pocket" . . . talks too much . . . talks just enuf . . . talks too little . . . "makes time" even where there is none . . . struggles to derive new dimensions of personal time and rhythm . . . dreams, both figuratively and literally, of new perceptions of space-time-psyche . . . works on social change

projects, encourages such projects . . . learns to distinguish between heresy and conspiracy in participating in a variety of
UGS institutional projects and UGS student projects . . . helps
students educate adjunct professors . . . helps educate adjunct
professors . . . delights in seeing a student develop his/her own
processes and really become the chairperson of his/her own
committee . . . battles the fatigue of some 25-hour days . . .
keeps the sensitivity of keeping blue-skying as a necessity (. . . a
drop-out journey of 45 seconds, or a day or a week) . . . learns
new rhythms in contrast with the MWTF, 10, 11 class attendance rhythms . . . strives to retain the vision of UGS as a
genuine alternative in graduate education . . . works for col-
leaguiality as a second observer-reader-listener core consultant
. . . focusing on a critical task, that of being "keeper of the process" while retaining flexibility, sense of humor and cosmic,
social and personal perspective. . . . (It ain't easy!)

FROM ROLE TO PHENOMENOLOGY

It is my contention, to state it most bluntly, that faculty members in
external degree programs paint themselves into *a particular role* . . .
at their peril but, more importantly, at the student's peril.

Faculty, facilitators—again, call them what you will—in programs like UGS are *not* teachers in any traditional sense. They do
not lecture in a classroom context or give and grade exams and papers in anything vaguely resembling traditional modes. And they are
not counselors in the normal sense of that description. While they
must be sensitive to another person's need for counseling, either
academic or personal, they assume the role of counselor at the peril
of creating dependency relationships that are inconsistent with self-
directed learning. They are not academic administrators, even
though they have to process papers that normally might be handled
by a specialist in the bursar's, registrar's, or admissions offices.
Rather, they must perform a variety of functions at a variety of times
and places. And it may be virtually impossible to *know* in any definitive sense what role one may be expected to assume next. This is why
it is often so difficult for a person trained in traditional graduate
programs or for a person who has taught in traditional modes to
move into this new set. The phenomenon almost defies definition,
and it may be easier to say what the faculty roles are *not* than to say

what they *are*. Sometimes a core wakes up in the morning with a set of objectives or tasks for the day but goes to bed that night without having achieved them because it has been necessary to move quickly in some emergency situation that consumes every skill he has.

It is my own view that persons serving in external degree programs serve themselves and their students best when they avoid self-definition in role terms, for instance, saying "Now I am a teacher." or "Now I am a counselor." or "Now I am an administrator." Also, in reflecting upon a given day's activity, articulating any of these roles in the past tense, "I was a teacher today," etc. is equally self-defeating—for self and for students. Rather, if one can see him or herself as *person* doing a variety of things—thinking, feeling, knowing, serving, sharing, caring, relating, always stressing the ongoing process—then he or she has a better opportunity to survive and be healthily helpful while working with students who, incidentally, might best be perceived as colearners or colleagues in the learning process. In short, there is need to move from self-perception as assuming a role or roles to awareness of the phenomenological situation(s) in which one is involved.

THE PROBLEM, HOWEVER...

There are many difficulties with this, of course. The faculty often has as much difficulty as students in moving from rhetoric to risk, especially if one has been *the* professor or *the* counselor or *the* administrator in conventional educational modes. And the situation depends as much upon *being perceived* as upon self-perception. I learned this the hard way during three or four Peace Corps Training programs in which I was not only making policy and executing it but also serving a judicial role in determining whether or not prospective volunteers should go overseas. *I* knew that I was a good guy! *I* knew whether I was making policy, administering it, or deciding the fate of a volunteer, but the volunteers had difficulty perceiving me as *I* perceived myself. Although they might feel the urge to sit up all night to share a concern with me as sympathetic listener, they were not sure that the information I got in that context would not be used *against* them (the paranoia was deep!) when I donned the robes of judge!

The situation is not too different in external degree programs. Students want clarity about the role of the facilitator because it is a bigger risk *not* to know. Better the awful truth than the horrifying ambiguity from whence, of course, comes the view that maturity in such programs is the ability to tolerate ambiguity. I have come to believe that persons do not belong in external degree programs as faculty unless they are willing to deal with questions pertaining to personal congruency. In specific terms: if a prospective faculty member feels the urge to dispense information about some subject matter field and needs a group of persons to whom to do it in order to maintain self-respect, ego, or status, then she ought to forget joining such an enterprise as a university without walls program at any level.

If a person finds herself saying one thing but being perceived as doing something else, the cues will be perfectly clear in these kinds of educational contexts. And this spells trouble. In fact, those responsible for such open education programs might well develop a series of questions, encouraging both prospective faculty and those already involved to test themselves. From this might come a profile to help with decision making, to wit:

- Am I willing or not to be open and/or transparent about the major details of my life and/or beliefs?
- Do I or do I not say one thing when in fact I believe something else?
- Am I willing or not to face myself when I am criticized or do I "close ranks" in some way that reflects a characteristic defensiveness?
- Do I need some kind of routinized schedule to give order to my life? What is the extent of this need, or lack of it?
- Can I serve multiple roles or even no role at all in a kind of phenomenological sense without being anxious?
- How do I feel when abused or lashed while knowing that such abuse is unjustified?
- What is my Patience Index?
- Can I identify with the frontier of another person's learning objectives and/or personal perspectives for achieving goals?
- What is my ability to tolerate ambiguity?
- Do I have some kind of method for ascertaining what cues I throw off and what I do about it if there is incongruency between my actions at different times and/or my behavior and my verbalizing?
- How many faces do I present to the world?

Too much has been written about personality analysis, behavioral congruence, transparent selves, and the like to require further elaboration here. Also, some of the great literature of the Western world, from Homer to James Joyce to Virginia Woolf and Anais Nin, have dealt in depth with such issues. This is to argue that learning programs such as UGS will surely fail if they are not sensitive to the faculty's developing congruent selves.

For one reason or other I've spent thousands of hours counseling, interacting, and listening to more students than I can imagine. Among their most common complaints: "My professor won't listen or *do* what he *says* he'll do." This is no less true for persons working in experimental programs than traditional. Recently I was talking with a former student about a colleague whom I'd known long, long ago; let us call him John Jones. My friend, the former student, was still livid about his relationship with Jones. "My God!" he exclaimed, "I never knew which Dr. Jones I was dealing with: the ugly, blunt man, the kindly saint, or the brilliant pedagogue!"

I am reminded further of a statement from a small midwestern college, experimental in thrust, in their search for a faculty member. Their prospectus, in part, read:

> We are looking for a "super teacher"—that one person in a thousand that "has it." We must have a person that can show by his own life style that learning may be a joyous experience, and he must be able to communicate this joy to students. This is our one concern. How much you've published or want to publish is irrelevant to us if you are not an outstanding teacher.[7]

It doesn't take a student very long, regardless of his relationship with faculty members, to know whether or not a teacher is excited about what he is doing, conveys joy in working with the student, and believes in what he says.

STRUCTURE AND CERTAINTY

In many ways, of course, it is much easier to be a faculty member in traditional programs. Both students and faculty know the schedule in advance. The professor can, within pretty wide latitudes, determine the substance of the course, and set conditions under which work is done. And in many respects, clearly defined, written requirements are necessary if one is working with hundreds of students. For the first seventeen years in my own teaching life, I was relatively comfortable with syllabi outlining reading assignments, guideline questions, and examination schedules. In many ways the syllabi held the courses together. And if 150 of us came together Monday, Wednesday, and Friday at two o'clock, ostensibly we knew what our common foci were. Hence, this is not to knock that procedure where large numbers of students are involved.

Recently, however, I gained some perspective on the distance I had come in my own beliefs and some of the fundamental problems which students face when a former student sent me a list of classroom policies he received upon assuming a position in a medium-sized midwestern university. The document seems worthy of quotation in total, minus the instructor's name, for those of us working in experimental education often forget the value and the danger in submitting students to such rules:

Attendance and Tardiness: While there are no specific regulations, repeated absence and/or tardiness tends to hinder your progress and may affect your grade. Regardless of your absence, you are responsible for all class assignments and lectures, etc. Reoccurring absences will be reported to the Office of Undergraduate Advisement.

Late Work: Work is accepted late (except for final projects). However, one-half letter grade is deducted per class meeting. For example, an "A" project which is due on Monday but not turned in until Wed. becomes an "A-".

Approval of Work: The instructor must approve *and INITIAL* the final design idea before the finished presentation is begun. Designs which have not been approved will not be accepted.

Assignments: Problem sheets will be handed out at the beginning of each new problem. DO NOT LOSE THESE SHEETS. If you are unable to find your sheet, obtain the instructions from another student.

Tests: NO MAKE-UP TESTS ARE GIVEN UNLESS ARRANGEMENTS ARE MADE PRIOR TO THE TEST DATE. If you are unable to reach me, leave a message with the secretary!

Grading System: Tests and projects carry equal weight unless otherwise specified. All grades are given a number equivalent: "A" equals 12, through "F" equals 1.

The numerical average of all projects	= 70%
The numerical average of all exams	= 20%
The instructor's evaluation	= 10%
Your grade:	=100%

Please feel free to consult with me during my office hours.

By open learning criteria, such regulations as these seem at best puerile and at worst ridiculous. But, of course, the "quest for certainty" goes on. Having no rules whatever can be dangerous, and many innovative programs, including free colleges of the late sixties, founder on those shoals. It is quite another matter to find faculty members drifting toward rules (even process rules) such as those quoted above. Another self-test for faculty involved in university without walls programs is to measure the distance such rule making has come since the beginning of a given program and then ask, "Do I feel comfortable about it?" If the answer leans toward "Yes," push the red light!

Some Generalizations

Faculty moving from traditional programs to innovative ones where the student is expected to be self-directed should:

- be self-directed him/herself or be accused of the Jekyll-Hyde syndrome.
- anticipate pressure toward lifestyle changes and/or attraction toward such changes.
- enjoy the prospects of personal growth, for it is next to impossible to enjoy another's growing self-awareness without finding it contagious.
- weigh "opportunity cost" of such involvement against any neutral or negative prospects, whether spelled in dollars, inconvenience, awkward periods of adjustment, pain, disorientation in space-time psyche.
- recognize that a vast number of competing ideologies and consequent methodologies, as well as world views which co-exist, must be mastered even to be criticized.
- realize that one cannot attract self-directed persons into such

programs without finding every brand of psychological quirk, social fanatic, rugged individualist, in short, a variety of personality types who must at least be heard if they are admitted to the program, whether one wishes to work with them or not.

- learn to pack guilt in mothballs and develop more sophisticated notions of relationships between anxiety, risk, guilt, fear, sorrow, pain, no matter how sophisticated one currently feels.
- look seriously at one's views on humor, irony, and paradox because such attitudes may be part of both the psychology and the politics of survival.

This book taken as a whole in a sense spells out these notions, yet some of them, the last for instance, are discussed later in more depth (see Chapter 11).

SOME PERSONAL BIASES AND PROCEDURES

Interaction between teachers and students where the role of the professor, teacher, advisor, or mentor has a clear history is relatively stylized. And by the time that most students reach college or graduate school, they know the proprieties of that interaction. And even when there is a rapidly changing set of relationships, as for instance in the late sixties and early seventies when it was great sport for youth to put professors and administrators against the wall, interrelationships were probably more predictable on both sides of the classroom desk or seminar table. As my above description, "What a Core Faculty Does," and my views on moving from rhetoric to risk suggest (Chapter 2), so much of the interaction between a faculty person and a student depends upon situation. It is one thing to chart a program requiring two or three years to complete, but it is quite another to deal with compass, tide, and ocean current readings when the student asks whether to zig or zag in trimming the sail in a program in which he ostensibly serves as his own captain! The first time in UGS that a faculty member hears such a request, he may be inclined to ask, "Didn't John have his ears open at the colloquium? or read the brochure? Should we have admitted him? If I respond directly now, does this mean that I am conning myself into further dependency situations? Or does he need a direct answer now so that I can be more indirect next time?" In asking and answering such questions, one may have to deal with one's own patience, one's anger, one's propensity to dispense knowledge, one's tendency to talk rather than listen while the student finds an opportunity to move on to his own devices, or one's reliance upon limited knowledge of the person or the field in which the question is asked. Also, one may have to deal with the paradox of being too close to a student to see him.

Yet one knows that every such question cannot be dealt with in such depth. Usually, there is not that kind of time. Furthermore, to deliberate each such request, even in a program such as UGS where there is tolerance for slow answers, may lead to partial paralysis, as the student waits while the faculty member delves more deeply into the convolutions of her own inability to make up her mind! There's an old saying that if you leave a letter unanswered long enough, it doesn't require an answer. Maybe in external degree programs where correspondence is a major means of communication (though they are *not* correspondence courses), there is perhaps more self-direction on the student's part because instructors are not immediately available to give on-the-spot answers. At least that's a hunch that could be tested by some enterprising empiricist!

Regardless of one's response to a student's questions, faculty members do find themselves living more closely with the consequences than in conventional programs. I've sometimes remarked, "The fewer students I know, the more letters of recommendation I have to write!" College students often discover themselves in a "lonely crowd." Conventional classes, grades, and papers *tend* to create walls between faculty and students. Talk between student and professor tends to be stylized, masked, or so linear that there is little room for lateral thinking and movement, especially if persons are involved with cognitive topics. Such interaction may serve both students and educators very well in mass circumstances.

But returning to the faculty member's response: when the faculty comes to know a student well, knows the student's many sides, lives, dreams, ambitions, family members, and so on, the consequences of an answer seem much more complex. Hence, the faculty member takes risks when committing answers to writing. One person's answer may become another person's code, thereby stifling self-direction. Also, in those programs where both peers and adjuncts serve on a student's committee and a strong human-support network of interacting peers exists, an answer may run like chain lightning through the system. Likewise, a nonanswer. As a result, a faculty member, in UGS at least, had best confront his ability to deal with his own anger, learn what happens if he is naive enough to be conned, deal directly with the guilt he may feel if caught being stupid, know how to cope with blind spots. If one doesn't come to grips with such matters but chooses to set forth in search of scapegoats, then how is he helpful in a program promoting openness and self-direction as a channel toward learning? Nor will "stewing in one's own juice" for any length of time solve much![8]

INTERFACING WITH OTHER CORE, ADJUNCTS, AND THE WORLD

If a student's committee in UGS is to be a learning team and the core is generally perceived as representative of the institution, then, of course, the core has a special responsibility to explain the program or parts of the program process which a student cannot, will not, or has not described. Furthermore, until adjuncts become fully familiar with UGS and are convinced that the process is viable, they often look to the core for credibility. This is one reason, of course, why the core must have doctorates themselves, an issue described below in connection with excellence and credibility.

This, then, throws special responsibility on the core, a responsibility not normally present in traditional structures where a professor is a professor is a professor and a course is a course—of course. How core faculty in UGS or facilitators in other programs cope with the problem of credibility depends upon the person. Quite beyond routine appointment and supplying standard literature, anybody willing to become an adjunct professor is usually interested in the institution as well as the particular student. Hence, in addition to participating in the student's certification and terminar meetings, the core may arrange special meetings with individuals to review a student's program, help the adjunct catch up on such topics as the status of accreditation, or perhaps share a mutual interest for further exploration. An occasional publication is sent to active adjuncts in an effort to engage them in the concerns of the institution as much as possible. In a sense, like all persons engaged in learning activity in UGS, they *are* the institution.

In the beginning, we may have relied too heavily upon students to effect the liaison of adjunct and institution. Working from a dispersion model, with students literally scattered from Nairobi to Niagara and Bangkok to San Juan, the logistics of getting any number of adjuncts together in one place to discuss any issue was virtually impossible. Also, consistent with a philosophy of student self-direction, it seemed especially appropriate that the student should explain to adjuncts the nature of UGS as an institution, the nature of the process, and our fundamental educational assumptions as an organic approach to a learning program. As I will show later in dealing with strengths and weaknesses of the program, the assumption that the student could or would do this may have been a bit fallacious. Sometimes it worked; often it did not; usually, the student and core needed help from peers to effect credibility at an early meeting of the committee. Often the core was pivotal, especially if an adjunct had difficulty with the twin notions that the student was chairperson of her committee but that peers on the committee held coequal responsibility. Putting all of this together in any given committee was no mean achievement; we experienced failures par excellence amid some very enlightened and exquisite successes.

Difficult as it may have been and continues to be for a student to learn how to construct and manage a committee, it is no easier for the core, especially if an adjunct perceives the core as filling the normal committee role as chairperson. Dealing with that perception, of course, is not half as exasperating as finding a student at the end of his work continuing to refer to the core as "the chairperson of my committee!"

Interfacing with other core is a complicated question considered more fully in the context of organizational development. Both students and core have had some difficulty, for instance, dealing with a procedural step added after the program had been in operation for three years, namely, asking a second core to review a student's program and Project Demonstrating Excellence as a consultant to the first core. Although introducing such a step was designed to promote quality assurance and develop collegiality, the second core was not given the power to block a degree. Therefore, gaining acceptance of the procedure as one *not* involving a veto was somewhat difficult, to say the least. Including the veto, whether by core or the traditional external examiner at the end of a program would have, of course, destroyed fundamental concepts of student self-direction, advice, and dissent of the committee as well as trust and confidence in a more open alternative to the doctorate (see Chapter 5).

For the core, interfacing with the world is not so different a prospect than it is for the traditional professor except in a few respects. It certainly takes more explanation if one is asked, "What is your field?" or "What are you doing?" "Aren't you afraid you'll be ripped off?" "How many of your students are castoffs from other programs they can't cut?" And so on, ad infinitum. Also, since we do not measure out our lives in courses, credits, and hours, it is often difficult if not impossible to translate what we do into conventional terms. And, if one encounters a professorial colleague who is so puristic about graduate work or his own field that he can't hear, one is tempted to shrug one's shoulders and leave the ramparts, wondering, "Did he really want to know what I'm doing?"

SUMMARY

One needs the speed of the roadrunner, the courage of the lion, the slyness of the fox, the tenacity of the bulldog, the persistence of the tortoise, and the quickness of the artful dodger in order to serve an open university well. It also helps to have the endurance and the capacity for the loneliness of the long distance runner. If one has the agility and speed of the computer, it also helps! Serving students as a facilitator, knowledge source, friend, and counselor and relating organically to another's learning goals is at once one of the most exciting and the most demanding tasks any human could assume. But the opportunity for tying into creative human networks to achieve personal growth and understanding and a philosophic vision is rare and of infinite potential.

In many columns of *The Humanist* magazine and in *Humanistic Frontiers in American Education* I have discussed ways and means for becoming more humanistic in approaching such tasks.[9] There is no point in repeating those discussions, but it is my conviction that persons working in these capacities may fulfill their potential as well as profound student needs by moving toward openness, toward fallibility, toward ambiguity, toward spontaneity, and so on. Those who catch *that* vision surely will have little difficulty communicating the joy of living which the small midwestern college was asking for in its quest for the "super teacher."

4 Writing: Spontaneity and Growth

Do we know enough about the quantity and quality of learning that results when persons log their experiences? Though we may be aware that learning occurs, do we usually know how the writer perceives it as learning? Probably only a few learners are aware of the personal value of writing processes or are sufficiently self-aware to build on the fundamental insights a log can provide. In spite of my own experience, I cannot predict precisely what I will learn when I begin to write a paragraph or deliver a lecture, but I have gained enough knowledge from the process to have confidence in the very *act* of sitting down at my typewriter or standing before an audience.

Being ready and open for that learning moment perhaps makes the listening more acute; I remember a vivid moment in a class on American political thought in the spring of 1964 when we were discussing Walter Lippmann's *Public Philosophy* as related to Woodrow Wilson's thought. In an unpremeditated way, I asked, "Are we today perhaps fighting to make the world safe for hypocrisy?" The students laughed, and for a split second I wasn't quite sure what I had said. Such experiences have made me increasingly suspicious of the well-prepared extemporaneous speech! And although I do not consider myself anti-intellectual, I can resonate with the view expressed in Robert Persig's *Zen and the Art of Motorcycle Maintenance* when he speaks of "the ghost of rationality."[1] In short, one plays the rational script with a certain kind of peril and, of course, vice versa!

Many authors have asserted that one learns to write *by writing*. But more importantly, I think, a person also gains insights about the self. This contention raises many questions; for instance: Is the process merely developmental, falling into some Skinnerian, Piagetian, or Kolbergian pattern?[2] Is it kinesthetic, effecting a release from some muscular or mental blockage? May it be derived therapeutically, somehow or other related to ploughing into or even playfully exploring the unconscious? Is learning, therefore, therapy or vice versa? And how much relates to self-constructed, personal-identity mythologies that reinforce societal ones—or vice versa—or something in between? Is the logging of experience, dreams, or whatever more like a dialogue with the self, hence effecting a kind of psychological dialectic that sharpens issues, resolves conflict, clarifies thought-action involvement in the world? These and many more questions should concern all colearners, students, and faculty in such educational enterprises as are discussed here.

I do *not* wish to address each of these discrete questions; rather, I want to raise a host of issues, share a hunch or two, and discuss some tentative views on the phenomenon of using such interaction devices to enhance learning, growth, and creativity.

In the fall of 1969 during a conference with an Antioch-Putney student, Johanna Halbeisen, we fell into a discussion about logging experiences. She shared some of her undergraduate experiences, indicating how fortunate she felt to have been required to keep a log of her learning processes. Before long we were both talking excitedly about our views on logs and were so enthusiastic about sharing our views that I suddenly said, "Hey! Johanna, let's write a duologue and share it at the conference we're having next month down in the Ohio hills!" It was a kind of "Ah-ha" response, and we rushed along on the momentum of our mutual enthusiasm. We agreed to compile a collage of our insights; I would write the first paragraph, she would write the last. We would write an equal number of paragraphs and simply splice them together, my first, her first, my second, her second, etc. to the end. And that we did! The result seems worthy of including here since we in Antioch and Union Graduate Schools have used it widely with essentially constructive results. Also, graduates of these programs, as well as those in other free-form programs in both secondary and higher education, also have tried it. Although set at a particular moment of time, the concepts are obviously undated.[3]

A Duologue

R. Once upon a time, 1965 in fact, during the neolithic era of the Antioch-Putney Graduate School, log writing was required of all
Antioch-Putney students. We said, "We don't particularly care
what you say, how you say it, what form it's in, but just write.
Naturally, you can turn in what you wish. We have just one requirement: you must share it with one member of the faculty, and if
it is to be entirely confidential you should write on the cover of it:
"Not to be seen by anybody but *So & So*." That was six academic
years ago. Now, log-keeping is optional, but it is my contention that
it's a valuable way to learn. In fact,

> There's somethin' about a log
> that takes you out of the fog
> those rolling sentences
> are pure repentances
> makes you feel less like a dog.

J. What is a log?—the almost-caught-it-on-paper . . . a file folder of
papers, bits and pieces . . . explosions . . . the hate letter that was
never sent . . . wonderings . . . wanderings.

R. Log-writing can include anything you do, from the very intimate to
the very public. And after all, if you're doing it *for* self-catharsis, *for*
developing self-motivation, *for* improving your ability to clarify, *for*
the record, *for* sharpening your communications skills, what does it
matter that it contains only those things which you're *against!*

J. What is this art of log writing that we haven't taught. Is it something inborn or can you teach it? Encourage it? Is it something you
have or don't have?

R. After reading one student log in 1968, I wrote a note to the author,
remarking:

> After a somewhat sporadic beginning, to about page 10 or so, I
> read most of the rest of your log at one stretch . . . I prefer to
> read them that way in order to get an overall view in one time
> span without much interruption. I wonder if you've reread your
> log in that way? I think you'll not only sense the achievement,
> but you'll also sense your freer spirit toward the end of the log.
> I just loved the section where you and Pat decided to cut a
> seminar and go to a movie . . . but I wonder if you should have

felt guilty, or about being guilty? Isn't this the guts of the problem of freedom, to act and accept whatever consequences which may come . . . even guilt of feeling guilty?

Last July 11, I recorded the following in my dream log:

> I'm steering a small barge along a Dutch canal, having trouble seeing because somebody is standing in the one clear aisle where I can see what's ahead . . . lots of boats . . . going side-wise and thinking I'd hit shore or other boats, but always coming out OK . . . coming to locks, waiting . . . eating a meal on the shore during the wait, losing my shoes, finally getting into and through the canal locks, but losing my passengers back at the stopping place . . . wondering if there is any way to walk back to get them; suddenly they're with me and the canal scene becomes an American Humanist Association Board meeting with Phil in charge of some kind of session where there's a protest with a physical education teacher who wants the minutes of the meeting amended. Then Phil gets five bottles of wine out of a locker and goes into an inner sanctum where the Board is ostensibly meeting. See him pick up the five bottles and head for the group, but never did see the group in session.

J.   My log isn't a unit. It doesn't even want to come under one name, "log." It isn't a notebook with a beginning and an end . . . it isn't in one place, but in many . . . seven . . . or ten. It's several notebooks that stop and start, each in a different language. It's a pile of carbons of letters to friends. It's a folder of poems, collected in various moods, written in various moods.

R.   The diary form is not very satisfactory. About two years ago, in fact on October 23rd, 1968, I started to emulate a friend in Putney who saw some value in making a page for each day of the year, then systematically recording what he had been doing that day. He had made an entry each day for ten years. I was quite impressed by his tenacity as well as the possibility of gaining some value from this approach to log-keeping. But I held out only for a couple of months, for the system became pretty sterile, to wit, (October 26, 1968):

> Began as sunshine, ended in rain; began with a Greene County program in process, ended with the government (interns) at Xenia and the Beaver Creek group dismissed—much phoning and puzzlement; how to fight ghosts? A busy day of conferences and seminars and (Maryllyn's) good food a vital aspect of tonight's seminar (6:30–12:30).

The first line the next day:

Up so late with seminars last nite, slept 'til 9 today. . . .

J.   Once I made a log of a year by recalling the song or music titles I associated with the time periods.

R.   A log can express you; a log *is* you; a log reflects being; a log *is* being . . . and being can range the full gamut from logical, linear, cognitive, exquisitely rational beauty such as $E = mc^2$, to the wildest and most delightful ambiguity in a haiku such as one which I included in the thing I recently sent you on haiku:

> Americans scramble
> up glistening cobweb ladders
> which dry in noon suns.

With a little work (which I didn't have time for) I could date this haiku; also, by referring to another kind of one-line log which was a kind of progress report to myself during my leave last year, I could tell what else happened to me on that day. But better that the cobweb (outside my study window on the Maine coast that summer day) have me happen to it!

J.   It's a giant jigsaw puzzle, with half the pieces missing . . . the half I never could write down . . . missed . . . lost. No. It's five or six puzzles, none of them complete. I challenge you, (or me) to piece my life together.

R.   Logs can be letters and letters logs, if they are perceived in that dimension. All it takes is a piece of carbon paper and some onionskin to build a first-rate log, whether to share or not to share. The main value of a letter-log or a log-letter: you are addressing it to one other person at a given moment of time. And assuming some existential quality to any letter, drawing a knife edge into the future, the letter CAN be a revelation *of* you *to* you as well as you to another. In retrospect you may not recognize the you, but to admit the recognition may be a sign of growth, *you* to *you,* an internal evaluation as it were not somebody judging you from the outside.

J.   It is shy . . . it doesn't want to be talked about as a unit—or as anything. Its many parts are written for others, even if, like the hidden notebooks, they are never read. There is only one who can key them all in . . . if she chooses.

R.   On the letter-log again for a moment: back there in the dark ages (or *were* they so dark and so many light seconds away?), as I say, back there when we on the Antioch–Putney faculty required the log-

writing as a kind of evidence, for extrinsic as well as intrinsic reasons, one person asked if he might put his log into letter form. He
said he had a friend who would understand; and since I also knew
the friend, it would make a neat three-cornered dialogue. Fine, I
said. And he went forth to write. . . .

J.   It wants different forms . . . sometimes I can only scribble . . . an
outburst on the back of an envelope, in the middle of some notes.
Letters are typed. The conversation thus flowing as fast as thoughts
and fingers allow, the carbon recording for future reference.

R.   As I said a moment ago, we went forth to write. And he did right
well at it, too. Letter after letter came off his typewriter. . . .

J.   You can pound something into the ground, reflection on reflection
weighing you down. Logs are dangerous in that way. This, even this
very writing, is on the verge of a circular chase . . . on logs. When to
stop? Reflection on reflection sends me screaming on the page,
pounding fury, sinking spiraling down . . . off the edge of the paper.

R.   So, the letters came off his typewriter. And he shared them with me
every couple of weeks . . . and he was a bit anxious about feedback.
"Were they OK?" he kept asking. So, I read them, used the substance of the lines (for he wrote reactions to books, nature, people,
ideas, feelings) to make comments in the margins . . . and we held
hour-long discussions on what he was thinking and how he was
thinking about it. In fact, it was one of the most memorable dia-
logues with year-long continuity that I've had in A–P. And interestingly enough, before a couple of months had passed, he moved out
of the letter form and began to write with incredible sophistication
and clarity . . . pouring his thoughts right into the typewriter. The
early flow became a veritable cascade. And he included newspaper
clippings, ditto handouts from seminars, whatever interested him.
He must have written six or seven hundred pages; I never counted
them. And when he finished his work with us, he said that the experience was one of the most valuable during his fifteen months internship.

J.   There is something that wants saying . . . somewhere under something . . . it is struggling to be heard . . . and not to be heard . . . it is
shy of exposure, fearful of light.

> He thought my views
> were very snide
> it seemed I'd hit
> his holy pride.

Our yes-no motions
put us in boxes
parliamentarians
slyer than foxes.

J.   I am looking at a log I made for credit for a year-long Humanities independent study. It recalls a year of struggle with painting, poetry, artists, (professional and otherwise), teachers, requirements, and discoveries. I have interspersed the descriptions of each quarter's work with sketches, ink prints, linoleum prints, poems to fit and help describe the learning of that time. Last summer was one of discovery about poetry and poets. . . .

R.   The above doggerel came from my Harpers Ferry log . . . a meeting log.

Ferry Log. About a year ago I hit upon an idea to protect me from being murdered by boredom and stupidity at committee meetings and retreats (but not at advances, of course!) I often try to catch a picture of a feeling, a situation or a countenance in four simple lines. Point is you can do it almost by free association. And in many ways it may say more about a meeting than the official minutes. Best of all, it doesn't have to make sense, for instance (still from Harpers Ferry):

Why so glum	Rap the gavel	Scribble madly
pale and drawn	call a meeting	in your notes
let off steam	shoot the syrup	but never miss
with a yawn.	in your greeting.	those crucial votes.

J.   Some collected poetry from various parts of my log:

> To Those Without Pity
>
> Cruel of heart, lay down my song.
> Your reading eyes have done me wrong.
> Not for you was the pen bitten,
> And the mind wrung, and the song written.

R.   And one such conference was even more memorable than Harpers Ferry for what I wrote during the meeting. It was a very tense session, motives were being questioned (in what was supposed to be a humanistic framework), masks were being put on and taken off with Halloween-like rapidity. My log that weekend, polished slightly on a 727 jet as I returned home, consisted of fifteen or twenty poems. It was obvious that the good guys and I had been screwed, but we didn't enjoy it! The most biting:

> Committee Meeting Progress
>
> We came
> we fought
> we fornicated
> to make the world
> safe for hypocrisy
> and to pee up
> our neighbor's back
>
> then move formally,
> "Twas really Chanel No. 5."

J.   My Humanities instructors didn't value the log form; they preferred researched papers. Maybe for this reason I got no response to my log when I handed it in; I wasn't even sure it had been read.

There is a copy of the letter I wrote to my Basic Drawing teacher at the end of the course. There are three character sketches of people I met during the summer. . . .

R.   So a log can be what *you* want it to be or *not* to be. Yours is the choice. It can be energetic, lethargic, a meandering stream on a summer's day, a hurricane, lazy, a silk cocoon on a mulberry tree, a play, a poem, a haiku, a dialogue, trialogue or polywog; it's a chance to see, hear, taste, touch . . . to fear, exult, exclaim, proclaim, propane . . . to jump a thousand leagues across the moon or damn the men who put us there and spoiled the romantic summer nights . . . to cuss, to fuss, to muss . . . to discuss being and nothingness or Sartre's book *Being and Nothingness* . . . to ring a bell or go to hell in a wheelbarrow; who will know that you wanted to go in a Mercedes?

J.   Perhaps my experience with the log for Humanities, its reception, or lack of one, makes me particularly hesitant to generally hand over any of my pen-biting and mind-wringing for someone else's inspection.

Yet, there's something very strong inside that says mind-wringing should be shared . . . with someone.

SUBSEQUENTLY

Obviously, there is often great practical and psychological resistance to logging. Some may have kept a diary earlier in life and discovered how sterile it can become. Also, it is scary to put some things down on paper, things one might feel he'd best keep locked in the closet of memory. Yet, as May Sarton indicates in her insightful *Journal of a Solitude,* "at some point . . . one has to stop holding back for fear of alienating some imaginary reader or real relative or friend, and come out with personal truth." Although she is concerned more about such resistance related to the evolution of the artist, her next observation has as much application to the artist of learning (all of us) as to creative writing:

> If we are to understand the human condition, and if we are to accept ourselves in all the complexity, self-doubt, extravagance of feeling, guilt, joy, the slow freeing of the self to its full capacity for action and creation, both as human being and artist, we have to know all we can about each other, and we have to be willing to go naked.[4]

But humans as social creatures in any culture take inhibitions into their systems with their mother's milk, at each day of school, and through tribal customs or national anthems. That's what socialization is about. Therefore, it's not easy to ask a person to disrobe, even if that person is *the only person* in the whole world who sees, touches, hears, tastes, smells, or even intuits that nakedness.

Quite apart from the question, Does logging work for the individual, regardless of who reads or listens? there are, of course, significant ethical questions that any institution must ask: Does any school have the right to delve into such privacy questions? Should logging be required or optional? If used as part of the evidence to support accredited courses or learning sequences, then who should be responsible for verifying the evidence—an entire committee, the school's faculty member—who? Also, should any part of that evidence become part of the public record? Furthermore, at the psychological level, what if log-keeping becomes a snakepit, a chamber of horrors, or a Pandora's box? Who is responsible for picking up the pieces? Is the faculty of the institution sufficiently skilled psychologically to cope with such a situation? What are the dangers of amateur psychotherapy or psychiatry? Are there legal implications? Are faculty facilitators sufficiently mature themselves to deal with the phenomenon, both institutionally and personally? In short, while it may be argued that *all* human interaction or *all* institutional activity carries such implications and risks, it must be argued that one exponentially increases the dimensions of potential learning and danger. In other words, it is much safer to stay on cognitive turf. The phenomenological also can be evaluated, but such tests don't answer the questions posed by either the idealist or the pragmatist.

I have weighed the pros and cons of encouraging such processes and have moved from the required log to the optional, so that an individual student may decide whether or not he or she wishes to participate. My conclusion: urging the risk is worthwhile so long as one openly discusses the nature of such risks. But it has taken me more than a decade to reach my present viewpoint, to have the insight to ask such questions as suggested here, to develop enough fundamental understanding of alternative therapies and psychological theory, to develop enough experience in working with individuals to trust my ability to perceive what may be happening at the knife-edge of a student's advancing perception. I am a bit frightened when I encounter an unwillingness to cope with some of these questions, or discover a naive trust that everything will turn out all right, or stumble into a lurid curiosity in and willingness to tamper with another's psyche. External degree programs may be no more likely than traditional programs to create mayhem with students' psyches, but external programs have a special responsiblity for being responsive.

SOME RESULTS

In the past decade I have seen the logging opportunity used most creatively in the evolution of human personality and experienced it as a significant means for achieving individual self-verification and self-confidence.

I have had many extensive exchanges of correspondence with students who preferred writing directly to a person rather than confining their thoughts to a lonely piece of paper. In one instance a UGS student did both, writing thousands of pages about his reading, his agony over his values-wrenching employment, his fantasies and fiction writing. On top of that, we exchanged nearly a hundred letters each during a forty-month period.

In the UGS context the log frequently has become the basis for books, articles, and poetry that have been shared with committee members before becoming part of the public record.

In working with more than a thousand graduate students, I have found joy in seeing so many increase self-confidence, achieve self-verification, and strengthen identity via the logging process. It leads me to conclude that the course of study common to all students is Search for Identity 101.

SOME METHODOLOGICAL CONSIDERATIONS

As the duologue suggests, a log can acquire many surface characteristics, yet it is not always easy to convince a student that a log doesn't have to be a diary. Sometimes handing him a copy of the duologue helps; sometimes it turns him off, especially if he is unwilling to adopt that "willing suspension of disbelief." Furthermore, as a former colleague once snarled, "Whoever heard of a graduate student getting credit for keeping a journal?" to which I responded, "After all, whoever heard of the Union Graduate School prior to 1969!" Obviously, gaining acceptance of the view that the log is a viable learning tool is difficult.

In UGS, as well as in many external degree programs, there *is* one requirement that helps a student get started. An individual's credibility depends on documented learning sequences, but it is difficult if not impossible for a person to remember so great a congeries of experience (books read, TV shows seen, lectures attended, etc.), so some record is necessary. Hence, the log is practical though not required as part of the documentation.

Another aid to the beginning student is a matter of pure persuasion through the voice of experience. In one's initial interaction with the student, whether in a routine academic counseling session or at a colloquium, the log is introduced as a viable option for recording experiences in whatever form a student wishes. Here, of course, one may cite specific instances or recommend reading someone else's log. In those instances where a log has become part of the public record, as in Michael Van Horn's *The Phoenix: Babblings of a Man Going Sane,* one has a better example to cite. But here again it is sometimes difficult to encourage the neophyte skier to start down the slalom slope!

More important, perhaps, are the reviewer's comments once the person begins, whether that beginning is a tentative letter of sharing or a page or two from somebody asking, How's this? This is the critical juncture. In open-learning programs and to self-directed people, telling somebody what to do may seem like a cruel contradiction. However, I am convinced that it may not matter so much *what* is said (so long as it is essentially positive and supportive) as *that* it is said. My firmest self-principle practice is to *support* any endeavor of self-expression; hence, as in face-to-face interaction, a person must know I am listening. In that listening, another's self-concept can be enhanced if he sees himself being valued, being needed, being useful, being seen (smelled, tasted, etc.)—in short, *being*.[5] It reinforces the belief in traveling, even if one never arrives. Consequently, I respond to any and every statement that arrives as logging (dialoging, too)—even if only to say that I'm "tied hand and foot and cannot respond to your ten pages until I get off the current treadmill." When I do respond, I rarely use declarative sentences; rather, I prefer questions, although they, too, can be destructive. But if they are open-ended ones that lead the student toward more confidence in his own perceptions, a climate is prepared for future interchanges.[6]

Privacy is also a critical matter. Without explicit permission to share any letter or log, the buttoned lip is the best policy. Sooner or later a slipped comment, positive or negative, will reach the writer of log or letter and erode trust. Also, if a student makes her log part of the learning record but does not wish it to be in the public record, appropriate steps must be taken to safeguard that sacred trust.

Another technique I've discovered to be helpful is suggesting that the student read her log in solitude at *one sitting*. Many times I've advised, "Take your log out on the hillside or the beach, away from the phone, barking dogs, family or other distractions, and read it at one fell swoop. You'll be amazed at what it will reveal to you." What it reveals, of course, is the person perceiving her own life as though from a distant perspective. If she has written out of her own experience, then she's bound to see how she has or hasn't changed. And scary as that might be, seeing oneself in action as though one is an outside observer is most insightful. It may be both kaleidoscopic and horoscopic! Usually the person doing this writes back, phones, or comes in person to say, "I can hardly believe it!" Since reading May Sarton's *Journal of a Solitude*, I have urged others to read it in virtually one sitting or at least in one mood period in order to gain a swooping view of her life as well as her backward glances at its scope. Ira Progoff also provides many sophisticated insights regarding ways to gain retrospective vision.

By the time a student colleague works with me for a week or month, she tends to expect the unexpected, for I am simply myself, being whatever I am. While this has often shocked my faculty associates and in many ways made my life hell with colleagues holding preestablished criteria for professional propriety, it has nevertheless made living and working with students exciting. It encourages some of them to be themselves; hence one person knows I'll laugh and dream up a mad response when he sends me a fabricated "secret" army memorandum in which a Commanding General instructs his lieutenant colonel "to detain and interrogate the individual(s) listed below because of efforts to place seditious and un-American statements in the U.S. press: Dr. Roy P. Fairfield" and the huge red letters DEAD are rubber-stamped over my name! Or three other compatriots fabricate a "Letter Award" in which I've been given the school letter in "Creative Dittoing." My files also contain a letter, legible only in strong light, since it's typed on black paper. Just as they may expect the unexpected from me, many know that I feel the same for those who catch the bug!

TRUE PRACTITIONERS

It is both fun and insightful to encourage students to expand their own self-awareness and hence self-expression by means of learning to pun and to write various forms of poetry and mood pieces. The latter may include the former when students share their reflections on the world in free-swinging or impressionistic letters to their committees. And core faculty mood pieces tend to generate similar expressions among their students.

Piet Hien's grooks also encourage a new way of seeing. By free associating about moods, bits, and pieces of dialogue in a colloquium or other formal meetings, one can turn situations and the "in-betweenness" of human intercourse into delightful doggerel. For instance, at one colloquium meeting several years ago I noted on the left side of my yellow pad that a student making a presentation "says he wants to be a College Development Officer." Opposite that note, I wrote:

Took me a year	Be a director
to hear his verbs	admit and enjoy
nouns and pronouns	take fullest control
mixed with herbs.	be man and not boy.

By sharing these observations with him, we opened up a dialogue which continues today.

The haiku, too, is a form of poetry generating new ways of seeing. Somewhere in my log I scribbled, "Cast haiku on the water, and they come back in more sensitive form." 'Tis true. At one colloquium I carried on a four-week dialogue with a woman as we both penned haiku on the same sheet of paper, and today I receive letters from her reflecting a continued extension of her sensing. Also, by sewing puns and haiku into my own mood pieces or as P.S.'s in personal letters, I reap a veritable harvest of haiku from around the world.

OTHER ANGLES OF VISION

It seems appropriate to mention other ways in which I respond to logs. Although I dictate most letters, I've come to feel that responses to logs must be more personal; hence I do them on my own typewriter, and usually my first draft is the last one—errors and all. The communication seems more direct, more spontaneous.

I'm currently experimenting with a form I call the poem-letter. Somehow through such communications I seem to catch more levels of meaning and feeling than through straight linear prose, and more times than not, the person to whom I am writing responds more quickly.

One instance: it involves a woman who adopted a second family and discussed in her log domestic entanglements, the frustration of being torn between counterpointing hopes of motherhood and professional womanhood. When her concluding logs arrived, I read them at virtually one sitting, after which I wrote:

Dear Ann,

How measure such a journey
no teaspoon small enough
or ocean large
to catch the tears
of joy or love or fears

or see it through
kaleidoscope of daily sensing
the hurts
the pats
the visions
of might-be
mixed with strawberry milkshakes
television operas
and the murky clouds in nightmares
who won't stop running
for garbage to be ground down
kitchen sinks
for dishes to be washed
for fights to be stopped
close enough to edges of ambiguity

or weave it in a fabric
more variegated and as gossamer
as that which old Ulysses' wife
wove every day
knowing 'twould be torn out
that night while she waited
and waited and waited
warp and woof
woof and warp
threads solid
threads as thin as the finest spider web
tying life into knots
that disappear in a cup of tea
or midnight kiss . . .

The day Ann received this note she phoned at midday to say Thank You.[7]

A VERITABLE CORNUCOPIA

In short, my propensity to share takes many forms. I know myself well enough to know that it is mostly spontaneous. I float fables, short stories, a few dream logs, do-it-yourself screw-it-up kits, xerox copies of newspaper or magazine articles, logs of trips that usually include grooks, haiku, or free verse that I've written during a trip or anything that interests me or I think will interest others. And both daring and sharing are reciprocated.

After a three-day trip from home to Minneapolis to Denver to Milwaukee and back, for instance, during which I participated in three certifications, a minicolloquium, and lots of conversations, including one three-hour session at the Denver Museum of Natural History, I could not resist the temptation to share a variety of reactions including those I had while one student and I tried to imagine what such prehistoric monsters as diplodocus, now only varnish and bone, might have fantasized about *their* lives, sex, and environment! Also included: our eavesdropping on a couple of kids looking at a mummy, and my feeling as the DC–10 taxied to the runway heading for Chicago:

> Cynical smiles   We taxi thru lights
> these attendants   such deep blue they challenge stars
> clowns now acting   over the Rockies.
> thru living trance.

And of course, that's at once the beauty and the horror of life: its complexity and the universality of its simplicity.

So I shared my retrospective log, all six pages, single-spaced, with some eleven people under the general caption, "Some Monologuing About Some Dialoguing and Logging." Predictable: appreciative responses and more perceptions about learning from our common experiences.

Some negative responses from sharing mood pieces deserve recording, too. One person, unresponsive to mood pieces mailed to the entire graduate school population, asked to have his name removed from our mailing list, even though he wanted to continue as a student! Interestingly enough, he was a colloquist at a colloquium that I could attend for only two days, so I talked with him no more than half an hour or so. But it is true that as both Antioch and Union Graduate Schools have become larger, have an increasing number of graduates, and are surely too large for all faculty to get to know all students very well, they have become more impersonal (see Chaper 5). Also, it becomes increasingly difficult to gain general acceptance of methods that may work best among small and more intimately related persons. Busy persons such as our students, who are bombarded with third class mail, often don't read *any* xeroxed, mimeographed, or other duplicated materials. This, of course, is a general problem in our "bizzy-dizzy" society, though it is discouraging when persons in external degree programs sometimes fail to respond to what we are obviously doing for *their* good! (see Chapter 11). Yet, as one fablist observed, "The world would have been saved long ago if it hadn't been for its saviors!"[8]

SOME PROSPECTS

Those who are true believers or practitioners of the kind of interaction discussed here must gain enough affirmation to have the courage to continue; nobody can be involved very long in an exercise in futility or "the dialogue of the deaf." Yet, little response is required to make it seem worthwhile qualitatively, even though the quantity of such results may be forever unknown. When one graduate confided, "I liked the poem you included in your recent memo, so I cut it out and slipped it into my mirror," I had a warm feeling for what he said because I knew he was genuine. Imagine my shock of recognition a few weeks later when, upon visiting his home, I saw it in the mirror in his office!

Another danger of such sharing pivots around the fact of being perceived as something bigger than life when, indeed, you yourself know that you're only one person with toes of clay. I keep hoping, however, that persons who see my many-sidedness will be less likely to paint me into a role corner and will interact with me situationally. Most of the time it works if the joy of such learning is not smothered by the threat it poses.

So I suspect that I shall continue sharing insights, opinions, and concerns both wholesale and retail, having come to believe more firmly that Darwin had a point when he said that a key to evolution was the surplus of seeds. By scattering seeds widely (though not wildly), some of them are bound to germinate. By working in a variety of gardens, as I encourage UGS students to do, both they and I can survive psychologically even if some of the seedlings, bushes, or even giant redwoods die, are destroyed by fire, or suffer lack of nourishment.

My own confidence in self-expression was increased by writing the first draft of this chapter, even if some parts of it were ambiguous, vague, even presumptuous. Perhaps other colleagues and co-learners in external degree programs can only respond to the heavy psychological questions by trying some forms of self-expression and self-definition. There is no question that such logging and sharing sharpens issues, resolves conflict, and clarifies thought-action involvement in my own world. I cannot ask others to accept my experience as theirs. I can only suggest a trying to cope with the why of human existence.

5 Charisma to Bureaucracy: Inevitable?

At the crescendo of the student dissent movement and about the time we were preparing for the first Union Graduate School colloquium, John Fischer wrote a one-page article for *Harpers* entitled "Preface to the Catalogue of Curmudgeon College." Obviously angered by student protests, Fischer's Curmudgeon presented some tough policies:

> No student should be compelled to attend a college he doesn't like. . . . Absolute freedom, tempered with occasional expulsions . . . no dormitories . . . no sports program. . . . All students are welcome to sit in any classroom as long as they like. . . . Any attempt to sit in the administration building will be treated as criminal trespass by our town sheriff . . . (6'3," 280 lbs.) . . . President Curmudgeon . . . hires and fires the faculty . . . feels no obligation to take their views seriously. . . . As he observed in his now-famous paper on collegiate governance: "The true scholar is inherently incapable of running anything. . . . Students participate in governance the same way that customers participate in the governance of Macy's. If they don't like the goods offered, they can go to Gimbels."

He went on to say that when it comes to pot, LSD, and liquor:

> What a student ingests on his own time and in his own quarters is his own affair. But if he snores in class, breaks laboratory equipment, gets busted by the police on campus, freaks out in the halls, or otherwise disturbs his teachers and fellow students, he gets shipped out on the next plane.[1]

Many educators who kept records of their anger index during that period of their lives no doubt identified with Fischer's President Curmudgeon, for they were, indeed, "trying times."[2]

THE MATRIX AND SOME QUESTIONS

The Union Graduate School was founded by men and women who recognized the need for new pathways to learning. But our motivation was informed as well by some terribly dehumanizing forces that generated the Free Speech movement in Berkeley and reached a peak with the Kent and Jackson State shootings and the Cambodia invasions of May 1970. In late 1969 and early 1970 when we attempted to build a structure with a minimum of structure, a school where the student had a voice in determining the conditions that would shape his or her own destiny, we were well aware of the Sturm und Drang of the country in general. Furthermore, Timothy Pitkin, Sam Baskin, and Goodwin Watson had been vitally involved with innovation in higher education: Tim as president of Goddard, Goodwin at Columbia as early as the thirties, and Sam at Antioch. Also, the Union committee responsible for some of the early spadework and Judson Jerome, the major draftsman of the original proposal, had been associated with innovative institutions or programs for some time.[3] I had worked with Peace Corps Training Programs for two years and at Antioch-Putney for five. Our experiences revealed the many paths open to us as well as those that might prove less fruitful. This chapter proposes some central questions with reference to the organizational development of UGS; however, in perspective, these questions seem relevant for any innovative institution attempting to survive in what seems like a hostile world. One cannot talk at much length with founders of such institutions as Goddard, for instance, or read the life histories of Summerhill or Black Mountain College (to say nothing about working for such institutions) without a keen awareness of fundamental questions:

- Should one seek outside funds to launch such programs or generate money from within in such a way as to make them viable and independent? Should one ask for assistance from traditional institutions of any kind?
- How does one manage the delicate balance between publicizing the programs (in order to obtain clientele) and assuring performance consistent with publicly stated objectives?
- If one is overly concerned with self-preservation in an experimental context, what are the risks inherent in such a paradox? Should we, rather, build in self-destruct mechanisms to

preclude hardening of the arteries? Is Max Weber's observation that institutions move from "charisma to bureaucracy" an ironclad law of organizational development? Are there any ways to soften, slow, or divert that movement?

- Are there other dehumanizing forces in learning situations besides the defenses of specialization and territoriality, forces from which students invariably suffer?
- To what extent is it possible for the consumer (student) to participate creatively in the evolution of humanistic learning?
- To what extent should educational programs become "subversive activities," following the spirit of the Postman and Weingartner dictum?
- Do external degree programs such as UGS perhaps hold out more hope for radical institutional reform (to accompany learning reform) than any individual associated with such programs has any right to expect?
- What practical gimmicks or procedures does one need to invent or incorporate into such a program to insure survival when interfacing with the world?
- To build such institutions can one find persons whose egos are strong enough not to get in the way, whose commitment is strong, whose stamina enables them to endure or design blue-skying for themselves to create enough distance for personal survival?

Our questions at that time may not have been phrased precisely like this, but concerns included these major issues.

As coordinator and director of the program, I interjected some of my own experience-shaped beliefs, to wit:

- We should reject outside funding and rely on tuition; we should be tough-minded enough to execute a policy wherein a student pays in advance or is invited to leave.
- We should keep a very low profile, working through and around the interstices of power, geography, economics, politics, and specialization; in short, we should be legally "subversive."
- We should do everything feasible to blur distinctions between faculty and administrative functions and between faculty and student roles in order to minimize growth of us-them syn-

dromes which seem so devastating in American education; more positively, we might think of ourselves as colearners, colleagues, and coworkers in this enterprise.

- We should remain as open as possible for the invention of new ways to perform old functions.
- We should find persons to serve nominal administrative and faculty functions who express *commitment* to this mode of learning structure, even if they lack a national reputation.
- Human response-ability should be the vision of human interaction, regardless of the learning situation.

Such beliefs were not part of any systematic credo. Rather, it was a matter of representing and defending such viewpoints whenever and wherever necessary. Some future historian of UGS will no doubt find ample opportunity to test my claims with the oceans of evidence in UGS files and human memory.

IN RETROSPECT

As I read a vast number of official UGS documents in a retrospective search for insight about our organizational development, I was struck by a number of questions:

- Why is it that one's early insights in an enterprise tend to look either brilliant or terribly naive?
- What, where, and when were the *turning points,* for better or for worse, and what interventions might one have introduced to prevent pursuing the *wrong* trails?
- How many of the changes over the years were a function of increasing size? of increasing complexity? How many were a function of geographical dispersion? How many were a function of a rather decentralized and shared model of power utilization (McGregor Y, rather than X)?[4]
- At what point did the vision of the founding parents of UGS seem so radical to later participants that anybody holding those viewpoints was perceived as reactionary?
- How much charisma can last how long in evolving an innovative institution in contemporary America? How much charisma is too much? When does it get in the way?

I have no illusions about answering these questions definitively. In many ways, it's much more fun to ask a question than to answer it. But I hope that relating these queries to some of the salient features of our evolution may be helpful to others involved or who may become involved in their own organizational evolution, regardless of the field of endeavor. But first, let's put a few of these questions against some insights of C. Northcote Parkinson and Friedrich Nietzche.

In Parkinson's delightfully insightful book, *Parkinson's Law*, the author reminds us that "it is known that perfection of planned layout is achieved only by institutions on the point of collapse . . . that perfection of planning is a symptom of decay."[5] The UGS founders, therefore, can congratulate themselves for not having planned too carefully at the program's commencement. When we locate that point in our existence at which we succumbed to pressures to structure, or what I call "the propensity to codify," we might mark that point with a red flag; it could be the point where deterioration began.

Or let us look at a Nietzschean insight; at one point in *Skirmishes in a War with the Age*, Nietzsche remarks, "Liberal institutions straightway cease from being liberal the moment they are soundly established: once this is attained no more grievous and more thorough enemies of freedom exist than liberal institutions."[6] Conceivably, we could test the trend of development in any institution of higher learning by comparing its statement of goals with its own self-evolving concepts of stability, status, or seriousness. When, for instance, those associated with UGS perceived the achievement of accreditation as the *summa bonum* of our development, we may have victimized ourselves in the Nietzschean paradox. Such a dilemma is reflected in the measurable distance between the attitude of students at the first colloquium, when only two out of twenty-nine wanted accreditation, and the twelfth colloquium three years later, when thirty-three out of thirty-five wanted it!

Also, let us look at the phenomenon of forging change. Without question, UGS was designed as an instrument of change. Our objectives were to develop a genuine alternative to the Ph.D., an alternative that *might* encourage more conventional institutions to change their ways, an alternative whose graduates would be concerned about reweaving some of the patterns in our social fabric. In that sense it was a revolutionary thrust—but informed by the psychological insight that individuals rarely make lasting changes unless they are willing to change themselves. But a paradox is evident here, as suggested by Garry Wills's view that "There is no machinery for change. It comes about unexpectedly. It comes about through an individual, through a small group, through prophets. And you can't program prophets, or recruit them. These people just run up and invent their own way. That is the way that change happens."[7]

In stressing the right of the individual to design his or her own program for changing the self as part of an institutional design for effecting social change, we may be involved in a fundamental contradiction. This contradiction, however, becomes most poignant when those UGS students and faculty who are part of psychological self-change thrusts (Zen, transactional analysis, altered states of consciousness, etc.) encounter social change advocates (militant feminists, Marxists, ethnic activists, etc.). That the respective individuals and groups have every right and reason to clash one cannot deny. The question here pivots around consequences. What happens if any group attempts to exert or even seize power to change the direction of UGS as an institution? On the one hand, the psychologically oriented people take a dim view of exercising such power within UGS, thereby abandoning the field to the social change planners; on the other hand, the latter tend to disdain the former and know that when it comes to organizational development, might rules the day. It's not too farfetched to say that it's Buddha versus Alinsky, or Maslow versus Marx. Despite a self-directed learning environment, will the group in power have the courage to let the other group be?

One is reminded of the crucial situation the Constitutional Convention faced in Philadelphia when challenged by potentially destructive factions, defined by James Madison as "a number of citizens, whether amounting to a majority or minority of the whole, who are united and actuated by some common impulse or of passion, or of interest, adverse to the rights of other citizens, or to the permanent and aggregate interests of the community."[8] The American Constitution insures the continued existence of the faction while maintaining the whole social fabric through complex and variegated checks and balances. The test for UGS may be similar: have we organized a student's learning context (with peers, adjuncts, and core on the committee) and the institutional matrix wisely enough to guarantee individual and group freedom to learn as well as the continued existence of the school?

Early in our life, Ben Thompson, an Antioch professor, suggested as he arrived at a colloquium, "The motto of UGS should be 'power to poetry'." A preponderant number of those now in the program might be more comfortable with "poetry in power."

CREEPING BUREAUCRACY

Institution builders may find it difficult to measure how far they've traveled down the bureaucratic road no matter how much they intend to avoid such a route or fate. Rather than oppose every tendency toward bureaucracy, I agree with Max Weber and later students of bureaucracy who have pointed out repeatedly that bureaucracy is the way things get done in a mass, urbanized, technologized society. Without utilizing infrastructures such as transportation and communications systems or credit and other fiscal systems, it is next to impossible today to operate any institution whose clientele is national or transnational. A critical question crops up repeatedly; namely, how much must one's own microsystem conform to a variety of macrosystems and still maintain its own integrity? If one is determined to maintain that integrity as an educational institution, one must constantly inquire: Do we want Veteran's benefits? Must we participate in federal grant and loan programs or seek accreditation? Must we develop a program dependent upon air travel credit cards or, for that matter, the jetways and highways at all? And if one's status depends upon involving persons who have doctoral degrees, how can one live with the paradox that more traditional "docs" are producing more radical "docs"?

In *Zen and the Art of Motorcycle Maintenance,* Robert Pirsig suggests one acid test. On the motorcycle trek that becomes the vehicle for his philosophizing, Pirsig comments on his partner John:

> He felt that institutions such as schools, churches, governments and political organizations of every sort all tended to direct thought for ends other than truth, for the perpetuation of their own functions, and for the control of individuals in the service of these functions.[9]

Another of Pirsig's viewpoints may be fundamental to understanding why humans so very often become caught in their own self-perpetuating tyrannies:

> The true system, the real system, is our present construction of

systematic thought itself, rationality itself, and if a factory is torn down but the rationality which produced it is left standing, then that rationality will simply produce another factory.[10]

Anybody who has been involved in developing an institution—public school, private hiking club, business, church, or whatever—knows that it is easy to apply some kind of rational system to persuade others to conform to recommended viewpoints, codes, or rules. Hence, it seems probable that any institution advocating a liberal, radical, or freedom-seeking end is virtually bound to reinvent autocratic reasons for *not* acting in accordance with its own goals. Or, to use a favorite illustration, sooner rather than later those in higher education will reinvent Leviathan State University with its constellations of provosts, assistant provosts, department chairpersons, vice chairpersons, janitors, assistant janitors, deans and deanlings to the farthest reaches of the multiversity.

If one starts amoebalike, as UGS did, one can, of course, watch separation and digestion closely enough to see what is separating and digesting.[11] Or, to use another metaphor, if one starts from ground zero, one literally can count the administrative memos or formation of committees to determine what the rate of ascent is, perhaps devising a self-destruct system at some preestablished altitude. Also, one can account for the number of times a particular policy formulation is *revised* and can double-check whether or not the revision is longer or shorter than the original (it will probably be longer!) to establish a perspective on bureaucratic evolution. One may gain self-perspective by examining one's attitude toward the files: Are they sacred? Why? Why not? One day I found myself addressing a memorandum (on a *printed* form) "To the Filer" because I literally did not know which of several women might be filing. I said to myself, "Whoa! What's happening here, *this* . . . in a relatively small and humanistic school?" The filing had become depersonalized! Another check: Do you find yourself saying, "Well, it's easier to keep the files this way than it is that, so let's do it the easy way." The easiest way may be more administratively feasible, but is that feasibility consistent with humanistic and innovative education? For instance, employing a second core as PDE reader was a step designed to improve the quality of UGS student programs (see Chapter 6); *requiring* that reports from the second core to the first core be filed as a matter of routine was a purely administrative stipulation that violated the original conception, as it had already been agreed that what the first core did with the report was his or her business! We must guard against easy slippages into bureaucratic administrative techniques. And yet these evolutions in external degree programs like UGS are probably minor, however symptomatic, as compared with some larger and deeper trends. I was surprised in a delightful and constructive way when a student visitor to an admissions meeting read off a list of clichés and slogans that we had used (underwhelmed, cognitive dissonance, fractionalized therapeutic sessions, etc.) and went on to remark, "It's interesting that even in innovative programs such as UGS, we develop our own jargon!" One needs such checks, for the little hillocks which we erect may trip us up more quickly and easily than a Mount Blanc or Mount Everest.

SOME DISTINCT TRENDS: AN OVERVIEW

Regardless of the causes or even noncauses resulting in various changes in any institution, time and distance do permit thumbnail sketches of trends. The initial organizational proposal for UGS called for the location of centers at several Union member institutions. In fact, some of us did a great deal of spadework on that plan, but there seemed to be little enthusiasm for such development during our early years. In retrospect, this may have been fortunate. By using a central headquarters for administration and a guerrillalike approach to the location of colloquia, we avoided the negative aspects of territoriality. Except for our entrapment in a couple of Antioch student strikes, which seriously inhibited some of our administrative functions, we managed to avoid local institutional squabbles that could have sucked us up like a straw in a tornado! But we risked being destroyed by our own success (see Chapter 1). There was no doubt that we were implementing an idea whose time had come, for the number of inquiries and applications was close to overwhelming, especially because we wanted to respond humanistically. We might have become too big too fast. Fortunately, all persons in the decision-making process agreed on the basic issues. Furthermore, we agreed to hold the student population to approximately 300 and the full-time core faculty at approximately 10 full-time equivalent since our promise to the Ohio Board of Regents called for an approximate 30:1 ratio (see Chapter 8). Yet, pressure to regionalize emerged as some members of the core wished to move out to serve students more adequately, to develop closer and more functional relations with adjunct professors, to locate other material and human resources, to cut travel costs, and so on.

Although the notion of regionalization was incorporated into the original model and part of Sam Baskin's long-range hopes for the Union, my own experience with every brand of territoriality shouted warning. In fact, in early 1972 I wrote a note to my colleagues, asking in part:

- What are the motives for such a shift?
- Is such a shift consistent with the fundamental goals of UGS?
- What is the most appropriate timing for making such an organizational shift?
- Who should be involved in deliberating such a shift, and who has the power to implement it?
- Which regional or decentralized model is most consistent with the objectives of UGS?
- *Assuming* some kind of decentralized model:
    - Can we avoid the usual power struggles over power, over money, over decision-making policy? Are we willing to take the time to discuss those struggles and compensate for their probable consequences in light of a few models; namely, that discussed by *The Federalist Papers*, those suggested by the University of California, General Motors, Antioch, others?
    - Would admissions be centralized or decentralized and what difference would it make?
    - Are we willing to live with the possible (probable ?) increase in cost of such a program?
    - With the regional model, would the student have any choice of core faculty, especially in the early phases? Would his choices of committee members be as wide as they are with the centralized model?
    - Would the criteria for particularizing any aspect of core faculty contribution be more than a formality for the larger program if the core faculty were to become primarily keepers of the process?
    - With a completely decentralized model, would a coordinator/director or dean for the total program even

be necessary? Could he coordinate *and* serve as core faculty? Is that possible or desirable? Are other models of coordination or organization feasible? How about a model of several UGS centers, each *completely* autonomous to avoid overhead expenses for a centralized office? to avoid power and prestige struggles? a confederative rather than a federative model?

In considering the possible applications of such questions to other enterprises at other times, these questions still seem pertinent whether considered from a psychological, territorial, or other perspective. For whatever reasons, some of the core outstationed themselves but did not fall prey to territorial traps. Only after accreditation was there a new move to adopt the regional model but with the recognition that national and regional models must coexist so that students in any given territory would be free to choose the process that best fit their needs. The notion of autonomy holds as well. Only time will tell whether the relationships between the various units of UGS will be federative or confederative, although we talk about being *one* graduate school.[12]

ADMISSIONS COMMITMENTS

Consistent with an early decision to maximize a participatory (consumer- or person-centered) decision making in UGS, Goodwin Watson and I incorporated students into the admissions process within two months of the first admissions. Any students in the Yellow Springs area who cared to join us were free to do so. We simply transported that idea to the first colloquium and invited volunteers. That pattern continues to this day. Within the first few months, ethnic minority input was manifest; also *both* female and several minority viewpoints were represented during the first two colloquia. Hence, participation of minority and women students in UGS reflected this self-conscious effort at representation long before an affirmative action plan was adopted in early 1974. These processes also enabled us to hammer out admissions criteria incorporated in UGS literature.

Although we debated at length over criteria, quota systems for minorities and women, and procedures for informing rejected candidates about our decisions, our admissions procedures seem to be the most humanistic when compared with several others in which I've participated over the years. Obviously, such procedures are slow; they rely heavily upon the good will and the vision of student volunteers; they demand a heavier commitment from participants than from other UGS persons. Although persons serving on a committee for the first time may be inexperienced and hence unqualified, the maturity of UGS students and the essentially consensual process of deliberation seem to get a person tuned in rather quickly. Although employing objective criteria uniformly to all applicants may be impossible, core faculty participants (and two are always present) effect continuity; furthermore, it is imperative that we do not practice self-deception about objectivity. While one committee might possibly accept an applicant whereas another might reject him, the most extreme viewpoints are somewhat leveled by the nature of the deliberative process.[13]

CORE FACULTY DEVELOPMENT

As observed earlier, UGS was launched by core persons with many years in experiential and innovative education. But we knew from the outset that we needed to give serious thought to the criteria for employing new persons. The responsibility of a core faculty member, as stated repeatedly, hardly resembles that at traditional universities.

In our efforts to establish criteria, we formulated many job descriptions over the years. Also, because we have encouraged all UGS personnel to participate in the decision-making process and because we desired to make minority and female representation real and not token, the task of adding core faculty and finding administrative leaders has been arduous. Furthermore, our effort to gain some field distribution among a relatively small number of persons has intensified the difficulty, even in a depressed job market.

Any innovative program cutting new pathways in higher education must confront the difficulty of finding persons who can feel comfortable in transdisciplinary situations, in situations demanding a person to serve in different roles concurrently, and in learning sets where one's major task is sometimes that of standing out of a student's light! Judging from lists of criteria (see Chapter 3), Christ, Buddha, and Socrates wrapped into one person could never fulfill some student and faculty expectations! Increasing in five years from two part-time to six full-time and fifteen part-time faculty obviously strains daily communication. In addition, our geographical dispersion model, with some of our core literally a continent apart, makes telephone and letter communications imperative. To enhance core interaction, we hit upon the ratio of 10 faculty and 300 students as an optimal size for UGS, but the rationale for that relationship has eroded with our development. These trends, of course, do not make us necessarily any better or worse, any more or less vulnerable. Perhaps one survives best, both institutionally and individually, simply by accepting them as current facts of life. We have evolved from a small group of persons sharing a vision to a second and third generation with good potential for developing colleagiality with both student and core colearners. And rather than tearing ourselves to pieces over illusions, ideology, and power, which is the wont of most university faculties, we should focus on the vision of self-directed or person-centered learning and direct our skills and energies toward whatever colleagiality is healthy. Assuming our organizational pattern is sound (whether centralized, decentralized, or partly each) and assuming that the student committee pattern is sound, the vision of UGS may continue for many years into the future. If, on the other hand, we succumb to internal power squabbles, battle over money, status, and territorial prerogatives, or descend to the common mendacity that all too frequently characterizes faculty interaction (usually in the name of professionalism), then we'll know we've been successful in reinventing Leviathan State University!

In a system encouraging openness between a student and her committee, openness between core who are ostensibly engaged in achieving the same objectives should diminish the normal paranoia, professional jealousies, and petty squabbling among faculty. I would assume also that mutual trust would be a logical and human expectation among such educators, yet I am not sure that this is perceived as "a consummation devoutly to be wished" among UGS colleagues. Or if it is, we are not terribly sophisticated about ways to effect that goal because the official records of faculty meetings seem little different than those of more traditional educational institutions, despite an occasional skylight to the sun.

ADMINISTRATIVE TRENDS

As suggested earlier in this chapter, creeping bureaucracy may be

inevitable in American institutions that develop from relative small-
ness to something larger, that interface increasingly with state and
national agencies, that tie their microprocesses with those in the
macrosystem. After all, such growth creates more fiscal transactions,
more individual student records to file, more phone calls to field,
more reports to file, and more of this and many more of that! This
requires division of labor, more office staff, and more coordination
of that staff. Also size is as much a function of complexity as large
whole numbers in this kind of learning context. Although our processes are relatively uniform (admission, colloquium, form committee, certification, learning contract, and terminar), the number of
ways to execute such processes is virtually infinite since each program is custom-made. And again although we encourage self-direction, students perceive that they need help at many points along the
way until they learn to find their own perceptions credible.

During the first five years of UGS existence, we were fortunate
to have an administrative coordinator who was not only committed
to fulfill the vision of UGS but also capable of dealing with an
incredible number of details and student needs. Betty Jo Pool mastered the difficulty of coping with an unusual number of phone calls
and letters while maintaining some sense of confluence between
academic objectives and the administrative execution of details that
buttress academic programs. By gradually attending colloquia and
assuming responsibility for communicating the nature of UGS processes to each new group of students, by assuming some responsibility as peer on a number of student committees, and by attending admissions and faculty meetings and assuming identity as core, she acquired a holistic comprehension of program and student needs. During the last year or so of my tenure as coordinator/director of the
program, we were, in effect cocoordinators.

My own views of administering such a program hinge on the belief in a participatory model stressing joint rather than unilateral de-
cisionmaking. It was my earliest intention to put myself out of a job.
This does not indicate neglect or fear of decision making on my
part; rather, I thought that UGS would be stronger if many
individuals participated in the everyday operation of the organization. This belief explains my commitment to student-faculty involvement in admissions, student committees, governance, colloquium
planning and execution, and other ad hoc committees dealing with

UGS issues. At the time of our accreditation gauntlet, I conceptualized this in an organizational diagram, attempting to relate our participatory model to the more hierarchical model of the larger Union organization (see Appendix B). There was, of course, little appreciation, understanding, or acceptance of the way in which Betty Pool and I had evolved a functional organizational pattern in which administrative functions were more attuned to academic objectives. Not only did the North Central accreditation team argue that we needed to clarify administrative roles (see Appendix C)[14] but not long after my resignation as coordinator, the language referring to my successor became "director."

In short, the evolution of an increasingly impersonal and bureaucratic administrative trend has seemed almost inevitable, yet I believe the administration has for the most part remained functionally humanistic because those of us involved still *know most of the people* in UGS. It is still small enough. The administrative functions are now sufficiently established and specialized to guarantee continuity. I was successful in putting myself out of a job, as I perceived the job I wanted for myself; future administrators in UGS may not have that option. In the latter sense, I may have failed!

Another vital area of administrative change relates to curriculum trends, the monitoring of which are the responsibility of both administrative and faculty persons. Indeed, we have restricted student execution and recording of the various steps in the curricular or academic process. For instance, after some terribly unrealistic pressuring from students to hold certification sessions shortly after a colloquium, we adopted the six-month rule: no student may hold such a session until half a year after entering the program. This provides students a much more realistic period for involving adjunct faculty and peers in their direction. Also, about two years into the program we urged students to formulate a step called precertification, which may consist of any form of communication, including the circulation of a tentative learning contract, a meeting with the committee, a conference phone call, or whatever. It makes the certification session much more functional as a working session. We also found it necesary to introduce the learning contract, signed by all committee members, to protect students from slippery memories and further hassling down the road of contract execution. In addition, we standardized the terminating phases (still allowing for both substantive and temporal flexibility) to obtain the right number of copies, permit time for the second core reader to react, and provide students an opportunity to develop an adequate program summary. Moreover, seeing that the various administrative steps are clearly and accurately recorded and in the files as evidence has been a major administrative task. Attending to such details are, of course, part of the practice and politics of survival.

In my judgment any institution that neglects such details, both in interfacing with students and with the wider educational world, does so at its peril. The ticklish and paradoxical problem in individualized learning contexts is to standardize unobstreperously, so that collecting data, filing reports, etc. by any person in the entire learning transaction does not become an end in itself, an all too easy eventuality if *numbers* of persons rather than *persons* become the focus. The challenge rests in adopting new procedures at midcourse in program development without succumbing to the temptations of routinization, abstractification, and dehumanization.

Whether or not we have succeeded probably depends upon one's angle of vision. From a core faculty viewpoint, such changes have been a mixed blessing. We knew that to survive we needed to tighten both the academic process and the reporting thereof, yet we were well aware that it's all too easy to get lost in the paper and neglect the student's learning. From a learner's viewpoint, an increasing number of graduates and active students bemoan the increase in volume of paper reflecting this trend—newsletters, procedural changes, and other matters regarding accreditation, affirmative action, and governance actions. Whether or not we will maintain a proper balance or fall into some Parkinsonian trap remains to be seen.[15]

COLLOQUIA

The original design and implementation of UGS provided for two modes of entry; one could start with a colloquium or begin with independent study after a conference with a core faculty member. We tried the latter for a couple of years. But the need for more predictable entry figures for budgetary purposes and the adamant reluctance of some of these "independent" persons to attend a colloquium to fulfill their residency made that option counterproductive. Hence, with rare exception, students now enter via a colloquium.

As stated elsewhere in this book, a UGS colloquium normally has been a four-week, intensive workshop session in which about thirty students, the core faculty, and a variety of consultants consider UGS processes, personnel, and program prospects.[16] The one expression most commonly used to describe a colloquium is "mind-blowing." Although it is difficult to characterize any one colloquium since each is different for each participant, some trends are perceptible. By varying the length of colloquia, the core has become more flexible in accepting whatever happens. And while most colloquia follow reasonably predictable cycles (initial anxiety, development of mutual assistance strategies, increasing willingness to subject UGS plans to scrutiny, concern for returning home to ordinary lifestyles), experimental models provide new opportunities for perceiving students evolving new modes for changing their learning styles. Also our changing student population (more ethnics, more women, more social change advocates, more disciplines reflected) has moved us away from planned encounter sessions to more concern for social change activities. Also, our mode of organizing colloquia has changed. We've moved from utilizing large numbers of visiting consultants to greater use of students and graduates as resource persons, from tight preplanning to more flexible during-colloquia programming. And, while accessibility or nonaccessibility of core at colloquia has generated anxieties of many dimensions, we've probably learned enough about "how to do it" to program core through any given colloquium with more calm and constructive results.

No matter what happens at a colloquium, both students and core usually make it superb grist for their learning mills. The files are filled with such student reactions:

> After many attempts, I have decided that it is impossible for me to separate my colloquium experience from the rest of my life since I entered the UGS process. All of my life's areas (values clarification, new friendships, academic growth, lifestyle, occupational development, personal relationships) have been either dramatically changed or totally confused by my UGS experience. The people I met take many forms. Some are shadows which occasionally dart across my mind. Others are so burned into my life that the things I do are often done for them to observe, silently, then comment upon!

The core, effecting the major continuity from one colloquium to another, has learned to relax with some of the inevitabilities, contradictions, and paradoxes. The student with the loudest demand and protest doesn't necessarily want it. The well-known consultant is not necessarily the most helpful. The twenty-four-hour day is rarely enough for the instant communication that colloquists often expect.

With encouragement from the North Central evaluation team, we are experimenting with new forms. In 1974, for instance, we decided to learn what happened when the same group came together for two ten-day colloquia, six months apart. We guessed that commitment to the process would be stronger, that it would give group members an opportunity to gain more perspective on one another over a period of time; we speculated that keeping the group small (fifteen) would encourage more communication. For the most part, our hunches were correct. Furthermore, this model, according to the participants, had some of the following advantages:

- Time to grow during the six months, then share that growth and flow with it positively;
- Less pressure to force a committee into existence;
- Easier to attend in light of job and family commitments;
- Time to digest material and become better acquainted with UGS processes;
- Different mood in each colloquium a distinct plus: structuring of first group meeting (April), nonstructuring of October session so each person could seek those he/she wanted to utilize more intensely as a resource, and easier to concentrate energies for ten days than thirty.

In the summer of 1976 we experimented with a colloquium featuring two graduates as coconvenors and encouraged students to bring their families.

Something happens when one assembles a group of UGS students; it's a chemistry that I don't fully understand; nor do I think it can be captured fully on video or cassette, written report, poetry, statistical evaluation, or emotional or intellectual osmosis.

ADJUNCT PROFESSORS

From an organizational development viewpoint, it's difficult to perceive the phenomenon of our use of adjunct professors in students' learning contexts. They have not been that integratively involved with UGS as an organization, but they have been involved and committed to the individual student's learning programs. More specifically particular adjuncts have:

- Driven or flown across country to meet with a student's committee for certification and terminar sessions;
- Sat up all night to read a PDE or visit a school or other action project;
- Invited students into their classrooms to share ideas; to home and study for lengthy conversations to share knowledge, concerns, or ideas about a given subject; to accompany them to professional meetings or a local bar for dialogue;
- Introduced students to friends, associates, and other human and material resources.

Or, as I've attempted to say, more impressionistically, an adjunct

. . . serves as tutor, consultant, facilitator, colearner for and with a Union Graduate Student in order to further a student's program . . . in this role he/she may be as formal or informal as is necessary depending upon circumstance, situation, relationship . . . serving on a committee may involve meeting with members of that committee periodically but at least during certification and terminating sessions . . . student and adjunct must decide the nature of communication between one another, among various members of the committee, and with the institution through the core faculty on the committee. . . .[17]

Despite all the activity of adjuncts in UGS, their interactions have not acquired any institutional characteristics. Most relationships between core and adjuncts or students and adjuncts have been ad hoc or situational. Although ongoing UGS personnel and even a few adjuncts expressed the viewpoint that adjuncts should receive more attention, the dispersion model of UGS has precluded much development beyond peripheral communication. The adjuncts should be commended for their consistent support and understanding of our fundamental belief in student self-direction and for their acceptance of the problems of geographical dispersion. Very few have resigned; many have expressed the desire to take on more responsibility. Most have never been paid commensurate with their worth. Although we have been leaning toward formalizing the contractual relationship with UGS as a school, whether this clarity will effect stronger commitment is unknown. The basic commitment, after all, is to a student learner.

HUMAN NETWORKS AND BLOBBING

At the time of the first colloquium in June and July 1970, no precedent existed for implementing an idea such as UGS. Fortunately the imaginations of those present were the human potential inherent in a person-centered and participatory model.

One student, Don Polkinghorne, was fresh from two years of experience developing a new freshman program and unique administrative structures at Goddard College. He was bubbling with enthusiasm for what Goddard was calling "the blob approach" to learning and administration. Actually, it was a brand of *ad hocracy;* students, administrators, and faculty formed "blobs" to discuss, decide, and implement. When no longer needed, they self-destructed, so the college didn't have to bear the deadweight and dehumanizing quality of standing committees. We considered that idea for several days at the first colloquium and concluded that it was a good model for UGS. And despite its dangers, its potentially volatile and somewhat unpredictable nature, it continues. Students have participated in the learning committees, fiscal affairs, admissions, employment of core faculty, the accreditation task force, National Policy Board, and minicolloquia organizing; in fact, it has been a rare UGS decision-making situation in which students have not been involved. By the end of the second year of operation, a careful summary of endeavor reflected the fact that 82 percent of the 139 students from the first five colloquia had been involved in some piece of UGS action beyond their own particular program.[18]

More important, of course, has been the quality of human networking. As I so frequently say in acknowledging student contributions to peer programs, every time a UGS peer participates creatively and supportively in another's process, UGS becomes a little stronger. This is also true when a peer graduates but remains on a colleague's committee as peer.[19] Although an occasional UGS student takes on too much or hassles over procedures or lets a colleague down, for the most part peer support has been monumental. Peers have performed many of the same functions as adjuncts and core and, in some instances, have done them better. Usually closer at hand, usually effecting more trust, usually more aware of his or her learning colleague as *a total person*, the peer is often in a better position to support a colleague than other committee members. By assisting a colleague, the peer also gains more insight about UGS processes (with less presence of threat) and his or her own learning strategies or problems. So, peer learning becomes more viable as it becomes more credible. Furthermore, we must always keep in mind that UGS students hail from many walks of life, often have had several careers, and are frequently in contact with vast human and institutional resources. Hence, peers are a bubbling spring of plenitude. Those not geographically isolated *exploit* such interaction in the best sense of that word. And there is certainly no social pressure to interact.

The lines of peer connection tend to flower from a given colloquium, but area meetings and minicolloquia (which the core sometimes spark when traveling about the country) tend to be cross-colloquial. It is fun, as core, to attend such meetings and watch persons from different colloquia recapture the momentum they felt at their particular colloquium as they compare their own work with that of their newfound peers.

Persons who feel good about these human interactions in and around the UGS process occasionally refer to their "tribe." One woman at one colloquium kept asking me, "Roy, who's your tribe?" At first I blinked; then, I indicated that members of my tribe were at every airport in my circuit-riding endeavors. But when I returned to the colloquium after a member of my family died, I knew from the empathy of that group that *they* were my tribe. In 1970 when UGS began, I doubt if any of us could have predicted this development.

EVALUATION

Educators in this country increasingly have tested and evaluated. The annals of education are filled with every test namable, from IQ to SAT and GRE, MMP, ad nauseum. And at least since World War II one would hardly dare write a proposal for a foundation or the U.S. Office of Education without building into it some kind of research or evaluation component. Of course, if one is to learn from mistakes, even if there are no external agencies looking over one's shoulder, some assessment of performance is required to answer a key question: "Are we *doing* that which we *say* we are doing?"

Responses have grown from discussions with every interested

party in USG. Evaluation has been a heavy part of every process: admissions, colloquia, committee meetings at certification and terminar, core faculty meetings, ad hoc sessions to deal with specific problems such as finances or student progress, and at both governance and Union Board meetings. Whether or not there is any pattern to the results may be difficult to say.

In asking students to report on their programs via a program summary, we ask for specific evaluations of their colloquium, committee input, internship, certification, PDE development, and terminar. In view of our need for potential communication to the world through this summary, we have structured our reporting procedures; hence, there is uniformity in the topics that are evaluated, even though each evaluation of each item may be uneven.

At several colloquia we have not only taped the group evaluation sessions, so that convening core could listen, learn, and change models, but we've also distributed questionnaires to participants in an attempt to gather some statistical data on the value of visiting consultants, core contributions, and other specific events. Although such efforts have not always been sophisticated in a technical sense, they have provided us some helpful profiles to govern future action. Under increasing pressure from students and our governing board, the faculty is encouraged to devise new modes of self-evaluation and distribute questionnaires among colleagues and students to gain perspective on their own performances (see Appendix D).[20]

When the visiting North Central accreditation team first suggested that we didn't have the personpower to do the kind of evaluation that should be done, they were probably both right and wrong (see Appendix C). Obviously, any sophisticated empirical evaluation *beyond* those of the friendly consultants[21] employed in conjunction with accreditation and the accreditation team itself would require a major effort, an effort which is now ongoing. But such an approach misses one major point. Most of the interaction between persons in the learning contract and between a student and his learning situation have a phenomenology that can be captured at best only in part. There is no doubt that more students should keep logs and that we would learn from them (see Chapters 4, 8, and 9). This also raises many ethical questions that would have to be resolved if subjected to public eye. The point is that neither UGS nor any other program of this kind can transcend the most superficial of externals if it does not weigh and consider the phenomenological; hence, our self-studies now include in-depth interviews and written profiles of our graduates to etch those dimensions of learning.

GOVERNANCE

Many tomes could be written about the phenomenon of governance. UGS governance was launched in the midst of the period of turbulent student dissent with the notion that every consti-tuency—core faculty, student, and UECU board—would have a voice. Although cast in the format wherein each group would have representatives, few of us were so naive as to believe that anybody really represents anybody else! Hence, in early June 1970, the UECU Board accepted the recommendation that the UGS board would be composed of two core faculty, a representative from each col-loquium, and four UECU board members. By the time of our first meeting in November of that year, the group consisted of two stu-dents from the first two colloquia, five UECU board members, two core, and two rotating chairs open to anybody in UGS wanting to voice an opinion. We also decided that students would be added un-til there were six; then, they would rotate one at a time as we held subsequent colloquia. Also, at the first meeting the group decided to become a *policy* board and not merely an advisory board.

The UGS minutes over the years reveal our concern with the whole gamut of UGS organizational, personnel, and fiscal problems. We were concerned constantly with the realities of the UGS Policy Board's role and its relationship to the larger UECU Board, which always assumed ultimate corporate responsibility. Unfortunately, this issue was more tense than necessary because students and core usually attended 100 percent of the time while neither UECU board members nor officers attended regularly.

By the time that "push came to shove" regarding such matters as the ultimate size of UGS, financial responsibility of UECU to UGS and vice versa, replacement of the initial coordinator/director, the launching of new units, and other important decisions, the Na-tional Policy Board (NPB) had:

- moved from consensual decision making to parliamentary procedure.
- elected a chairperson (student).

- increased the student term of office from six colloquia to two years.
- become primarily minority and feminist oriented in student membership.
- codified some of the power relationships in relation to the UECU (for instance, no core could be fired without consultation with the UGS Policy Board; an assessment fee for each student would be applied only *after* negotiation; the chairman of the NPB would attend the larger UECU Board meetings).

Naturally, the focus was on power; as militant minority and feminist views became dominant, many students and some core developed real concerns that the original learning visions would be obfuscated by the power games. From my own perspective I felt a deep sorrow when I heard persons at NPB meetings spouting fine rhetoric about saving humanity and improving the world but cutting to ribbons persons who expressed viewpoints characterized as sexist or elitist or racist (though such characterizations often were technically fallacious!). Careful listening to what another person said was lost in the fury over power manipulation. After one such meeting late in my own tenure as coordinator, I wrote a memorandum to my board colleagues, "Some Reflections Following a National Policy Board Meeting and Subsequent Reading of the Minutes."[22] In part it read:

Had there been time . . . I would like to have shared two *hopes* which have crossed my mind many, many times during each of the past several meetings:

- I keep hoping that members of the NPB will return home after a meeting, asking, "How did I happen to be there? What events led to my being at the NPB meeting? Was it chance? By design? By what? And what difference does it make?"
- I *hope* that somebody will come along some day interested in the social, economic, political, cultural, and historical evolution of the UGS National Policy Board, analyze it, share insights, etc.

I express these hopes as one having been trained in the methodologies of history, political science, sociology, philosophy and psychology . . . as well as one having evolved a deep concern for interlocking causalities, interlocking events *and* the phenomenology of experience.

Also during the course of the past several months I've repeatedly asked myself:

- How long will it take us to reinvent Leviathan State University?
- Are organizations doomed to develop administrative arteriosclerosis?
- With increasing student demand for structure and certainty of administrative responsibilities, can we maintain the level of academic free choice which seemed to be the vision of the founders of UGS?
- Was Max Weber right in positing the notion that institutions and people tend to move "from charisma to bureaucracy"?
- How or can we evolve trust relationships among UGS students, UGS committees, and all other UGS-related persons if our governing board is increasingly concerned about power checks and balances?
- Are we willing to cope with the ironies, paradoxes, and contradictions which evolve in an institution that stresses self-direction for students and formal accountability for the core faculty?

A student who has watched UGS grow and who always reads and responds to monthly reports wrote as follows:

I want just to say briefly once again that with almost every monthly report and NPB minutes I am depressed by the creeping bureaucratization of our program. I am sure that such indications, if you also feel them, depress you, too. Somehow the direction seems so insistently *against* the thrust from power to poetry. Maybe it was even the nearly intangible tone and stylistic change of the NPB minutes, which seemed so much colder. Surely it was the proliferation of committees and the tensions imposed by external demands. The tuition hike and the demise of the extremely helpful "package" depressed me. I guess it's like supercooling a saturated solution: all at once all the fluid crystallizes. I just want you to know that I am experiencing some real grief for UGS as it was. I am feeling harshly and endlessly reminded that it's something very different now than it was when I began. Richard Neibuhr in *The Social Sources of Denominationalism* described the nearly inevitable petrifying of sects into denominations. His observations are instructive for me as I look at UGS . . . and the world.

I find this a pretty powerful statement even if one may wish to discount some of the perception as projection.

How far I had spent my own capital with this particular group of persons is illustrated by their nonresponse.

As I indicated a couple of months later in a private memo to many friends concerned about trends in UGS as well as my own pain,

> I find myself in a strange place, so radical that I am reactionary in this growing place of conservatism. To save what? To save the paranoia of a few persons who have been mistreated or who ride like Sir Galahads in quest of the grails of certainty? And once again I learn of the laws of developing institutions: they *will* get more bureaucratic because those who seek power want rules and regulations, want psychological certainty, want checks and balances . . . no matter how many they have to destroy, face to face, in order to save the world for ethnics, the underdog, women, whomever . . . and they have so little sense of paradox and irony and humor, so puritanical and so right are they . . . and, of course, in writing this I am the only one who does not claim to be right in my own self-image! So where to now? Can the academic part of UGS survive before the onslaught of those who will force others to be free?

No doubt there will be rejoinders to this viewpoint expressed from other value systems and strategies. But even as any current generation of students and faculty work to evolve new governance modes so that each constituency may have a vital voice, I can only hope that they will accept the inevitability of change since all life is precarious; also that the essential genius of UGS is the learning blob which self-destructs. The latter, paradoxically enough, may be the most stable element assuring UGS continuity.[23]

6 Excellence: Hang-up or Opportunity?

Traditionalists in higher education continually probe at what they usually perceive as the major Achilles heel of experiential and innovative education, namely, standards of excellence.[1] And, interestingly enough, those of us immersed in it continually react as though we were vulnerable. (This chapter may be no exception!) Meet a former colleague or old friend and an occasional UGS adjunct professor, and more times than not the conversation comes around to that question; in fact, it sometimes becomes the dominant issue of the interaction. Of course, since most of us working in this field have experienced what commonly is perceived as "quality education" in traditional programs, experienced it at every degree level, we know that many assumptions made about that quality are open to question. Yet, we react; we're defensive; we argue, even when not convinced that humans are rational or ever settle much by logical debate. Since most of us have come out of argumentative or verbal settings, however, we continue like old dogs with old tricks. Nor can we seem to realize that it's hard to be heard across the backyard if we're arguing from different premises!

Despite all the tumult and shouting, questions of excellence usually boil down to a few basic assumptions:

- Students can/must be selected by some relatively objective criteria (SAT or GRE scores, rank order in high school or college classes, grade point ratios, face-to-face interviews, high potentiality, etc.).
- The faculty can/must be chosen similarly on the basis of a credible record of academic performance, publication, graduation from a well-known university (prominence equated with excellence), potentiality, etc.

- The overall ratio between student and faculty must be kept low or reasonable, the assumption being that low ratio means close and meaningful interaction and high accountability.
- The material resources (library, laboratories, dormitories, parking spaces) should be consistently adequate in terms of the expressed purposes of the school or degree program under consideration.
- Curriculums, courses, degree programs, professional or para-professional training must accomplish in fact what they say they do.
- The residency requirement must achieve its purposes.
- The regional accrediting association or other specialized certifying agency must be competent in judging whether or not one's total academic and fiscal operation is both accountable and excellent.

I won't attempt to argue each of these points; after all, billions of words have been written about them. Even the most casual perusal of educational journals, doctoral dissertations, or the books in any library will reflect seemingly interminable argument over program evaluation. And any innovative program that expects to be accredited must ponder these issues. Yet, as I query in Chapter 1, must the credible become accreditable? Wouldn't a truly innovative program probably eschew that convention? But most of the programs considered in this book have not chosen to eschew such an interface; they have faced up to fundamental survival mechanisms: survival (hence excellence?) depends upon acceptance; acceptance depends upon accreditation; accreditation, enrollment, and financial recognition by the U.S. Office of Education (though not necessarily the Veterans' Administration)[2] depend upon excellence. 'Round and 'round she goes, and where she stops nobody knows!

Hence, university without walls (UWW) programs at the undergraduate level, Goddard and Antioch at the master's level, and Humanistic Psychology Institute (HPI), Walden, Nova and UGS at the doctoral level have all had to consider these commonly accepted traditional assumptions. And sometimes our implemented decisions have been more appearance than substance.[3] Of course, we've hired faculty from the Harvards and Berkeleys; of course, we've found admissions criteria that minimize whimsicality or random factors; of course, we've tried to keep overall ratios of students and faculty low, even when it has required redefinition of faculty; and of course, we've written proposals, tapped federal funds, and stretched our imaginations to cope with physical facilities, curriculums, and residency perceptions. Nor is this to be ultracynical about such effort. Often our decisions have been too painful and too real to permit the luxury of indulging in self-denigration. Those of us committed to these kinds of programs and institutions probably will continue to find ourselves forced into responding to American educational infrastructures of finance and evaluation, calling for the patience of Job and the imagination of Picasso if we are to survive.

ALSO PAINFUL

I find it difficult to listen to questions from persons who know all the answers or who speak with such authority that it is almost useless to respond or to those who refuse to search for alternative perspectives on a problem. One also encounters a whole gamut of self-fulfilling prophecies, nonsequiturs, and irrelevancies. One is reminded of Plato's character Thrasymachus, an ancient cousin of Machiavelli, who defined justice as "the interest of the stronger."[4] Sometimes in the United States one merely substitutes richer for stronger to catch the flavor of an attitude.

Ponder these wearisome questions:

- How do you know what your graduates know if you don't test them?
- How can they know anything when they take no courses?
- How do you know that you have a quality product?
- If students don't specialize in one field, how can they compete on the open market?
- Since the Ph.D. market is poor, how can you justify granting more degrees?
- Aren't you afraid of being ripped off?

Our attitude, however, does not necessarily have to be one of defensiveness. As a faculty colleague once remarked at a colloquium, "We must be careful we don't judge our work entirely by our failures."[5] The tendency may be to do just that if one is trying something different. In fact, I want to focus upon that *differentness*. The sickening part of much criticism about excellence is the assumption that the same criteria should be employed for judging every student and every program. One frequently hears fear expressed that extended degree programs will lower or undermine standards. The assumption is, of course, that the critic's standards are high and that any change is a lowering!

Our programs are different in both process and result; hence, rather than moan because evaluating that differentness is difficult, one should attempt to determine the nature of both the processes and the means for looking at them. Educators should have expected to learn that lesson long before this, yet many seem *not* to have! We have not totally disregarded empirical research that is ostensibly objective, and we have not overlooked commonly accepted assumptions. For instance, in UGS we do occasionally use the GRE score if it is readily available, and faculty should normally hold a doctoral degree if they are involved in educating Ph.D's. If our policy is part of our survival kit, as it is in these two instances, let's admit it and move on to subject that phenomenon to question rather than avoid it or defend it upon some abstruse grounds.

EARLY ENCOUNTER WITH EXCELLENCE

Of course, designing external degree programs could not avoid the excellence issue. At an early stage in the UWW program, for instance, the organizers held series of meetings in which suggestions were made for assessing both students and institutions, suggestions that included evaluating competence, collecting evidence to support learning, appraising both cognitive and affective growth, designing procedures for periodic assessment of student progress, developing tentative narrative transcripts that would indicate both objective and subjective progress, and assessing a student's "noteworthy contribution"[6] to others. Surely, such criteria are not wholly absent when a conventional professor evaluates students in conventional courses; the learning gestalt is simply different and for good reason. We are attempting to transcend the limitations that occur when learning is removed from the stream of life. However, for many persons, the course-credits-hours approach is adequate for their needs, but we are simply encouraging students to develop new means and contexts for meeting their needs.

Nova, Walden, and HPI programs have had to face these issues at the doctoral level. Surely nobody can expect to receive a degree in humanistic psychology without an awareness of alternative psychologies. Surely nobody can expect to receive a Nova degree without attaining competence in the several educational administration areas. In fact, some professors in the Nova circuit even give grades, though the means by which students acquire information and through which competence is assessed are alternative routes. Surely a person earning a Walden degree, which is primarily in thesis writing, cannot expect to survive without coming solidly to grips with competence in alternative research methodologies.

I am more familiar, of course, with the evolution of the Antioch and Union Graduate School programs. In the Antioch program we encouraged students to evolve their seminar needs in light of available faculty or nearby resource persons; also we emphasized the accumulation of log materials or other evidence reflecting learning. For a long time we expected a major project (thesis) from each person as well as a supervised practicum, so we were concerned about quality control data that could be verified and for which we would be accountable.[7]

The evolution of viewpoints and procedures in UGS has in some ways been much more interesting because many of the methods and procedures of UGS run counter to commonly accepted criteria for evaluating doctoral programs. Let us, for instance, take a look at the North Central Association definition of the Ph.D.:

> The Doctor of Philosophy degree program prescribes no specific universal model. Each institutional program is expected to reflect generally accepted standards of doctoral training with the compatible professional and academic goals. The program involves attainment of independent and comprehensive scholarship in a selected field. Mastery of a substantial body of knowledge is combined with training in research. To this end, the program should consist of formal courses, seminars, discussions, independent study, and research designed to assist the student to acquire, as well as to contribute to, knowledge in his field.
>
> During the first year or two, a doctoral student may take a number of formal courses to advance his knowledge of his field, its scholarly tools, and its relationship to other disciplines. The scholarly tools consist of proficiency in foreign languages, statistics, or mathematics according to their appropriateness to the special field. Foreign languages are no longer uniformly required by all institutions for the Ph.D. degree.

Relationships of the special field to other disciplines involves the study of related and supporting disciplines.

Since the Ph.D. is primarily a research degree, the doctoral student should begin relating his total program to the research objectives shortly after entering the program. He should receive careful guidance in developing these capabilities through a sustained research project on a realistically limited, but important, subject. His efforts should culminate in the writing and defense of a dissertation. The research should be more than a mere compilation of information; it should make a significant contribution in its own right to the understanding of the subject; and it should be judged for quality by selected members of the graduate faculty. A significant block of time, and perhaps credit, should be assigned to the dissertation to avoid overloading programs with course work.

Following completion of the formal advanced study and satisfactory performance in comprehensive examinations dealing with the field requirements and central goals of the program, the student should be admitted to candidacy for the Ph.D. degree. The remaining time should be devoted to completion of the research project and compilation of the results in a dissertation. The final Ph.D. examination frequently consists mainly of a defense by the candidate of his research and dissertation.[8]

Cognizant of such criteria for determining excellence, we came squarely to grips with the implications of what we were doing very early in our institutional life. We made it clear—in both written and oral discussions—that the reputation of the program eventually would depend upon the quality of work that graduates did and not some hypothetical notion that because professors had Ph.D.'s or that the student-faculty ratio was low, the graduates would be good. In short, we expected the proof to be in the pudding, not the recipe for it!

At our very first colloquium in the summer of 1970, we spent an enormous amount of time talking about quality. How could we achieve it individually and as an institution? How might we recognize it if we experienced it? Were there any external tests of truth that we could use? And could we trust a sign even if we saw it? And how could we convince the world that we had a quality program when the processes themselves were being evolved? Why did we need accreditation if we wanted to do something different? And why did we call the UGS project a "Project Demonstrating Excellence" (PDE)? If the demonstration were clear, wouldn't excellence be obvious? Did *naming* it "Excellence" really make it excellent?

At that colloquium we distributed two documents that articulated our stance toward the issue. One offered the practical suggestion of seeking perhaps three recent graduates of first-rate universities to discover what those students might recommend for reading or courses. In fact, the hand-out concluded:

> It is likely that you will get better curriculum guidance from advanced graduate students than from adjunct professors, and usually without charge. The material covered by most required courses in your field can be assimilated through independent study. Some courses may be so stimulating and so much more the *man* than the books, that you'll want to enroll in or to audit such a course.[9]

Our second hand-out, a three-paragraph quotation from Aage Nielsen's *Lust for Learning*, concluded:

> . . . it is first and foremost not relevant how good a person my leader, or my parents [or my adjunct professors] or my peer group think that I am. Other people's opinions are good learning potential, but to bring them into my primary considerations is to delay or regress. Once I have established within me a direction and an understanding of how I want to be a good person, and after I have attempted to practice some of these ways, then I can move in with you under your standards without it hurting me. Then I can let you buy my time and my skills for a given period, and I will know when I need to go on to further my own pursuit of an integrated goodness and excellence.[10]

In retrospect, it is interesting, on one hand, to observe the core faculty urging UGS students to appeal to traditional graduate students' experiences and on the other encouraging them to appeal to the authority or vision of Nielsen. Our behavior seems paradoxical.

Since then, of course, the issue of excellence has been ever present even when it is unspoken. As in any other program that plans for survival, it is an integral part of the structure. As suggested at other points thus far, we have instituted various normative procedures. As outlined in my in-house paper "Quality Control and/or Health in UGS" (1971), "preventative-positive-reinforcing" methods would include, among others, careful admissions processes and colloquia designs to assure accurate but imaginative launching. The negative sanctions, what I called "corrective-negative-restraining" ones, may need more delineation:

- There *are* hurdles and/or requirements, such as the evolving of a program (including study plans, internship and project) such as a certification session, which cannot be held until there is consensus among the committee that it should be held.

- As "keepers of the process" core faculty have a special responsibility to encourage students to choose effective, committed, and creative committee members rather than persons who will simply scratch their backs or be in too much accord; also, core faculty have special obligations as coordinators of arrangements for both certification and concluding sessions, ascertaining whether or not a student has followed the processes outlined in the brochure and to make sure that all members of a person's committee will be present at any given session.

- As "keepers of process," too, during certification sessions core faculty must be sensitive to the kind of "contract" which students and committee members are evolving for a student's tenure in the program.

- As "master of alternative methodologies," a core faculty must not be timid about using his crap detector to point out what he perceives as spurious, fallacious, questionable, etc. as he sees any given product or process (pink is hardly green except under very special circumstances; nor is $2 + 2 = 0$ except under clearly defined logical conditions!) (suggesting: pick a methodology for doing something and it's well to master the integrity of that methodology).

- All committee members, if they are, indeed, friends of any given student, will be constructively critical rather than soft-mindedly and soft-heartedly rubber stampish . . . meaning, inferring, implying: that *any* member of a student's committee may have to be a "slower of the process" as well as a facilitator of learning if he or she sees that a student is trying to slide through, is hell-bent to finish regardless of the consequences and the implications for the next person and the total UGS process. In one case, over loud protests, we encouraged a person to postpone his terminar from April to May to July . . . and even attempted to effect further postponement when . . . at the 11th hour, 59th minute it was obvious that he didn't have his "thing together"; result: he held the session, was terribly upset and embarrassed when the committee reached a consensus that he had much more work to do; further result: this session, plus another pointing to several months of "clean up" work, led to the procedural change outlined in "Project of Excellence and Terminar" indicating that we shall set the dates of finishing sessions *after* all members of a committee agree that such a session will be a celebration rather than the traditional agonizing "oral" or "examination."

- It is assumed that the key concepts outlined in the brochure are in effect. Hence, we are attempting the impossible and *do* expect highly motivated, highly creative, highly competent, highly knowledgeable people to emerge from the processes . . . hence processes do include knowing as well as feeling, learning as well as opinion, study as well as action, meditating and speculating as well as articulating and date compiling . . . *as well as* connectors rather than *either/or* outlooks, if you'll forgive the paradox.

> We *must* have structure,
> the cat complained,
> we thought it sunny
> he said it rained.

EVOLVING CONCEPTS AND PROCEDURES[11]

At the expense of contradicting ourselves or being trapped in a variety of paradoxes, those of us responsible for the institution have written position papers that establish guidelines so students as well as outsiders may see how we attempt to induce and ascertain quality. Of course, it's a simple matter of fact that we have more experience, more data to use as a basis for judgment, and with more students, more pressure to be clear. Without question, the decision to seek accreditation forced us to standardize procedure and to clarify our position. This has special relevance along three axes; namely, determining what a Project Demonstrating Excellence (PDE) is, setting some exit policies, and establishing guidelines for developing a learning contract.

The PDE

In retrospect, I suppose, we could have chosen a happier caption for a student's major project. Anxious to open up the parameters of the traditional thesis or dissertation and to transcend the connotations of those terms, one of the founding fathers hit upon Project Demonstrating Excellence. We have stuck to it, and perhaps the caption keeps us focusing on the problem of defining excellence rather than neglecting it. Living with the difficult may in the long run enable us to survive, both psychologically and institutionally.

From the outset, the PDE was not to be confused with a thesis or dissertation, although some students found it more convenient to use such terms in communicating with their non-UGS professional colleagues. Also, we attempted to communicate to others that the PDE did not *in itself* necessarily stand alone; rather, it was to be considered as part of a *total program* that also included an internship and a study program. And where a PDE seemed totally incomprehensible to a non-UGS reader, we urged her to start with a graduate's program summary or comprehensive picture of work done during the tenure. In short, it was and continues to be our hope that a UGS program is a total learning thrust and not one chopped up into bits and pieces; we've seen enough of what T. S. Eliot called measuring out one's life "in coffee spoons."

And yet, interfacing with the world was still difficult. When one of our preaccreditation consultants asked me to pick out ten or fifteen PDE's and rank them in three categories (excellent, average, and marginal), I did so. The next day he remarked, "Strangely enough, your best ones look amazingly similar to conventional theses!" And I had to concur.[12]

But these kinds of struggles have been helpful to those of us concerned both with particular students and their learning, growth, and productions and with institutional development, evolution of free-form education, and fundamental learning questions. If the mind- and heart-searching struggles are painful, one needs be reminded of that old piece of doggerel:

> Writers strive
> while alive
> and get ahead
> when they're dead.

The same may be true for educators!

After launching upon the accreditation route (see Chapter 7), we evolved guidelines for both students and external examiners that focused sharply upon standards issues in and around the PDE, which undergo continuous scrutiny and revision. Although somewhat lengthy, its major contents are included in Appendix E. Appendix F lists representative PDE topics.

TO EXIT OR NOT....

According to an old saying, you can tell the quality of a school by the percentage of dropouts. Perhaps it originated with the celebrated dean of the Harvard Law School who opened each freshman class ceremony with the warning, "Look to the left of you . . . now look to the right of you . . . one of you won't be here next year!" This assumption has an interesting corollary; namely, if a person cannot make it in an institution of higher learning, obviously the student, *not* the institution, has failed. While this belief may have been modified somewhat by the realities of trying to keep students in elementary and secondary school, one encounters it so frequently in college and university circles that it seems to be accepted as a working principle, norm, or guideline. Surely it relates to the institution's self-concept.

A combination of this assumption plus our ostensibly humanistic approaches to both admissions and program development has created some very sticky questions. For instance, since we do not have grade and credit hour hurdles for a student to leap, how does the student know when he should exit? Or how does the institution decide to terminate a student? Since any dismissal for arbitrary reasons would be contested with a demand for evidence, in the context of academic due process, what kind of evidence would stick? Should all admitted students be guaranteed the degree? And what happens when those of us making policy introduce time limits, such as a minimum of six months to certification or a maximum of four years to graduation? Although these are inevitably tied to tuition schedules, should there be *any* time constraints placed on self-directed learning? We have struggled with the paradoxes, ironies, and even the humor and pathos of trying to answer these questions. (During our first four years of existence we asked only one student to leave; within days following his arrival at a colloquium, he left, formed an educational institute in his state, and granted *himself* a doctoral degree!)

In our early years, pressure from our governance board, student queries about drop-out statistics, and external influences prompted us to report occasionally on the phenomenon of exit, pointing out that we had encouraged some persons to "go interim"[13] or slowed the process for others who evidently were not going to make it. It seemed to us that those who accepted our conditions, tuition package approach as well as a tenure policy, and who then chose not to communicate might well encounter the four-year statute of limitations, then drop out. This was a more passive solution to quality and excellence problems.[14]

Not until the faculty began expressing some concern about students who seemed to be drifting did we begin to formulate a comprehensive process/progress assessment policy. This was a long and arduous task, requiring faculty and governance deliberations as well as the assistance of legal counsel. In essence, the procedure we developed provides for systematic quality checks at the colloquium and at certification, as well as the opportunity for core faculty to raise questions about the suitability of any given student at any time. If a student is dropped at any point, by a combination of faculty and students at colloquium or certification or by a progress assessment committee at any other time, the student has procedural due process rights to appeal the decision. Ultimately, the decision rests with the president of the Union for Experimenting Colleges and Universities. The procedure seems eminently humanistic, but one always hopes that sticky situations can be resolved by full faith and discussion rather than resort to legalistic means. And it is by no means certain that an institution is necessarily more excellent simply because an occasionally unfit person gets in and is thrown out!

DOES ANYTHING GO?

Despite our careful attention to admissions and learning formulation, despite our careful attending to every process step, and despite
such guidelines as those for the UGS PDE, the outsider tends to assume that anything goes in experiential/experimental programs.
Students, too, stumbling into UGS under false pretenses and perceptions or perhaps beset by change of heart or changed family-work
circumstances, sometimes flounder in external degree rhetoric that
sounds like anything goes. Naturally, this is easier to do where the
checks are not in a single hand (the professor, the chairman, etc.),
where one may try to play one committee member against another,
or where one can dismiss an entire committee to start anew. Yet,
what is theoretically possible seldom occurs, in UGS at least, *if* lines
of communication remain open. Peers on a committee, who are as
concerned about the quality of the UGS degree as any other interested party, often exercise the most constructive constraint. I am
always pleased, for instance, when I see this kind of peer interaction,
as in a three-cornered conference phone call or via the pages of an
extensive and thoughtful letter evaluating a prospective learning
contract, internship report, or PDE.

So, do we get ripped off? Yes, occasionally. Will it destroy us? I
doubt it. Is the phenomenon any better or worse than rip-offs in
more traditional settings? I don't know, and probably nobody can
answer that question. If we dwell on it, however, and make invidious
distinctions one way or another, we take our eyes off our fundamental task in the educational world, namely, to facilitate a student's
learning through a viable alternative to the traditional degree.

AN INTERVENTION?

Many institutions with undergraduate honors programs or graduate
programs use the external examiner as a way of preventing rip-offs,
poor quality, and incredibility. Some innovative programs also use
this technique to assist with these potential problems. In fact, we
sometimes used it in the early days of Antioch-Putney. Walden University has it well integrated into its total procedure. But in UGS we
rejected the concept rather early and have continued to do so. Bringing in the external examiner at the very end of a student's program,

which is the usual procedure, would be saying to the committee, "Look, we don't really trust the student and you to evolve a program that *is* excellent." And while we have come to live with many paradoxes in UGS, this is a contradiction that no doubt would destroy the integrity of our effort, and ultimately the institution. So we've found another way to approach some of the issues implicit in employing such a method, by introducing the second core reader.

Toward the end of one's program, the core faculty member of the student's committee, in consultation with the student, invites a core colleague to review *both* program and PDE. The feedback of such a review goes to the first core rather than directly to the student. The first core may do whatever he wishes with the report—even burn it—but normally it goes to the student, who may wish to modify his work in light of that report. He is not required to; nor does the second core have a veto.

This method was introduced when we were three years into the program ostensibly to effect quality and to develop colleagiality. Ironically, a couple of core voted for it because they said they felt lonely representing the institution by themselves. In my judgment, however uneven the procedure may be, it has served a variety of purposes. Nevertheless, working out the logistics to do this is sometimes terribly difficult, especially if the PDE is some kind of performance. In one instance, my colleague Caroline Shrodes flew from San Francisco to San Diego to attend a student-directed performance of the *Oresteia*. In another instance, another colleague, Phyllis Walden, attended Hugh (Brother Blue) Hill's mime-dance-music concert in Deer Island Prison, Boston, on the very day that the prison authorities held a shakedown and the prisoners revolted. That we were fortunate not to have become hostages did not occur to us until we went to the Harvard Faculty Club for luncheon and the closing numbers of Brother Blue's performance!

A Fantasy?

We have not had as yet the intestinal fortitude to implement what has been discussed seriously at a few colloquia; namely, to review all UGS degrees five years after graduation and rescind those given to persons who have not lived up to their potential for creativity, self-direction, and production! While intensive study of many of our graduates reflects high standards of excellence, both *in* UGS and beyond tenure, we're not claiming to be perfect . . . yet!

THE PUDDING

To return to some of our opening questions about excellence: Are our students selected objectively? No, but experience tells us that the techniques we are using do work for the most part. Visitors to colloquia and North Central evaluators indicate that our students are "among the finest they've ever met." Both our students and those in other external doctoral programs are designing and building new institutions, writing poems, plays, and books that are being published, sculpting, filming and painting exhibitable works of art, inventing patentable processes and materials, reorganizing university departments and schools, as well as changing curriculums. Many are on the very frontier of important social movements, such as the feminist, Black, Chicano, and Native American Studies programs. In many fields, such as medical and psychotherapeutic ethics, they are questioning conventional wisdom. In short, any mature consideration of excellence would find our students and graduates measuring up favorably beside those who reach the doctoral plateau via more traditional routes. A recent survey of graduates reveals that the majority of those questioned do not feel handicapped in competing or conversing with Ph.D.'s from traditional programs.

Moreover, we have kept the student-faculty relationship at a reasonably ideal ratio even while pioneering in a study to determine what is reasonable (see Chapter 8). We also are pioneering in new conceptions of residency (see Chapter 9). We continue to subject the results to both internal and external scrutiny via the very process of evolving student's programs. Furthermore, most adjunct professors in UGS *are* outsiders. Since they work for other institutions, they are in a good position to compare, contrast, speak, advise, consent, dissent—all of which contributes to our perceptions of quality. And each student and core faculty must become a master in the utilization of the resources needed to complete a program.

All the world's a classroom, and everybody to whom any UGS person relates is a potential teacher or colearner. By keeping our antennae extended into every conceivable corner and process in that world, perhaps we can avoid the rigor mortis that sets into most formal learning so early. Or, if we find ourselves dying, let us make the most of that. For instance, from one of the most wholesale evidences of death, that in which trillions upon trillions of shells wash onto a beach, one can learn much from the beauty of those shells! We must not fall victim to easy formulas in the name of accountability, operant conditioning, or competency-based this or that!

7

Process as Criteria: Designing New Accreditation Modes

One of the many leitmotifs in this volume is the issue of accreditation. While it is doubtful that most students in any of the new degree programs are terribly knowledgeable about accreditation processes, most do want accreditation. It's much like a seal of approval: it assures status and may even determine whether or not one obtains or holds a job or gets a salary increase. Students know, too, that their friends are likely to ask whether or not their "innovative program" is accredited. Hence, while they may be low in sophistication, they know that this status is desirable.

If anger could be pumped into barrels and used to fuel industry, no doubt enough would be generated annually over this issue in American education to keep the wheels turning for many days! Similarly, if anxiety could be bottled for similar use, the fuel tanks rarely would be empty. In UGS alone, as much energy has been spent talking about the problem as working on it. And some UGS students have become very angry that we expended one ounce of effort on it or risked being turned down; after all, to use their metaphor, "Why start a revolution and ask the enemy to furnish your guns?"

RATIONALITY PREVAILS

For all the feelings related to this issue, my sense of the innovative landscape suggests that rationality has prevailed. For all the fears and sweat that have gone into the struggle, for all the name-calling, and for all the haunting specters imagined, nontraditional educators now work in a better climate than that which prevailed as recently as five years ago. Patsy Thrash's fine survey of the phenomenon reflects a significant movement toward flexible policies and applications by both national and regional organizations. As the title of her survey, "Nontraditional Institutions and Programs: A Challenge for the Accreditation Process," suggests, accreditation officers throughout the country have been responsive to needs in postsecondary education.[1]

But before narrating some of the details of the UGS effort, let's examine some of the reasons why institutions seek it. Extrinsically, the federal government utilizes private accrediting associations in a legal way to determine criteria for eligibility of federal funds. The intrinsic purposes are reflected in the U.S. Office of Education's list of functions which the associations perform:[2]

1. Certifying that an institution has met established standards.
2. Assisting prospective students in identifying acceptable institutions.
3. Assisting institutions in determining the acceptability of transfer credits.
4. Helping to identify institutions and programs for the investment of public and private funds.
5. Protecting an institution against harmful internal and external pressures.
6. Creating goals for self-improvement of weaker programs and stimulating a general raising of standards among educational institutions.
7. Involving the faculty and staff comprehensively in institutional evaluation and planning.
8. Establishing criteria for professional certification, licensure, and for upgrading courses offering such preparation.
9. Providing one basis for determining eligibility for federal assistance.

Hence, there *are* reasons for seeking accreditation; and those of the U.S. Office of Education are not too different than those of the Council of the Federation of Regional Accrediting Commissions of Higher Education (FRACHE). The major problem, of course, is to devise means by which one can assess the key FRACHE objective; namely to determine whether or not "an institution has clearly defined appropriate educational objectives, has established conditions under which their achievement can reasonably be expected, appears in fact to be accomplishing them substantially, and is so organized, staffed, and supported that it can be expected to continue to do so."[3]

As anybody can readily see, it's not easy to ascertain what is appropriate, reasonable, and substantial. Almost any two persons or institutions of good will (however defined) might very well disagree on the meaning of such terms. What we in the innovative learning world must assure is the development of due process ground rules and their ongoing evolution when accrediting institutions implement another objective: "providing counsel and assistance to establishing and developing institutions."[4] The remainder of this chapter is the story of evolving such due process considerations as UECU sought accreditation for UGS through the auspices of the North Central Association of Colleges and Secondary Schools (NCA).

CLEARING NEW PATHWAYS

Following a year-long interaction between the two organizations in an effort to evolve a procedure for evaluating nine of the Union's university without walls (UWW) undergraduate programs in various parts of the country, a process that ultimately led to NCA candidacy status for UWW, representatives of the two institutions met in January 1973 to develop a strategy for evaluating UGS.

At this meeting two major decisions were made: first, the NCA accreditation team would be comprised of persons to whom both North Central and the Union gave mutual consent; second, the evaluation team would observe the program in action, studying the dynamics of its diverse parts and as a whole rather than perceiving the program primarily through the usual previsit self-study report or descriptions. We wanted the team to have an opportunity to see every component of the UGS process in operation. Rather than taking snapshots of the institution at a single moment of time, the team would take films of the program in motion. This seemed especially appropriate for a program stressing process, one sometimes identifying process as product.

PREPARATION

Staff members at North Central and UGS spent considerable time during the January-March period locating evaluators acceptable to both UGS and NCA. One of the guidelines set at the January meeting was that of including minorities and women in the visiting team. Upon finding and appointing mutually acceptable team members in early March,[5] UGS supplied them with background material—brochures and reports, data on the development of the program, including the history of significant changes, statistics, etc. During this gestation period we projected a tentative calendar of events and steps for the NCA team to observe.

Meanwhile at UGS, we established an accreditation task force comprised of core faculty, administrators, and students who were privy to reports that UGS's own private consultants had developed after close analysis of our program the previous winter.[6] The task force was national in base, but it met for a day at headquarters in Yellow Springs to study ways in which persons in the UGS process could be involved in developing summaries, position papers, and statistical analyses as needed over the course of the projected, year-long evaluation period.

Finally, the North Central team and the UGS task force met in Chicago in late March 1973 to develop the procedures and a calendar for implementing the plan. This was no ordinary meeting. All parties present were ultraconscious of our pioneer effort, its cost, and its implications, not only for the future of the Union Graduate School, but also for the future of accrediting institutions of higher learning in the United States. We had a most frank interchange. Many questions were raised:

- Was the UGS process for any given student such that the team should see the various steps in a particular sequence?
- Could the sequences be varied?
- Should all members of the accreditation team be present at all events?
- Would members of the North Central team serve in the role of the traditional evaluator or might they get caught in advocacy roles?
- Having launched such an accreditation process at a given point in space and time, what were the implications of looking at UGS persons and processes from a longitudinal viewpoint over a two to five year period?
- Should UGS develop a status report following North Central guidelines, at least in general, or determine its own particular set of guidelines adapted to UGS needs?

These questions were not answered completely at the March

meeting. In fact, they came up again in later sessions, but the North Central team, the North Central administrative staff, and the UGS task force engaged in an honest interchange informed by intelligence, experience, and broad perspectives on higher education in the United States. Although we were apprehensive, being sensitive to our ground-breaking efforts, several persons from both groups expressed satisfaction and excitement about the prospective value of the endeavor.

THE PROCESS

The first NCA team visit to a UGS event was designed to afford members an overview of UGS activity and to concentrate specifically upon our admissions procedures. Not only did team members participate in the three-day visit but also the North Central staff, and UGS faculty, administrators, and students as well. The sessions encouraged maximum give and take. Consistent with the maximum openness process and policy characterizing most UGS endeavors, we decided to "disclose all" frankly rather than package papers or processes neatly so as to be seen in a most favorable light. The NCA team also attended a regular monthly seminar sponsored by the coordinator for UGS.

The Admissions Committee and the North Central team did their homework equally well. Each person read all twenty-five applications (the number normally considered) before the formal session began. The Admissions Committee, consisting of four core faculty and five students, conducted its business in a fishbowl. They accepted two, rejected seventeen, and placed five in a "pending" category until more information could be obtained about them. At the end of this very typical meeting, we engaged in a frank interchange as the North Central team raised questions about those persons admitted or rejected, criteria for admission and rejection, and other related subjects.

AN ONGOING STEP

Consistent with one of the guidelines developed at the Chicago meeting in March, the chairman of the North Central team submitted a tentative report on the visit. We had agreed previously that the team would send a statement after each event to which various UGS task force members could react, submitting any commentary directly to the chairman. This procedure was especially valuable to UGS, for it gave us a film clip of what the NCA team saw and provided immediate feedback about ways and means of strengthening our program. Or, we could make no changes whatever, for we were determined *not* to compromise our fundamental philosophy and procedures.

THE NEXT FEW STEPS

Interaction between UGS persons and the NCA team and staff during the following four months was very intense. During a single day in May, the full NCA team observed two certification sessions in New York City. In early June the NCA participants observed a two-day governance meeting in St. Louis. Later in June, some members of the team attended a termination session in Chicago. And in July and August, all members of the NCA team devoted more than twenty days in attending our colloquia in Northfield, Massachusetts, and Sonoma, California. During the colloquia, again conducted in a fishbowl, the North Central participants could observe the UGS process closely and discuss any topic under the sun with seventy students, all full-time and some part-time core faculty members and staff, a few adjunct professors, and the entire membership of the National Policy Board.

In short, this year-long interaction between NCA and UGS was no superficial observation; it was an in-depth opportunity to see the inner workings of the Union Graduate School in all its dimensions, from the more formal steps of certification and termination of students to the more informal but challenging learning opportunities that inevitably result when thirty high-powered Union Graduate students meet at a colloquium. Here was an opportunity for the team members to interact with everybody in each learning phase. Here they could perceive the vision of the UGS founders in both macro and micro size, at both cognitive and affective levels. Both our strengths and weaknesses were evident.

SOME TENTATIVE CONCLUSIONS

At the close of each of these meetings, the North Central team chairperson and his colleagues were generous in sharing their perceptions firsthand, face to face . . . and frankly. Also, each UGS faculty person or staff member present at those meetings could respond as he or she wished. As mentioned before, after each visit the NCA chairman submitted a tentative interim report for any comments we might wish to make.

If these interactions all seem too formal, I would like to point out that there was in some respect a continuing dialogue between the chairperson of the NCA team and the UGS administrative co-ordinator. This was not only imperative from a substantive view-point, but it also enabled both the NCA team and the UGS person-nel to adjust calendars and schedules as necessity demanded. It also allowed us to modify the large chart in light of local navigational needs.

The NCA team honestly endeavored to see into every corner of our dreams, objectives, and achievements as well as into the ongoing processes for UGS students. Our hope was that the team would cap-ture the phenomenology of our experiencing.

DENOUEMENT

We designed the final, week-long visit of the NCA team to UGS headquarters to accomplish several goals. First, our task force felt that the NCA team should evaluate our rather unique record-keep-ing system. After all, we had spent nearly a year evolving it and needed professional feedback. This would test, too, whether we had met our consultants' admonition to design a mode for communicat-ing each student's process and portfolio succinctly and intelligibly.[7] Secondly, the NCA team had many unanswered questions pertaining to the evolution of the UGS parent organization, UECU, and the na-ture of its administrative organization and personnel. Third, the NCA team wanted to probe more deeply into a few areas where they were uncertain of the accuracy of their perceptions and tentative conclusions.

Hence, in early November we met for long and intensive days of work. The NCA team members were all present as were several members of the UECU board's executive committee and all full-time members of the core faculty.

At the close of this meeting, the chairperson of the NCA team met with the entire faculty and the president of UECU to summarize the team's perception of strengths and concerns (see Appendix C). The chairman's statement was hard-hitting but so eloquent that the UGS task force could only regret that it was not taped for future reference. Later, we expressed our views to the NCA staff that all such events, especially in dealing with experimental and experiential programs, should be taped so that both affect and content would be caught for use by members of both the institution and NCA.

Following that visit, the NCA team attended only one more event. Feeling that they had not really captured the innovative dimensions of a UGS terminar in the one they had seen, they asked us to locate another terminating session. In a few weeks one team member and an NCA staff person attended a terminar in New York City.

REPORT WRITING

Meanwhile, consistent with a March agreement and subsequent discussion, the task force met to develop a status study following all NCA team visits. Hence, after the November visit the UGS task force developed a self-study report that would afford any reader a comprehensive picture of what UGS is about. The rest of the script is a matter of public record. The NCA team wrote its own report and, following North Central process guidelines, made its recommendation. In late March we met with the NCA board for further questions and discussion. The board then voted us candidacy status providing for biennial visits and six years to achieve full accreditation.[8] And we are still on course in achieving this goal.

IMPLICATIONS

The implications of expending so much time, energy, and concern on such a process are indeed profound at a time when institutions of higher education are searching for ways to regenerate themselves. The project broke boundaries in that the two institutions could evolve such a process, what Patsy Thrash calls "sequential evaluation,"[9] with so much openness, integrity, and penetrating analysis. As Ben Davis, the chairperson of the NCA team, concluded:

> Both the North Central Association and the Union Graduate School regard the process they mutually created as one which is truly supportive of high-quality innovation, in that it enables the true strengths and weaknesses of the program to be seen clearly. Both institutions came away from this experience with enhanced confidence in both the accreditation process and the courage to innovate. The persons who were involved in these processes came away with mutual respect for one

another, as educators and as people.

Both institutions are stronger as a consequence of this endeavor. UGS changed some of its processes [without compromising its principles] because members of the task force and faculty listened carefully to what the North Central team was saying. The endeavor itself indicates that North Central changed, in that it was a willing participant in a new approach to the accreditation process, one designed to comprehend the qualities of a nontraditional program rather than measuring it with tools created for other kinds of programs. Nontraditional programs and institutions like UGS need this kind of hard, positive scrutiny from evaluators who value high-quality innovation. And in order to have it, both the educational institution and the accrediting association must be willing to devote substantial time and energy to building a working relationship of openness and trust, attacking hard problems directly, not hiding them, and perceiving one another on the same side, not as hostile forces.[10]

8 Faculty Load: Measurable or Mysterious?

Brash as it may sound, I don't think that anyone knows what constitutes a faculty load when dealing with external degree programs, universities without walls, and other open institutional programs! Although various ceilings, norms, ratios, hour contacts, and other traditional factors are usually considered *for the student,* the very nature of the learning gestalt makes it difficult to know what might constitute a "fair work load" for the faculty. Should there be a constant ratio of students and faculty? Should the faculty count student contact hours and add to them his "homework" time, that is, both paperwork and those professional activities needed to keep up with his job? Would it be wise to establish a fixed workweek and expect a faculty-facilitator to adhere strictly to those hours? And what about other personnel recognized as part of the learning syndrome; namely, adjunct professors, consultants, peers, and paraprofessionals? How does their work relate to the calculus of student-faculty load?

This problem has intrigued me for at least a decade. More recently it has perturbed me persistently since both my student and faculty colleagues in the Union Graduate School sometimes presume to know better than I what I am capable of doing! In addition to becoming angry about such presumptions, I have often felt whimsical. Ironically, we encourage students to be self-directed and to stretch themselves beyond all previously known capacity, yet we presume to set student-faculty ratios for the faculty and circumscribe other kinds of activity known as "faculty load." Even after recognizing the politics of institutional survival, I still perceive the current situation as ironic if not downright paradoxical. Hence, I will explore some of the basic questions related to the general issue of faculty load, focusing primarily upon the graduate level since I know that best.

145

More than twenty-five years of experience informs me that measuring teaching loads by student-faculty ratios is at worst absurd and at best a very rough approximation. For example, when I taught at Bates College (1947–57), the student-teacher ratio was about 15 to 1; with 5 classes, I should have had about 75 students, but in fact, I never had fewer than 140 and usually averaged 155. At Ohio University (1957–64) when the institution's ratio was about 21 to 1 and I had 5 sections, my load should have been about 105 students; in fact, I never had fewer than 200 and usually had between 300 and 425! At the Hofstra University summer graduate school (1956, 1958, 1959), the tuition collected for my courses might have reflected some approximation of load; however, Hofstra collected between three and four times as much as my salary! In Antioch-Putney Graduate School's first year (1964–65), the student-faculty ratio was 11 to 3, and I carried less than average academic weight, but during the next five years, I had two to four times as many students as the ratio might suggest as a normal load.

Since the mid-forties I have read the AAUP *Bulletin*, and more recently I have read the *Chronicle of Higher Education* for insights on patterns of union organization, but I've discovered few new angles of vision. Compilation of a student-teacher ratio seems primarily an administrative gimmick to appease some constituency, a means of dealing with an accrediting agency, or at best only one rough criterion related to budgeting. Normally it is used to set *lower* limits for class size or to chastise some professor for not carrying his weight. But has it ever been used to set upper limits, except perhaps with graduate faculty in the more prestigious institutions? I know of two specific instances in which graduate faculty, advising doctoral students in major universities, carried nearly 100 students at a given time.

CHANGE OF ROLE

Several factors, of course, change the learning environment in external degree programs, undergraduate or graduate. The standard units of measurement, such as courses and terms, tend to disappear. Learning becomes a process with the contract as the integrating factor. The professor, call him by whatever name, becomes keeper of the process as well as consultant, a rather radical change of role. And it's not so much a matter of measuring hours or numbers of students as a change of lifestyle. His working days will not necessarily fit normal working hours. Although teachers in extension or continuing education in large urban areas have been aware of such phenomena for many decades, the typical professor hasn't had to cope with such realities. Also most facilitators in university without walls programs are more genuinely concerned with the whole student, if that student wishes such attention, than higher education usually has been, and this requires a major readjustment. In traditional terminology, such programs are concerned with a student's cognitive *and* affective lives. Although higher education normally deals centrally with the classroom, the library, and the mind, perhaps tossing a sop to extracurricular activities, external degree programs do recognize life relevancy as legitimate, which opens up the matter of residency (see Chapter 9) and gives credibility and accreditability to experience as learning potential when integrated with more formal or theoretical learning. Such a departure from a professor's training or experience may be difficult to accept. Yet, if she is going to work with students who are open to connecting life and study and who are, in fact, assisting institutions to evolve such possibilities, then she must recognize it as a different ball game.

Such recognition has consequences. One of these is that daily objectives may not be achieved at all if a crisis interferes. For example, I recently visited an institution where two of my colleagues had spent the entire previous day helping to locate a student's husband, who had skipped town with their two children. How could the two professors "teach" sociology to this woman under such circumstances? One could moralize ad infinitum, of course, remarking, "That was none of their business!" or "That is somebody else's job!" or "They shouldn't have established such a dependency relationship with the woman!" But the existential fact was that the student had come to trust them and had asked for their help at that precise point of her life! She would not be shuttled to some administrative or social agency that *might* help her! It is a simple fact of life that older students have more continuing financial and family obligations, more entangling alliances, more *probability* of illness and other problems.

Nobody of course can be or do all things. Yet the historical faculty role of disseminating information among students, discussing it, and evaluating comprehension has expanded to keep pace with the knowledge explosion and increased specialization. Hence a faculty member must be more willing to say, "I don't know," more willing to develop a human resource network to complement his knowledge of material resources, and more willing to be accessible at odd times. He also must be willing to set parameters of time when he is inaccessible and not feel guilty about it! Also, since the best external degree programs are in a constant state of evolution, the faculty member must perceive his load as including organizational development or else live with the paradox that the nature of his learning-facilitating may be in essential contradiction with the nature of his institution. Although Max Weber was probably accurate as well as prescient in observing that institutions tend to move from charisma to bureaucracy, it is a weak soul, indeed, who will resign himself to it as inevitable. Hence, the true believer in such innovative programs seems to have little choice other than to participate in the shaping of the institution. In short, should we expect either students or faculty to be exhortative about self-direction if they must yield to hierarchical direction?

Other factors make faculty load difficult to quantify. Human interaction between students and faculty is essentially *qualitative*. For too long we have measured the depth and breadth of learning by clock time. The 55-minute hour, the 150-minute seminar, and the 15-week semester are all passé! When a student writes to say, "To show you how much influence you have had in my life, I have written my first haiku!" and then shares that insight, it is ridiculous to measure his and my interaction in terms of seconds, minutes, and hours! In the few seconds it takes me to read the letter and the few minutes it requires to respond, we may open up an entirely new universe for both of us. Putting any of this into faculty load terms is absurd. Even in mathematics and the hard sciences or other disciplines where knowledge accretes, the phenomenon of equating study time and knowledge gained is open to question.

Hence a faculty member may wish to perceive his load in terms of "earning insights" as well as "spending time." By changing his attitudes to include that concept he will find himself at the threshold of a constantly expanding universe where the laws of entropy dissipate! His psychic income becomes astronomical. While he may have to file load reports to give somebody, somewhere, a sense of "what he's doing," he'll probably perceive that effort in a whimsical, paradoxical, and ironic light as he evolves new mind sets, forms new habits (especially listening capabilities), and develops new relationships to and concepts of an institution.

SOME STATISTICS

I am not unmindful of the practical need to consider seriously the problems of planning faculty loads in conjunction with institution building, hiring and firing, budget balancing, and the like. Having now served as a founder of two innovative educational institutions and two voluntary organizations, I perceive such practicalities as survival mechanisms.

Challenged by students and colleagues for carrying too heavy a load, teased for being a "rate breaker" of the nineteenth-century variety, and failing in my attempts to develop a new faculty-administrative configuration, I set to work in 1972 on the problem of faculty load in an effort to define it, to devise some new angles for seeing, and to propose some guidelines for further research. At the outset, the problem seemed to defy all traditional classification and analysis. One simply could not add contact hours. And it was not easy to separate the cost of the various aspects of one's activity by saying "I spent X hours at lecturing, Y hours at administering, Z hours at this or that." The role definitions simply did not stand up; the strands of one's life do not separate into discernible patterns. Simply counting student noses seemed just that, simple-minded and simplistic. So, what to do? Maybe the problem needed restatement?

After some reflection and considerable free association, I concluded, "Why not state the problem in terms of 'weight' of demand?" Data collection wouldn't be ultraobjective, of course, but after half a lifetime of serious study in both natural science and social scientific methodology, I had concluded that objectivity is what I say it is. At least, I mused, this whimsical conclusion might save me from being too serious if charged with nonobjectivity! Why *not* determine load very much as it is, in terms of the weight on my intellectual, emotional, and physical energies. After eight years of work in two free-form graduate schools, I certainly knew that one five-minute phone call sometimes requires more energy than half a dozen lectures. Examples abound. Supervisors of student teachers often speak the rhetoric of liberal education but behave like tyrants. I also knew that an hour of listening quietly to a student's difficulties might be more difficult than a day of grading papers.

I began by setting up three categories: heavy, medium, and light. Eventually, however, after reviewing my load for several months, I realized that I needed a five-point scale as a place to put some of the in-between data.

I started with one other whimisical observation: theoretically, if one is encouraging self-direction in external degree programs, then a faculty member really shouldn't have very much to do. Also, if all persons took their self-direction opportunity seriously, their demands would be approximately the same. Yet experience had already destroyed that theory. Obviously there were both peaks and valleys of demand. When a student enters UGS, as suggested in discussing rhetoric and risk, she is more likely to need assistance in evolving a program. I knew, too, that the nature of my work undercut my assumption. In addition, during the terminating phases of a student's work, there were papers to read, films to observe, cassettes to hear, and action-oriented projects to visit.

Consequently, I was hardly through the first analysis of demand on my energies before I began to shape criteria for placing a student's name in one column or another. And I gave ample weight to that student who really gave me a hard time. At the end of the first thirty months of study, some of the load profiles became clearer.

At the *light end* were students who didn't communicate during the period being analyzed; obviously, such persons make low or no demand.

The *heavy end* is slightly more difficult yet not too difficult to differentiate from medium demand. For instance, if I fly to Saskatoon or Zurich (and I have) to participate in a student's terminating phases, that requires time, energy, and a considerable amount of planning, assuming I make a multipurpose trip (a budgetary imperative). Also, if I spend several days at a free school or on location at similar action projects, if I read a 1000-page log or 3000-page poem, or if I participate in an all-day certification conference, those activities, too, are pretty demanding.

Somehow medium or *average* demand becomes just that. In fact, I perceive it as a routine report, log, or periodical communication with a committee in which I share a normal expectation of responsibility.

The *medium heavy* demand is the most difficult weight to ascertain. It seems accurate, however, to assess that weight when a student sends a chapter or two of a paper, asks me to read a journal article or short book so that we may discuss the ideas in it, asks for help designing a questionnaire or a proposal for a grant, perhaps requests discussion at home or the office or a visit to the site of her or his internship. I determined *medium low* demand in a similar way, though going in the opposite direction.

Let us look at early results, perceived in percentage terms rather than numbers of students. This may enable us to make a few generalizations and speculate about further work to be done in a more wholesale way, although I would be the first to contend that the greatest value of the chart has been in its making (see Table 8.1).

Table 8.1 Student-Faculty Load

Time Period	Months	Heavy	Medium-Heavy	Medium	Medium-Light	Light
5/15–8/15	(3)	5.3%	20.3%	23.0%	23.0%	28.4%
8/15–10/8	(2¾)	14.2	11.4	35.7	15.8	22.9
10/8–11/25	(1½)	14.7	6.6	19.3	21.7	37.7
11/25–1/1	(1¼)	6.7	10.8	21.7	15.4	45.4
1/1–2/15	(1½)	6.5	13.8	30.6	18.5	30.6
2/15–4/7	(1¾)	7.9	10.6	33.8	10.9	36.8
4/7–5/7	(1)	21.5	12.3	30.8	10.8	24.6
5/7–6/7	(1)	11.9	10.4	28.7	20.3	28.7
6/7–8/7	(2)	12.5	16.1	26.7	17.9	26.8
8/7–9/15	(1¼)	8.8	7.0	21.1	26.3	36.8
9/15–11/15	(2)	14.0	7.0	24.6	17.5	37.0
2/1–3/15	(1½)	19.3	12.3	42.1	7.0	19.3
3/15–5/1	(1½)	18.5	13.0	31.5	7.4	29.6
5/1–9/1	(4)	23.3	23.3	35.1	5.0	13.3
9/1–9/30	(1)	11.1	13.3	46.8	4.4	24.4
9/30–11/30	(2)	19.6	8.7	43.5	6.5	21.7
16 periods Averages	(1.28)	12.9	12.3	28.4	14.3	29.0

Note: Percentages refer to percentage of students in my total numerical load in the given period.

The parameters of demand in the three main categories are as follows:

Demand in a Given Period	Percent of Students Making Demand		
	Highest Percent for One Period	Lowest Percent for One Period	Average Percent for One Period
Heavy	23.3	5.3	12.9
Medium	46.8	19.3	28.4
Light	45.4	13.3	29.0

Combining the two highest categories and the two low categories offers:

Demand in a Given Period	Percent of Students Making Demand		
	Highest Percent for One Period	Lowest Percent for One Period	Average Percent for One Period
Heavy	46.6	15.8	25.2
Light	63.1	18.3	43.3

In other words, in one period, late summer, nearly two-thirds of the students (63.1 percent) were hardly in evidence; on the surface that may seem irresponsible, yet perhaps it should be linked to the fact that I had indicated I would be on vacation at that time and would respond only to urgent requests. On the other hand, the heaviest demands were made during a five-month period that included a summer; that period, logically enough, reflects the nadir of light demand. Also relevant even in a program where self-direction is a high expectation is that most students "check in" in more than routine ways during the five-month period.

But let us look at some aggregate figures. Even assuming a modicum of statistical error and recognizing the dangers of extrapolation, I may expect about an eighth of my students (12.9 percent) to make a high demand on me during any given period; or, taking the two heavy categories together, only one quarter (25.2 percent) will exert very heavy pressure. Meanwhile, I may expect to experience a routine report from about a third of my students (28.4 percent) or hear in the most casual way from about 43 percent during any given period. Although such aggregates do not permit me to predict what may happen on any given day, my efforts in compiling such data have made me more aware of load in a qualitative-quantitative framework rather than merely quantitative.

A DIFFERENT PERSPECTIVE

The self-anchoring scale provides another mode for relating load and performance, and this analysis can be used regardless of job or numbers. By setting up a variety of goals or objectives within the context of tasks to be done or a role or series of roles to be filled, the individual can evaluate himself in quantitative terms[1] (see Table 8.2).

Table 8.2 Some Characteristics I Wish to Practice in UGS

Self-Rating
[Poor (1) to Excellent (10)]

	1	2	3	4	5	6	7	8	9	10
Accessibility to Students								x		
Promptness of Response to Demand								x		
Resourcefulness										
Human									x	
Material								x		
Knowledge								x		
Willingness to										
Make Demands on Students							x			
Flexibility to a Change in Student										
Perspective								x		
Willingness to be Involved with a										
Student's:										
Job								x		
Life								x		
Balance between Friendship and Objective Evaluation; Human Support;										
Promotion of Independent Relationships								x		
Willingness to Take Abuse					x					
Facilitator of the Personal Growth Dimension								x		
Ability to Listen								x		
Adapting Communication to Student Need								x		
Keeping up with Intellectual Interest and Skills						x				

What do these characteristics have to do with analyzing faculty load in university without walls programs? Take the accessibility dimension for example. If one has 25, 50, 75, or 100 students to serve, can one serve them all on *their* terms? Since there are many student perspectives on the multiple roles faculty fulfill in this mode of learning, one student may feel mistreated if he has anything less than a day a month, whereas another might echo the view of one UGS student who observed at the outset of his program, "It's your task to stay out of my light!"

Since many Union graduate students work full days and can only phone at night, I have consistently held an evening "telephone hour." I recently experienced a tinge of guilt (but more of sorrow) when I felt forced to change that hour from late to early evening in order to drive some of my reading and writing projects into a wider corner of night—and to preclude spending entire evenings on the phone with students from Berkeley to Bangor. But experience confirms that being open with students regarding one's own needs generates reciprocal respect. While I would hardly rate myself a "10" for accessibility on the self-anchoring scale, I perceive my own availability as pretty high. I value accessibility as a characteristic humanistic teachers should have if they are to be effective. Far be it to speak one language and act another!

Each of the characteristics outlined in the self-anchoring analysis might be subjected to the same quality-quantity discussion. Without question, to practice what one speaks requires time and, consequently, work—hence load! A few words about some of those items on the scale may help define general problems of load and suggest lines of further search for those wishing to take the matter seriously.

Self-directed students at any level of competence surely do not expect instant feedback from faculty, nor is it necessarily healthy to respond immediately. But many of my own college professors and colleagues have angered me because they did not return a paper or an exam or answer a letter for weeks or months on end—if ever. Assuming humanness is the capacity to respond, then surely in external degree programs that construct self-images of humanism, responsibility may be defined as response-ability. I recall a former colleague who tried to return all exams and papers within twenty-four hours. "Then," he mused, "I only have to do them once!" And that system really works if one isn't too compulsive about it. I attempted it when I had 400 students at Ohio University, and it was downright difficult to achieve. However, it certainly relieved me of a lot of pain and shocked the students constructively. Likewise, today, I clearly intend to answer all phone calls and correspondence within a week, even if to say via postal card "I can't answer for ten days or two weeks." Obviously, this is load; but also obviously, whether or not I can achieve my objective depends heavily upon my support system. Administrators who do not take an individual faculty member's philosophy of response into consideration when allocating funds for secretarial or administrative assistance really don't understand the fundamentals of load, human creativity, and the development of support systems.

Another for instance: willingness to be involved with a student's life and job is more than a matter of faculty attitude. If we are serious in developing experiential educational modes where work-study and experience-theory can be matured in optimal ways, then every consideration must be given to provide encouragement for industrial visitations, educational linkages, and the use of on-the-job personnel as part of a human network. Again, to perceive a faculty facilitator's role in narrow student-ratio terms without considering the support money and time allocations necessary for him or her to do a comprehensive job is absurd. And a faculty member must be encouraged to know how far to go in developing observational skills in visiting a job or internship site to make firsthand contact with those who may vouch for the student's learning. Fortunately, many men and women of the workaday world are being added to faculties to afford more perspective on work dimensions; unfortunately, too few professors have the range of workaday experience that would maximize their understanding of the ways in which work and study can be combined effectively. I am personally thankful for my own working-class background and six years of industrial experience. Frequent visits to industrial plants and constant conversations with plumbers, masons, boat builders, electricians, garbagemen, and educators from every level of endeavor also help me ride the frontier of my students' perception of work-study. Editing the book *Humanizing The Workplace* and engaging in at least one carpentering job per year also sharpen perspective, though in this, as in every other category on the self-anchoring scale, I still have a long way to go.

Regarding other points on the scale, I probably make impossible demands on students less frequently today than I did when my classes averaged ninety in number and, ironically enough, I had to perform to motivate them. But I've spent enormous energy in the past decade learning how to listen, learning how to respond to changing student perspectives, and learning how to be of use by taking abuse. This learning was part of my ongoing load, since I could not change my habits without experiencing some of the problems discussed in the context of congruency (see Chapter 3). And the time it takes to challenge students and make such demands, even if students expect it, may not be worth it. In fact, it may be counterproductive in those programs where students must be encouraged to relate their learning programs to life's expectancies.

And what about load as a function of so-called professional time? At precisely the moment when public schools increasingly encourage their teachers to devote time to professional days (surely part of load calculations in the public school sector), those involved in external degree programs may wonder what on earth a professional day is. Is there enough time for reading? Is there enough money for unorthodox learning outreaches, which might include a trip to Japan simply to climb Mount Fuji or catch a Zen insight, to the exclusion of professional conventions? Is there enough recognition of writing haiku, for instance, as a way of developing new ways of seeing? In short, how does one keep up with one's intellectual interests or continue to hone one's skills? Does *anything* go? Does *nothing* go? Or is keeping up something in between as legitimate or credible preparation for the next problem that confronts one as a learning facilitator in UGS or UWW types of programs? I have been both bold and conservative in rating myself with a "6" in keeping up on the self-anchoring scale, for I am not sure what keeping up means! In fact, it may be an outmoded concept. Once upon a time I felt both embarrassed and confused upon meeting a new person who immediately asked, "What's your field?" I knew that I was supposed to say history or English or political science, for that was the expected answer. Now I am delighted to respond with "humans!" And since I spend most of my waking hours interacting with or thinking about humans, perhaps this is keeping up. Those concerned with experiential-experimental education need to consider this matter in a context beyond conventional sabbaticals, professional meetings, degrees, and other norms. After all, being professional may guarantee only mediocrity!

A TYPICAL TRIP

Elsewhere I have discussed in more detail the uses and abuses of faculty in UGS as well as some of the phenomenological implications of these learning modes. Believing, however, that illustration may be more vivid than explanation, here are the salient features of a recent five and a half day trip. I was away a total of 125 hours, living them as follows:

Contact with students		
and their committies	67 hrs.	(54%)
In Transit	24 hrs.	(19%)
Personal/Sleeping	34 hrs.	(27%)
Total	125 hrs.	(100%)

The trip included two certification sessions, four terminars, and twelve individual or group conferences for a total of eighteen meetings. Is this typical? Yes, for full-time core faculty in the Union Graduate School. Is it sane? Hardly, if one perceives sanity in conventional work terms. So how do you figure a load? And how many roles does a faculty member serve on such a trip as this? Surely, one is learning facilitator par excellence, for it is amazing how many persons one connects to other persons in weaving together this human network known as the UGS. Also, in such a perambulating life one encounters ideas, programs, proposals, plans, and people whose programs, proposals, and plans are not "written up" or publicized for months and years. Further, since this kind of trip requires working nights, weekends, and holidays (because most members of Union Graduate School committees have full-time jobs), it throws into a cocked hat any consideration of a normal workweek and normal salary scales; also, the workday may be four hours or sixteen. And, if one flies east to west across three time zones, a working day may easily stretch to twenty hours! For these and other reasons, faculty in external degree programs must devise personal means of self-rejuvenation. In this way perhaps one can avoid justifying Dr. Alexandr Zuckerkandl's assessment: "The object of life is to get through it."[2]

SOME CONCLUSIONS

In short, I contend vigorously, maybe even contentiously, that most measures of load used in conventional programs are virtually useless for extended degree programs. I also feel that persons in experimental, experiential, innovative, self-directed (pick your term) learning modes need to be more conscious of the problem. With the advent of unionization and the normal evolution of institutions into bureaucratic modes (see Chapter 5), innovation is threatened if those involved in developing such programs do not shape the parameters of their own work lives. This is neither an antiunion, nor an antibureaucracy pitch; each phenomenon has its own place in getting things done, hopefully with some equity, in a complex, industrialized, technologized, urbanized society. However, we need not paint ourselves into a corner or be guilty of conflictual contradictions by accepting normative definitions of load. Enough evidence already is available to suggest that we are forced to make the world safe for hyprocrisy. Need we add to those illustrations?

Stated more bluntly, students, faculty, and administrators in innovative programs should work concertedly to evolve new perspectives on this complex problem, for the very existence of some programs will depend upon the way in which the data are translated into budgetary and operational terms.

Tentatively, I am convinced that load is a function of individual human commitment to students, program, life, the world! One person's burden is another's joy or freedom. Just imagine anybody prescribing student-faculty load for such people as Socrates, Anais Nin, A. S. Neill, Eve Curie, John Dewey, or Alfred N. Whitehead! Load, further, is a function of one's self-concept, one's sense of being old or young or in between, experience, and health (both physical and psychological).

Load is also a function of one's support system. Whereas we once might have said that he who has the mimeograph machine can control the revolution, in the experimental learning context we might say that he who has a dictaphone, secretarial assistance, and a duplicating machine can control his own life in working with, supporting, and interacting with as many students as he wishes to. Furthermore, if one has easy access to cassette recorders, video equipment, and movie projectors, one can expand into those learning networks where such equipment long ago opened the options for students. If, on the other hand, locating equipment is difficult, how can the faculty options be opened? While it might be argued, in Parkinsonian style, that equipment will be expended as it becomes more easily accessible, that possibility for expendability should not be ruled out simply on the grounds of cost or irresponsibility. A university president once told me that I could teach 200 as easily as 50 or 100 to which I responded, "It all depends upon what we are trying to do. Once beyond 30 or so, if it's simply a matter of dispensing information, you may as well open up the auditorium and teach 3,000!" In short, don't we have to adapt means more appropriate to new learning situations and bury all conventional wisdoms about load in the context of classroom contacts?

We need to consider seriously the possibility that faculty can contract with students, with colleagues, or with institutions for the nature of the load that is comfortable in the context of salary, fringe benefits, and other emoluments. Again, we must subject conventional wisdoms, such as those developed by unions, NEA. and the AAUP, to severe scrutiny so as to consider the wider parameters of experimental-experiential learning. With an increasing number of faculty willing to work less time for less money, or share a single job with someone else,[3] or divide the calendar year in unorthodox ways, with these changes both here and imminent, we must invent new configurations that tie time, place, function, and outcomes together in a wider variety of possibilities. This may make it more difficult to administer, but administrators must exist for learners or work in cooperation with learners and not vice versa.

The more imaginative a person in experimental-experiential learning is, the more bankrupt and irrelevant do such questions as "What's a faculty load?" or "What's a student load?" seem. This paradox is even more cogent when considered in relationship to phenomenologies of learning (see Chapter 4).

Another way to say it:

> Ask about load
> wrong-headed slant
> who asks that price
> of soldier ant?

9   Who/What Resides in Residency?[1]

The history of residency in Western higher education is the story of Sturm und Drang. Over the centuries students have fought with citizens in town-gown battles. They have fought with both parents and administrators as institutions of higher learning assumed in loco parentis prescriptions, postures, and presumptions. Also, they have battled with one another and with faculty—to say nothing of soldiers, military recruiters, and state authorities.

For the most part, American residency has been a peaceful phenomenon when contrasted with what students throughout the world have experienced; yet dormitory pranks are legend, and it is a rare residence hall, fraternity or sorority house, or nearby boardinghouse whose walls could not tell truths stranger than fiction.

Perhaps it was in the late 1960s, with the rise of more politically aware and vocationally demanding students, as well as a different lifestyle among two or three college generations, that brought the residency requirements of American institutions under closer scrutiny. Also related to this relatively new phenomenon in American education are the high amortization costs on state university campuses and the rapidly diminishing student populations. Although I have not made an exhaustive analysis of college and university catalogues, a spot check reveals that some kind of residency is a standard requirement in most schools for most degrees. This constitutes little difficulty, perhaps, for students within commuting distance of a college or university, but it creates a major problem for persons living farther away. In an era when energy is harder to come by, whether or not there is a crisis, it is reasonably clear that the *concept* of residency, as well as the requirement, needs some rethinking. No doubt the university without walls programs in this country, the

Open University in London, and the variety of external degree and continuing education programs in several of the states tend to force the issue.

At its best in a traditional university or college, the residency requirement may develop a whole constellation of values. Persons of different sexes with different value patterns, ethnic backgrounds, creeds, etc., will share thoughts and experiences as part of the learning process. Also, assembling a critical mass of persons in one location makes it feasible to develop libraries, classrooms, athletic facilities, concert accommodations, etc., to facilitate learning. Perhaps such centralization led to the phrase *"a community of scholars."*

It is safe to assume that a large percentage of persons engaged in higher education will always be assembled in residence halls of one kind or another and engage in various kinds of joint activity such as concerts, games, bull sessions, or symposia, the net effect being reinforcement of the value and the phenomenon called "residency." It suits many persons well. But I propose to argue against the parochial notion that *requiring residency necessarily* results in learning, vocational preparedness, human progress, and institutional stability. I suggest another prospect, wherein a person might achieve similar goals without necessarily being in residence.

OF COURSES

At the same time that the notion of residency is up for grabs, the notion of the college "course" is also in question. This has always been true in many countries where a student is expected to be her/his own programmer and must at some time pass examinations to reach the next step of the ladder. In the U.S. the notion of attending a certain number of courses in order to achieve residency has, unfortunately, become a norm. Universities without walls, the open university, continuing education, and external degree programs do threaten the easy symmetry and mathematics of adding up course credits to constitute residency and hence graduation, whether one actually lives on a campus or commutes to a college or university. Some of the innovative thrusts, even when they use learning contracts or CLEP exams, cannot escape the dangers of that symmetry and mathematics.

We need to develop some different guidelines and concepts for both course and residency.

The use of the learning contract gives us the possibility for a new conceptualization. Also, various kinds of advanced placement tests *may* challenge conventional wisdom. But even then, as suggested by the word *dangers,* there is a tendency to translate experience into discrete entities, usually called courses, which then are added up to a requisite number of hours to fulfill residency or graduation requirements. Even at avant-garde institutions such as Goddard and Antioch, where narrative transcripts usually etch discrete entities called "courses," a student's wisdom, knowledge, and experience are translated into courses with hour values ascribed to each. The same is true of other institutions that use the narrative transcript form. The assumption is that, once given bits of wisdom, knowledge, and practical experience in a particular field are translated into quantifiable and identifiable entities, these quantities then can be added, subtracted, multiplied, and divided in such a way as to be intelligible to those who will read transcripts for their own particular purposes—in a credentials-oriented society.

There are currently many efforts under way to translate life experience into course titles that can be transcripted to satisfy the demands of our materialistic society. In fact, the Educational Testing Service sponsored an entire conference at Princeton on this topic, and the Cooperative Assessment of Experiential Learning continues the effort. Such endeavors are certainly worthwhile and surely challenge the conventional wisdom of listing courses in catalogues, assigning professors to those courses, then telescoping all effort into a letter grade and a given number of quarter or semester hours. It is no wonder, however, that a large number of the world's most creative people have eschewed such effort. Nor is it any wonder that a generation concerned with transpersonal psychology, Zen, Jungian dream analysis, Herman Hesse, and a variety of communal living styles challenges this approach.

In a credentials-oriented society, we inevitably chop experience into various discrete parts. We must, however, challenge this process whenever possible.

ACID TEST

Returning to the matter of residency: perhaps we should start with outcomes. If we want students to be "turned on" by professors, concerts, vocational ambitions, work experience, vivid sunrises and sunsets, dream memories, etc., such outcomes might very well be the measure of whether or not a person is gaining residency.

Perhaps residency might be seen in two categories. As long as some kind of institution must serve as an accrediting or facilitating agent, no doubt students must gather in some place, call it what we may, in order that they meet other students engaged in a similar process. Such a residency, which might be three days, three weeks, or three months, thus enables students to become familiar with persons in the institution whose task is to develop frameworks in which students can evolve their own self-directed programs. Such needs are psychological as well as a matter of convenience. No doubt most human beings *need* some kind of event to shape and to sharpen both loyalty and commitment to a particular process. No doubt, too, most people need to associate such events with a place and a time. In other words, if students are going to commence a learning endeavor, there is some psychological necessity as well as social economy in effecting a gathering of persons at an event or occasion that can be called residency. Also, somebody in charge has to blow the whistle to start that event.

If, however, we are serious about what I have facetiously called competency-based self-education, then the major task of any given institution is to develop "the courage to [let] be." At the event in question, perhaps the whistle-blower's major task is to encourage students to evolve a variety of learning contracts which constitute courses as well as a variety of learning "sets" that constitute residency. Students should be encouraged to vary such courses or sets to include every known learning situation, from the most linear to the fuzziest gestalt, from the safest or simplest (in the learner's experience) to the most experimental or risky.

Some Illustrations

Instances of implementing these ideas have been discussed or alluded to in various parts of this book. The master's programs of Goddard, for instance, find students launching their work in one-week seminars and extending it while they continue with their occupations and meetings in regional settings for evening or weekend workshops. Walden University requires students to attend a month-long summer program to acquire proficiency in research, to look seriously at contemporary problems in American education, and to evolve a design for a thesis. After that, Walden students work with an advisor near their homes and complete their theses via individual conferences, phone calls, and correspondence. Nova's Doctor of Education program in educational administration unites students for intensive month-long institutes and then organizes their work in regional clusters. The Doctor of Philosophy program sponsored by the Humanist Psychology Institute also launches students at short conferences, held in various parts of the country. In short, these and similar programs in this country challenge the traditional procedure of residency as a continuous phenomenon. We in the Union Graduate School are, of course, concerned with this challenge.

Although the original planning for UGS called for an eleven-week residency, we held our first period of residency as a six-week colloquium in Denver, Colorado, in June 1970. By the end of our second colloquium, we had dropped the continuous residency requirement to four weeks with considerable assistance from our students, a highly motivated and experienced group of "terribly busy" people, and with some input from the former director of the adult degree program at Goddard. We did, however, retain the other two weeks of residency, although we weren't quite sure at the time what they might consist of. During the next four years of our existence, we held fourteen four-week colloquia in which normally a student was expected to attend for four weeks or twenty-five straight days.

At one point in our evolution, however, it became necessary to define residency for the other two weeks we expected from our students. At one propitious point, pressed by an anxious student who wanted to know what he "needed" to do to fulfill his residency requirement, I remarked, "Residency is whenever two or more Union Graduate students and/or core faculty gather together in the name of the Union Graduate School!" Although it may have seemed like a wisecrack at the time, it held a germ of truth. During the course of the past several years, our students indeed have assembled in small groups and in an incredible variety of places and occasions. Although there is neither a quantitative nor qualitative compendium of the ideas evolving from such meetings, we do know that these sessions have been creative. Books have been born, poetry written, ways around the UGS system devised, and no doubt Cupid has bent a bow or two in such encounters.

Another positive generalization is also possible: not only have we talked about colloquia and minicolloquia facilitating a human network of persons to provide support and resources and to advise and consent (or dissent), but in fact our residency requirements induce such a network. As discussed elsewhere (see Chapter 5), UGS is an enormously significant human network, defying computerization but truly humanizing. That such a network will even constitute a serious threat to the variety of establishments in this country is doubtful, but it is an important yeast in the social culture. This network, aided by the telephone, cassettes, video, and the mails—to say nothing of closer contacts—constitutes a rich human resource. So many UGS students are on the frontier of their particular discipline or vocation, or are attempting to link in unique ways a variety of disciplines that they do not realize how far out they are until they look back to see how few are following.

In short, by providing a rationale for an infinite variety of human contacts and by imposing fewer constraints, such as classrooms, campuses, or lectures, upon the imagination for exploring the nature of such human relationships, we are encouraging another test of learning and freedom.

Naturally, there are drawbacks:

- We frequently get tagged as a degree mill on the basis of this external fact of short residency even though critics *do not* or *will not* take the time to explore the total nature of our program (other external degree programs have similar experiences).

- Some students, especially if they are located in remote regions or in areas where there are few UGS students, feel uncomfortable and even guilty for *not* going to class, *not* encountering fellow and sister students, in short for *not* doing those educational acts which for sixteen to twenty years they have been conditioned to do.

- Other students, perhaps content with "business as usual," do not make the best of the opportunity, or perhaps continue their "rip-off" ways in a society where cheating *may* be a norm.

- Some core faculty feel a bit uneasy about the seeming nonaccountability of the two-week period or the fact that it is not quite as systematic as residency in traditional institutions; and yet, there are other faculty who believe enough in the *concept* that they recommend that core be required to spend a minimum of two weeks a year with other core, an idea which may be increasingly relevant as the total Union Graduate School effort becomes more geographically dispersed.

Perhaps the agonies and prospects for further evolution of non-residential residency can be summarized in a series of questions:

- How can we convert those experiences we know to be credible (namely, human interaction in which learning takes place) into creditable and accreditable phenomena in a credentials-oriented society?
- In a society where everything is added, subtracted, multiplied, and divided, how can we make credible the phenomenology of experience, a phenomenology often consisting of insights and perceptions three or four layers deep in concurrent events?
- Is it possible to reverse a trend that is at least a couple of centuries old in American higher education wherein residency often consists of "calling of the roll," where there is little sense of community or cooperative learning possibilities—a phenomenon that may guarantee payment of the mortgage but often promotes frustration and alienation without much promise of learning innovation?
- Will it be possible for us to divorce the concept and requirement of residency from the concept and requirement of taking courses without perhaps bastardizing both or developing new ticky-tacky boxes that will only satisfy registrars, parents, prospective employers, or prospective graduate schools?
- Is there any way to convert the fluidity and richness of human experience into descriptive prose sufficiently intelligible that we can avoid the normative implications of the language? In short, can we make transcript construction genuinely creative writing?
- Can we learn to distinguish more carefully between experimental and experiential in order to avoid the semantic confusion that often exists when these two terms are used in tandem, concurrently, or seemingly interchangeably?
- Can we invent some stunningly new means of evaluating

human growth and learning without destroying either the evaluator or the evaluated? Will this perhaps help us perceive students as people rather than objects?

- Is it possible to develop institutions that are not institutions in the normal sense, institutions that recognize the flow of human existence without trying to bottle it up, advertise it, and sell it? If we evolve such institutions, must they necessarily threaten more traditional institutions?

By rethinking the matters of course and residency, we perhaps get to the heart of certain key questions: the relative merits of structured and nonstructured learning contexts or the nature of the credential-granting society. Surely there are no easy answers, but asking is important.

While I am fearful that formularized competency-based approaches to these questions will lead us into dehumanized modes, more educational jargon and cant, and shadowy valleys of *un-freedom*, I am optimistic that the several graduate programs discussed in this book will continue in the next decade to struggle with such problems in an effort to find constructive answers, even if such answers are only tentative.

10   Creative Solvency?[1]

So much has been written about money as "the root of all evil" that there may be nothing new to say. But without question, the squeeze on educational spending has made it difficult to follow traditional routes in starting innovative programs. Many sources have, quite simply, "dried up."

In the Antioch and Union Graduate Schools, students and faculty must locate internships, loan funds, scholarships, and jobs—in short, traditional funding—for their tuition. I've deliberated at length upon both my experience in establishing these schools and the possibilities for more constructive and imaginative funding for self-directed learning projects. Hence, I shall make a few observations, mention three creative solutions that I've witnessed, and raise some questions about the future.

SOME STATEMENTS

Although scholarships have been necessary for many students (including myself) to make it through college, and surely legislation for veterans since World War II has democratized higher education, is there any evidence of a rising tide of gratitude to the colleges and universities to and through which those funds have been funneled? Have any of those assisted devised imaginative new ways to extend those egalitarian forces? If so, who? where?

Students doing graduate work in this country seem to *expect* to have their way paid by somebody, somehow, perhaps a consequence of larger numbers of students remaining in school for longer periods of time.

In my judgment, fellowships, loans, and similar means of financial assistance may be as destructive and patronizing as they are helpful. Where such fellowships, as in the case of athletics, are tied to make-work or even make-believe work, the situation breeds cynicism. Such cynicism is hardly creative, and it invariably leaves a residue of unfulfilled expectations that is potentially crippling.

The teacher assistant (TA) syndrome, as a kind of slave labor, also breeds cynicism and alienation, as many in the educational world learned through the Free Speech movement at Berkeley and subsequent student dissent.

Consider, too, that Third World students are encouraged to incur debts to the tune of $10,000 to $15,000, although their traditions and experience do not include such cavalier ways of deferring gratification. Can such situations generate anything less than long-term anger and alienation? As one UGS student who served an internship in a financial aid office at a large urban community college remarked:

> A specific illustration that I came across was a young man, twenty-seven years old, physically able, attending school full-time, receiving three educational grants totaling $1,900, receiving public assistance, sharing an apartment with a friend, and seeking an additional short-term loan. This young man, as many like him, has no understanding of the basic economic law of limited resources and unlimited wants. He lives in a cul-de-sac secluded from the realities of life's hard knocks, and his behavior reflects a total ignorance of the rules of the game. It is a make-believe world we have created, one that seems designed for failure from the onset and from which we cannot retreat with dignity. Yes, open admissions is working on paper, but my gut feeling is that the open admissions graduate cannot be competitive with his better prepared counterpart. He, because he has been demand fed, cannot function as an economic being, able to make wise choices in our very complex society.[2]

Or, take the housewife who becomes imbued with feminist hopes or fantasies about her own self-verification, freedom, and renewal. Can she achieve a sense of worth if she has to beg or borrow from a husband or a former husband? Or incur long-term debts to a bank, school, or the federal government?

In short, can any of the traditional ways of funding a learning program, especially for innovative persons, be employed without seriously jeopardizing the human dignity that the self-directed person ostensibly hopes to retain or develop? Furthermore, isn't it paradoxical if the self-directed person looks to others, whether college, foundation, or persons, for his or her funding?

SOME ILLUSTRATIONS

During a decade of involvement with master's and doctoral students working largely on their own, or at least independent of parental support, I have seen many unique means of funding that are in the tradition of self-reliance and rugged individualism. Some students have done it via the internship route; others through work-study programs; many via a cooperative and coordinate family effort; a few by means of unbelievable self-sacrifice of food, proper shelter, and transportation. Surely where counterculture persons are involved, the readiness to accept a drastically lowered standard of living has been both cult and cultured. One male graduate student exchanged his baby-sitting services for the apartment that he and his wife occupied. All of this is in the best American tradition of self-help.

Some students I have known at several institutions obtained their tuition by involving themselves in petty larceny, gambling, and pushing drugs. A few have used lottery winnings. To this day, whenever I see a person haul out $500 to $1,000 in green cash, I wonder.

But the question remains whether those believing in self-direction of their educational lives are consistently innovative in finding new ways to pay their tuition, room, board, books, and other fees in the face of decreasing educational funds. If not, why not?

Let me mention three constructive situations:

- A man I'll call Jim Edwards was recounting his own financial dilemma, indicating that he might have to drop out of school. So, I mused, "Say, Jim, you have a mother, a wife, some daughters (and one of the daughters was present). You've taken care of them all your life (he was about fifty); why don't you give them an opportunity to help you by starting the Jim Edwards Educational Fund? I'll bet they'd be glad to team up so you can stop worrying." Within a month one of the daughters was working on the fund.
- Several women in the Union Graduate School, aware that their sisters were not equally affluent, began a fund to assist others not quite as fortunate as they. Although small, the

fund has already enabled the less affluent to participate in learning activities that would have been otherwise difficult if not outright impossible.

- An artist friend and former student, imaginative and bold, is planning a billboard campaign in which he will advertise in a major southern city for the funds to complete his graduate education.

The history of *all* education is the history of struggle at a bewildering variety of occupations that would run the taxonomy from A to Z in any job dictionary. However, I would not claim that hard work and suffering were good for me and, therefore, is good for you. Suffering and learning do not necessarily go hand in glove. And I would not support the Andrew Carnegie or the Ford Foundation policy; namely, that an individual student or institution should pay with a certain percentage of his sweat if he is given a certain percentage of funding for an education. I do, however, wish to pose some questions.

SPECULATIONS AND FANTASIES

Can a self-directed person afford *not* to consider seriously the implications of funding from another person, institution, or agency, since usually some toll in dignity, dehumanization, or self-destruction is exacted?

When a self-directed, innovative person follows the credit financing route in a credit card society, what are the *human* implications (even though the economic ones may find him or her using cheap money to pay back dear money in a steadily growing inflationary economy)?

If borrowing is necessary and one's family is willing to loan money, even at a very low interest rate, is it so bad for a twenty-one-year-old student, or one who is fifty, to borrow from family? (Simple as it may sound, many persons I've counseled had never thought of borrowing from parents *with interest;* it was a gift or a right or nothing!)

Should a self-directed learner, taking for granted his or her desire or right to design an educational program, *not* take for granted the challenge of designing a mode of paying for that innovation via a route consistent with his or her learning? While one has to avoid the

"When you're up to your ass in alligators, you forget you came to drain the swamp" syndrome, nevertheless, those truly concerned with human learning may well consider funding routes organically related to their learning perspectives. In fact, a total value scheme will probably grow more coherently from that route than by following one wherein learning schemes run contrary to the funding, like a student I once knew who gambled for tuition to study ethics! And surely anybody pursuing marketing or economics competence who designs an organic approach will emerge much more capable, both professionally and personally, of dealing with the world.

Have we even begun to use our imaginations in coping with these problems? While there may be a certain brazenness in advertising oneself on a full-sized billboard, as my friend is doing, isn't the whole area of self-advertising a virtually untapped field? Or is there any way to promote the "who I *really* am" reality to counter the "who I know" syndrome?

Have we even begun to utilize the cooperative potential of learning and human networks? The women in UGS who are cooperating to assist their sisters no doubt must be cautious so that their efforts will not foster expectations of gratitude or other dehumanizing values. Yet, as the new communal movement in this country since the mid-sixties has revived our vision of cooperative living and as wifely sacrifice since World War II has pushed many a husband through school, here at least are paradigms of possibility from which many variegations are possible. Too, energy shortages may force closer and more economical living patterns, to the benefit of students.

Can we *as a people* afford to continue policies and practices that deny large segments of the population education for as long as they want to study? How much are we paying for "free" public education that goes so far and no farther? How much are we paying, not only in cash but also in lost or unfilfilled human dignity? And isn't this cost borne by those persons wanting traditional education as well as those who want to innovate? Surely, alternative motivations for learning are as viable as alternative modes.

In sum, the person seeking an alternative approach to learning for self or others should not indulge in the luxury of cursing offices of education, banks, fund-raising officers, shortsighted parents or some other scapegoat. Those believing in innovative and imaginative approaches to education must launch a new era of imagination and innovation.

CLASS BINDING

Gerhard Falk of SUNY Buffalo describes a related problem that no democratic society can avoid; namely, will the increased cost of graduate education and decline in financial support increase the probability that future doctorates "will become the preserve of the rich and that ability alone will count for little in the academic marketplace?"[3] David Gray asked this question years ago, pointing out that the heretofore uniform residency requirements in graduate schools almost guarantee exclusion of working-class persons.[4]

While in the aggregate this is still a real concern, the increasing number of external degree programs at the graduate level offers hope. Furthermore, when a blue ribbon national group, such as the Panel on Alternative Approaches to Graduate Education, makes a major recommendation in this area, its status may help it be heard. As Benjamin DeMott reported, one recommendation was that

> Course sequences, residence regulations, and other institutional requirements should be adapted to meet the needs of students with family responsibilities, adult learners, professionals, those forced to pursue their studies intermittently, and others whose admission to graduate education and preferred patterns of study differ from those regarded as standard.[5]

Another almost inevitable pressure: an increasing number of persons are "working for a living" and studying concurrently. In one study involving nearly 25,000 students at sixteen institutions, 90 percent of the men and about 65 percent of the women were doing so.[6] Also, an increasing number of undergraduates are awarded credit for experiential learning.[7] Having had this kind of opportunity, as those directly connected with extended/external degree programs are well aware, students are not likely to return to formally programmed curriculums. Furthermore, affirmative action programs are pressuring many schools to follow the British Open University and Empire State models by deliberately seeking more minority and women students.[8]

In short, while we are certainly far from realizing equal opportunity for all socioeconomic classes, nevertheless, neither undergraduate nor graduate students need necessarily be class-bound.

INSTITUTIONAL SOLVENCY, CHALLENGE, AND RESPONSE

Just as individuals may be challenged to devise creative solutions to maintain their own solvency, institutions may also be challenged.

Since World War II, both old and new institutions generally locate grant money prior to starting a new program. This could be documented, perhaps ad nauseum, from the annals of both private and public foundations and agencies. The standard procedures have little variation: get an idea, write a proposal, get a grant, implement; or, know of a money source, create the idea, write a proposal, get a grant, implement. Of course, some institutions have initiated programs to prove that they would work and then sought funding. Having been associated with the latter and having developed some idiosyncratic viewpoints since 1964, I'd like to mention some resources that seem not to get the attention they deserve.

Both the Antioch-Putney and the UGS programs derived minimal funds from the mother institutions. The former, with some federal money during the second year, became solvent the third; the latter became solvent the first year. The former readily obtained student loan money at the outset because Antioch was accredited; the latter obtained no outside funds whatever until veterans became eligible during the third year of operation. So it required some determination, skill, and creativity to effect such solvency. Some idiosyncratic viewpoints:

- If an idea's time has come and there is a market for it, it is not impossible to launch a program, even without a market survey.
- If one bets on people rather than money, it is more probable that a program will survive because those people will "hang in there" despite the odds.
- If the program is forced to "live off its income" and does not have too many frills, too much fat, too much financial overhead, then at least it will not develop faculty and students with the unrealistic expectations programs often have when they start with affluent crutches; better the "long and lean" approach, no matter how puritanical it may seem, sound, be.
- If the operational part of the program is in the hands of one not fearful of making decisions, not fearful of overworking,

and not sycophantic toward his/her superiors, a stubborn determination to survive may develop a kind of institutional maverick attitude.

- If the innovative program is one that is potentially threatening to some establishment (a faculty, a board of advisors, etc.), then a low profile should be part of its subversive thrust toward survival.

- If there is nobody around who combines accounting ability with insights about learning, then one should be found quickly in order to make that seemingly mundane translation of learning processes into dollars and cents.

- If one feels that America has lost its ethical idealists, then that whole area should be reassessed; any new and exciting idea, especially if it is calculated to "take on the establishment" will find persons rallying from unexpected places, "crawling out of the woodwork," offering services if they see a real opportunity to make a difference.

- If one approaches the vast richness of American society as well as the rich variety of the world, approaches them with imagination and openness, it is incredible how many free resources there are; regional Yellow Page compilations of such resources, to say nothing about such volumes as the *Whole Earth Catalogue,* only *begin* to enumerate such resources, all of which can become integral parts of a creative solvency; we have only begun to perceive the possibilities of the electronic medium, public libraries, and other public information systems; in short, we must approach such infrastructures with more angles of vision than has heretofore been done in traditional institutions. For instance, it seems absurd to build research libraries in New York City universities when the finest research facility in the world is available at Fifth Avenue and 42nd Street; better to subsidize student subway rides to the New York Public Library or subsidize that library than to build expensive research libraries and staff them.

- If one does not hesitate to draw upon the reputation of ongoing institutions, even using their credit lines if absolutely necessary, then that kind of support buttresses both academic and financial daring, so long as one recognizes that one is drawing upon a kind of unearned increment and recognizes a debt to be repaid in kind. To wit: the Union for Experimenting Colleges and Universities is a consortium with an enormous amount of incremental and status capital which makes possible some programs often perceived as impossible.

- If one approaches these matters related to creative solvency from a humanistic viewpoint, then one *may* be able to avoid historic slave-driving syndromes.

I would be the first to admit that such viewpoints are not popular! That they contain my own biases and values is evident. They are a combination of my vision of human potential and freedom as well as my experience over more than a decade of working in a variety of institutions. Others may have their own views and solutions. But the important thing is that there *are* solutions.[9] Just as there is nearly an infinite number of galaxies in space, a similar number of possibilities exist out there in the interstices of our own society.[10] Creative solvency and creative independence to evolve new learning situations for the infinite needs of humans are functions of one another.

11 Problems, Paradoxes, Processes, and Prognostications

Several UGS colloquia ago, two groups of students got together and made two decisions: first, a group of women asked me to bring some handicraft such as needlework to a meeting to help them break female stereotypes about handiwork; the other, mostly men, asked me to "lecture about some things I'd learned about education."

To the spokeswoman for the first group, I responded, "Why me? I'm a carpenter by avocation." And she replied, "Because you seem flexible enough to do it, and we think it would be good for you if you were to leave your yellow note pad in your room some day!"

To the spokesman for the second group, I asked, "You want me to *lecture?* You mean, *really* lecture?" His response: "Yes!"

So with professional assistance from my wife and emotional courage from Rosie Greer, the professional football player who wrote a needlework book, I learned a simple bargello stitch while watching a World Series game that very evening. Next day, as I left for an afternoon meeting, I picked up my yellow pad plus my little plastic bag filled with blue and white yarn, needle, tiny scissors, and the project I had started the night before. I also carried butterflies in my stomach!

I then positioned myself on the floor in the middle of the crowded room where my efforts would not be missed. As the session began, I slowly, quietly, and nervously unveiled my project and began to thread the needle. The speaker stopped her presentation and somebody remarked, "Roy, I didn't know that you did needlework." I responded, "But of course!" Somebody else asked, "For how long?" And I replied, "Since last night." Laughter nearly broke up the session, but we moved on. I proceeded with the needlework. After the meeting the spokesperson for the group came across the room and silently kissed me on the cheek.

The second request, despite the paradox involved in lecturing to a self-directed group, was an easier assignment. After all, most of my student and professorial life had been within conventional academic settings. Yet what does one *say to* a group of experienced persons who presumably are designing their own learning programs? Is there anything transferable or applicable in the lecturer's learning, the usual assumption when one lectures? Or should I simply say a few words about what I had learned and let it go at that? But I was determined to do as requested, to lecture, with no questions until I'd finished. And I was determined, too, that the lecture would be long enough to make my affective points as well as cognitive ones. Furthermore, I organized my lecture, "Some Things I've Learned," in decalogue form; after all, we had ample opportunity to follow up my ten points with plenty of midnight wine and dialogue.

1. One of the most difficult things to evolve is the courage to *let* be!
2. I have no desire to be a member of any college or university department.
3. The closer one is to the center of power, the less one has.
4. Learning is a function of size; also the spoken word is a bummer.
5. Idealism is a bummer.
6. To be of use, you must take abuse.
7. Every student's major field is identity-searching—nobody has a corner on the market of being oppressed.
8. Relevance *is* relevant.
9. The higher one's profile, the less the likelihood of getting things done.
10. The central task of the learning process is to structure those conditions wherein there can be a self-discovery of paradox, humor, and irony.

Unfortunately, my father died the next day, I had to leave the colloquium, and little discussion of these points followed. I feel the way the spirit of Schubert must feel about the Unfinished Symphony.

Those who have read this far will not be surprised at some of the topics in this list; I've mentioned them before. And yet, perhaps they need reiteration and a bit more commentary but in a random rather than systematic mode.

As anybody in extended learning programs knows, teachers, administrators, or whoever is *in* charge tend to assume that this means *taking* charge. That's the way Western civilization and Western education have been! Even in person-centered programs, students show up for counseling and attend a colloquium or another type of group session to start; naturally enough, they've paid their money, and they expect something in return. In UGS, for instance, at the second colloquium, students rapped the core faculty's knuckles because we did not tell them "what to do." And how should one react to a student's retrospective remarks about a colloquium?

> The first few days were filled with new people and swinging mood shifts. I was glad to be there, I liked most of the people, I was angry that nothing seemed to be happening. I was impressed and depressed by people and processes connected with UGS, and I was experiencing myself in a new situation. Finally, after awhile, the dust cleared, and I began to really make use of the program.

Nondirection, indirection, and shifts in direction are not easy to administer or to absorb! Is this a problem or opportunity?

Nor is it difficult to enumerate a variety of other paradoxes, some of which have been discussed before:

- Students charging administrators in doctoral programs for being *elitist*, since such programs tend to attract persons with money or at least those who have bachelor's and master's degree programs.
- Students, faculty and administrators, seeking structure in self-directed programs, believe that rigidifying the process will reduce anxiety, paranoia, and fear, when any true analysis of the situation would suggest the need for sorrow in a society that markets the belief that there is security in structure, sorrow enough to effect a mood with which to deal with anxiety, paranoia, and fear!
- Persons and programs seeking an interdisciplinary thrust at the very moment that ethnic and feminist groups of every size and description are erecting boundaries to establish clearer identity, just as nations tend to become more nationalistic and chauvinistic at the precise point in their political and

economic lives when cross-national efforts might reduce the tensions.

- Persons still fearing their own anger and other emotions because they have been taught that they must not or cannot express them.
- Students programming their interaction with the use of outside rules rather than inner, thereby imposing restrictions on faculty that students themselves would protest. (For instance, why should a student determine that a faculty member should work only so many hours a day or carry a certain load if the faculty member feels that he or she can do more or must not do less?)
- Persons confusing busy-ness with patience I've heard all too many persons say, "I'm a patient person" when indeed they might have said, "I'm too busy to think about my UGS program." Their busy-ness leads to guilt about things *not* done but doesn't necessarily lead them to consider the true value of patience.

It's not easy to deal with the paradox that schools such as UGS, Nova, Goddard, and Antioch are often perceived as secure places from which to peddle risk. Consider, also, the paradox that believers in these kinds of educational programs may have to develop "a willing suspension of disbelief" in order to achieve trust; or that striving (as Zen would have it) is the root of our educational evils; or that offering support need not necessarily lead to dependency; or that if you are strong enough your ego won't get in your way; or that there may be a genuine closeness in keeping respective distances when any two persons are working together in these kinds of learning situations; or that the Hawthorne Effect and Heisenberg Principles may provide stronger places to stand than relying upon clearly articulated curricula or processes; or that process is a more solid place to take a stand than geographical place when establishing these kinds of institutions; or that accreditation or other symbols of acceptance are potentially erosive of learning potential; or that commencement in any institutional context is more likely psychological "finishment"!

Too many paradoxes for one gulp?

Yet anybody encountering such paradoxes may well ask: Are

you playing games with us? Isn't each paradox like a hydra-headed monster: chop off a head and several more spring out of the neck! That's probably so. In fact, one of the most insightful parts of Robert Pirsig's *Zen and the Art of Motorcycle Maintenance* is a poignant reminder of such a truth; the author's hypothetical character, Phaedrus, coins a law: "The number of rational hypotheses that can explain any given phenomenon is infinite." He goes on, with the modern history of scientific evolution to support him, observing, "What shortens the life-span of the existing truth is the volume of hypotheses offered to replace it; the more the hypotheses, the shorter the time-span of the truth."[1]

ANGLES OF RELEVANCE

No serious consideration of problems, paradoxes, processes, and prognostications of external degree programs can avoid other odd angles of vision. For instance, few workshops on writing are about writing; rather, they are about a person's life gestalt. Perhaps that is why colloquium is a good way to describe how we launch students in UGS; we're concerned about graduate work in a *total life matrix*. And accepting a situation in which we hope there will be an evolution of congruence in a student's several identities and an acceptance of that congruence is seldom easy. To be even more specific: for most persons, the purpose of working for a degree is to fulfill some kind of mental picture, which, regardless of its complexity, is usually quite static. Like concepts of excellence or perfection, such pictures can be helpful and destructive at the same time—if all those in the learning matrix do not accept concurrently an existential evolution of learning.

Actually, this is merely another way of reviewing that collection of dilemmas so often put into juxtaposition; namely, being versus becoming, certainty versus probability, expectation versus realization, etc. Those working in universities without walls must give attention to self-concept first and then focus on so-called objective, external subject matter. We cannot deny the search for the relevant in anybody's striving but in the context of identity-searching.

PROBLEMS AND PROGNOSTICATIONS

The external degree program may be the wave of the future for a very large segment of the population that cannot or will not follow the usual public-private school programming that extends from K through 12 (and maybe K through Ph.D). Without question, however, this approach to education is *not* for everybody. In fact, the evolution of this approach to learning which increased in magnitude and variety beginning in the early seventies, may extend the historic strength of American education and society; namely, the capacity to effect variety.

I have mentioned many problems and predicted many outcomes in the preceding chapters. Our greatest problem in the future may be failing to deal with such problems. Here I simply want to reiterate, reemphasize, and perhaps regurgitate a few viewpoints. While my emphasis relates particularly to experience in UGS, I believe that applications and implications in other higher education settings are evident. No doubt the Edelstein report is only the first of a long series of such studies to which we can appeal when searching for empirical modes of evaluation.[2]

SOME OBSERVATIONS AND OPINIONS

External forces, such as guidelines from the Veteran's Administration, federal affirmative action programs, and no doubt many others to come, seem to reinforce the human quest for security. Ironically, the more obsessive the quest, the less is the probability of discovery! Without a doubt, most people have a difficult time tolerating freedom or any kind of self-made prosperity—economic, social, religious, or psychological. Rather, people find it easier to operate within structures of somebody else's making.

Any guidelines, normative perspectives, or rules to apply to persons in self-directed programs almost seem doomed to fail since they erode the freedom (and not license!) a person may need to accept failure. The evolution of any program (and there's irony in the need for a *program* stressing person-direction) probably will be in the direction of what is normal for the society. Furthermore, from a practical viewpoint, whether anybody will bother to look at *all* the *data* that accumulate in this kind of program is questionable, and whether or not anyone is competent enough to interpret what happens when another person is involved in the phenomenology of one's private experience is certainly open to debate. As stated before, a UGS program (learning strategy, internship, PDE) may *look* traditional, but out of what total life context did it grow? It is too easy to generalize or extrapolate from a particular observation, say, "It looks traditional" and thereby condemn it!

Yet at any particular stage of a program's evolution, who is qualified to make judgments about all of the human transactions in a total life gestalt? Surely a sine qua non of approaching such a problem in extended degree programs depends upon recognition of the humans involved—their perceptions, their evaluations, their evolving identities. I see, for instance, innovative programs falling into traps of illusion and delusion when participants believe that rules will secure or protect. I also see them caught in reactionary paranoia when so-called oppressed persons pressure for rules to protect them against oppression. In this sense today's oppressed become tomorrow's oppressors.

Using legal analogies, organizations such as UGS may destroy their essential uniqueness if they move from using developmental or common law solutions to a priori or civil code approaches (see Chapter 5). One may hope, however, that the philosophy, psychology, and application of academic and administrative due process will guarantee a modicum of openness. In other words, flexibility will depend upon the spirit as well as the letter of negotiation.

How long will it take us to reinvent Leviathan State University? When one relates this question to the pressures from many sources to guarantee legitimate feminist and minority equities, the picture becomes even more complicated. Furthermore, and perhaps fundamentally, confusion about open access, experimentation, and the experiential is obvious. Affirmative action seems to focus primarily upon open access. There is nothing necessarily detrimental about open access whether viewed from the perspective of civil liberties, human rights, or humanistic education. But the experimental is not necessarily innovative if the methodology chosen for the experiment results in bureaucratic inflexibility or if one remains unaware of or deaf to Robert Pirsig's insight that hypotheses breed hypotheses.

An experimental institution is not necessarily one that encourages experiential learning. In fact, an institution that takes the methodology of experimentation seriously, namely, one with hypotheses to test in the classical mode, will most likely be antiexperiential if experiential learning is perceived as stressing common sense or experiences.

Furthermore, open access does not guarantee either the experimental or the experiential if the persons who want it simply want it or have a highly structured viewpoint regarding the nature of life. In short, a structured psychology in all probability is going to preclude experimentation and respect for phenomenology or the innovative. If persons want open access simply to gain power to force open access (hardly implausible in view of the history of power-seeking in any era), they'll hardly fight for innovation. And usually those struggling to enforce their own ideologies are usually too serious to appreciate the irony, paradox, and humor of self-situation.

In my judgment those responsible for the future of UGS and other such programs can only make a difference if they face the implications of the interrelationship between the innovative, experiential, experimental, and phenomenological data that humans in those programs generate. Surely no governance board can deal with such issues by assembling only two or three times per year, especially if they attempt to make decisions in a parliamentary fashion. Such procedures invariably reduce information gathering and decision making to castrating yes-no contexts. When this occurs, the result, as we've noted in the legislatures of the world, is one of power-brokerage and negotiation. And that doesn't necessarily comply with the learning needs of individuals. Because this has been the normative pattern for both faculties and administrations in academic circles, student cries are usually lost amid the fury of clashing arguments.

In the UGS context, we have discussed frequently the possibility of adopting more self-destruct mechanisms, experimenting as it were because we had some hypotheses to test. For instance, consistent with the view that our graduates' performances will determine the reputation of UGS, we have proposed reviewing each graduate's work five years after graduation to determine whether the degree should be retained or recalled. The hypothesis to be tested is the viability of both our admissions and our academic processes. After all, if we claim and prove responsibility for adding a dimension to a student's life, manifest in such achievements as furthering self-direction, moving from rhetoric to risk, increasing openness to learning, etc., we could then say our process is worthy of continuing. If on the other hand, UGS students duplicate the attitude of most other doctorates by mistaking commencement for finishment, then, wherein should we struggle? As rough as such an experiment might be, it also might indicate that the degree of open access that we may have effected to increase the numbers of women and minority groups was worth the effort. Also, it would give us a clearer understanding of the relationships among open access, the experimental, the experiential, and the phenomenological.

Another self-destruct mechanism that we have retained is the system of committees (blobs) through which students build their academic credibility. It might be the single aspect that enables UGS to survive despite incredible naiveté over fundamental issues of power and representation. Let's look at representation first.

As suggested in Chapter 5, we often encounter the assumption that a peer, an adjunct on a committee, or a person elected to the governance board from a given colloquium represents that colloquium, represents women, blacks, or other special groups. Those in person-centered programs where individualized learning matrices form the structure must subject such assumptions to critical scrutiny. Such assumptions may have become part of the democratic and republican mythology, but I doubt that we can afford the luxury of perpetuating them in institutions featuring innovative, experimental, experiential, or phenomenological learning. To acknowledge such assumptions as myths enables one to avoid delusionary or illusionary attitudes; to treat them as common sense is unadulterated nonsense unless one is willing to invent another set of assumptions; namely, that feminists think alike, that minorities think alike, that all men think alike, ad infinitum. Frankly, I have not discovered such a monolithic ideology among UGS students of any race, sex, clan, colloquium, or creed. If anthropologists, psychologists, and phenomenologists have taught us nothing else during the past few decades, they have taught us to be more discriminating when focusing upon the *uniqueness* of an individual's experience as well as the *complexity* of that human experience. Furthermore, they have taught us much about the nature of the community, while political scientists have developed highly sophisticated methods for analyzing representation.

I find it very discouraging and demoralizing to perceive among well-intentioned individuals (including myself) a kind of self-deception occurring when people talk vigorously about representation, ideology, and similar matters. We merely promote self-deception, and this often perpetuates contradictions that are not always resolvable. For example, promoting student self-direction in community contexts (as at a colloquium) may be a fundamental incompatibility or contradiction; after all, a colloquium is only a temporary community. A guarantee of both substantive and procedural certainty, spelled out in UGS process codes and individual learning contracts, may seem to reduce risk where risk is demanded. To perpetuate the illusion of representation among a student population where that possibility is even narrower than in national politics is a serious contradiction that needs discussion, analysis, and action consistent with stated objectives. Also, why encourage students to obtain nationally prominent, traditional doctors as adjuncts to help them achieve a radical doctorate? And, indeed, is the core faculty an equal among equals (with student as chairperson) if she is keeper of the process?

Not surprisingly, one can find in innovative educational enterprises some of the same power struggles as found in the macropolitics of the United States. And there is no more "purity" in this context than in the larger community. Hence, we'll probably see the circle squared before we find any number of people in positions of power self-destructing the apparatus through which they came to power. Such revolutions in self-concepts do not occur very frequently.

In short, I sense that innovative institutions will become self-consciously innovative, and experimental schools will become self-consciously experimental, especially if experiential learning becomes more widely accepted. I also feel that extended degree programs, however flexible at the start, cannot avoid the gradual accumulation of guidebooks, handbooks, and policy statements as long as they expect to operate within the framework of accreditation structures, federal guidelines regarding money, and affirmative action programs. And the bigger and more complex they become, the greater the demand is for such statements, such generalizations, such leveling processes. Paradoxically, at the very moment when UGS or perhaps any other institution gains its accreditation or accepts money with strings attached, it may be signing a pact with Mephistopheles.

My tragic sense, however, tells me that both as individuals and as organizations we must continue to combat our own flaws; namely, our incapacity to tolerate freedom, our inability to eschew the quest for certainty, or our tendency to join the faddists who espouse accountability, competency-based systems, or other popular trends. If we choose to battle those forces in the context of heroic struggle, if I may continue the logic and insights of Aristotle's vision of tragedy, then we have a greater opportunity to know *existentially* who we are as individual human beings and as institutions. Furthermore, regardless of the outcome, we have a greater probability of achieving Maslow's vision of peak experiences and self-actualization *through the struggle.*

My sense of the pathetic human condition tells me that we are more likely to take another course; namely, things will drift while we hope that somehow or other they will come out all right.

The very fact, however, that I have not given up trying to articulate my viewpoint or to look at the options suggests my own bias; that is, that we still have the option of choosing. I think, however, that the time may be shorter than we think, despite my hope that these learning approaches are the wave of the future and also in light of the groundswell moving a larger number of people and programs toward extended degree learning. Surely, if the ideologues gain ascendance, they will effect one kind of tyranny or another. Pathetic drift will eventually find us caught in our own pollution of will.

So, perhaps it's best that we opt for the tragic vision, so long as we do it in the context of humans in the cosmos, humans struggling, coping with irony and paradox in a spirit of humor and good will.

12 Some "For Instances"

A person hardly turns around in extended educational programs without bumping into a "for instance." After all, we are dealing with everyday living-learning in all its complexity. And that's far from a cold statistic. If those of us developing such programs acknowledge that we are involved with diverse instances, even while inducing individual and institutional goals, we do not get caught in the delusionary mazes of proof. Obviously, statistical evidence should be considered, but it is a trap to get hung up on it. When one quantifies everything, what happens to the human thoughts and juices that do not slide so easily down that sluiceway? I once read an evaluation of the vocational education program in a state with a national reputation for developing a comprehensive approach to the problem, and it was, indeed, a wilderness of accountability jargon in its coverage of activity goals, process objectives, performance information, on-site procedures, and formative feedback systems. Having visited a school in that state, I wondered if the "monitors" who wrote the report ever heard the circular saws ringing, smelled the lacquer in the auto body paint shop, felt the fabrics in the upholstery classroom, tasted the food in the gourmet training laboratory, or saw any of the other events occurring before their very eyes. Also, I wondered how they might react to a student log or a poem reflecting enthusiasm for the multicolored world which that school is!

In short, statistics and generalizations have their place, but shouldn't we temper our enthusiasm for such abstractions by remembering the declension of the word *lie* as "lies, damn lies, and statistics"? Or, if that seems too harsh, keep our eyes on the both positive and negative instances. In one recent batch of mail, I received several letters that affirmed our UGS efforts, to wit:

One of the greatest changes that has occurred since I entered the UGS program was not merely the opening of doors for me professionally (which I expected to happen), but the indirect and unanticipated change in my, and my family's life style, values, attitudes, activities, and interests. We became activists—and I am damn glad of it. I never realized how involved and committed my wife and kids could be to social action and social change. Somehow the spirit of UGS got transmitted via me to my family and had the sort of impact that fired their needs to be meaningfully occupied in filling the vessel of time with important things. R——— finished high school as quickly as she could and got out into the world via UFW. My other kids got into an open school and are happier than they ever were. None of them give a damn about degrees and credentials now, and they are really living. There are problems—and there always will be. But we are closer than we've ever been before.

This person had graduated two years earlier.

Personal testimonials are much more difficult to deal with; yet they must be seen in the context of a reaffirmation of one's own efforts in a society where pandering and patronizing are often treated with cynical disrespect. An illustration:

Just wanted to pen a note of gratitude for your persistent encouragement and faith in seeing me through. . . .

You have the very rare ability of inspiring an individual toward self-reliance . . . foster creative self-sufficiency.

Or,

The New Year's approach always makes me a little reflective of people in my life I consider important. (About this time I imagine you are a little fidgety about what may come! And maybe a little embarrassed! Have no concern.) I have told you before of the special significance you have . . . and just wanted to let you know I'm thinking of you.

These are the kinds of remarks, of course, that men are not supposed to exchange in American society. But there are other perspectives. In the same mail was a letter from a man we had interviewed and eventually admitted to the program. He wrote to say he was no longer interested in enrolling and how he reached that decision:

You might be surprised to learn that UGS conveyed the very impression it claims to avoid. My interviews ten years ago at academic graduate institutions gave me the impression that they wanted me to enroll, that they welcomed me. . . . But UGS made it clear that I was only one of a large number of subjects to be interviewed. When that interview was over, my visit to UGS was abruptly over. . . The interview made me wonder why I had come. . . . And your insulting question about what I would do "when I grew up" was not at all mitigated by your apology that you asked it of everyone.

Further digging in that pile of mail brought a resignation from another student who had a continued and continuing hassle about finding means to explore his inner life. He said, in part:

> The Project Demonstrating Excellence which is my heart's true desire is *myself,* the mystical transmutation of my lower self—which is what I work on every day. It will take a few more years—at least!—to complete my true PDE and if it is ever completed I may well hide it from the committee of present humanity and reveal it only to the One True Humanist!
>
> Being in the program has been incredibly worthwhile if only that it has served to bring me into contact with a continuing series of amazing mystics . . . . And I consider the money well-spent for leading me to my wife!
>
> And so I say farewell to thee, most noble son of Saco, Maine! It is primarily due to Dr. _____ and yourself that I have gone to such amazing schools as M_____, Antioch-Putney, and UGS. With the great nurturance of such freedom to flourish, I have had a most incredible education which continues even on more intense and rewarding levels. When it reaches the speed of light, I might even, as the Sufis say, "learn how to learn"(!).

Then there is the example of a person who is disappointed and believes that my anticipated disappointment may mean disapproval:

> I regret very much, although my regrets are diminishing as I approach a conclusion to this project, becoming involved in a traditional research endeavor. I would have preferred a

phenomenological project, one more consistent with my concepts of UGS. Unfortunately, for many reasons, I chose this topic and method of approach. It is, nevertheless, a worthwhile piece of work and will be a contribution to the growing literature. . . . My role is researcher—collector and compiler of data, evaluator of conclusions—and perhaps, one who recommends change in existing practice.

INTERLUDE: PERCEPTION AS PROJECTION?

A many-tomed work consisting of such "for instances" would be easy to compile, for the varieties of human experience in extended degree programs are as much the objective of study as are the various topics on which students are working. Although the empirically or statistically oriented person might argue that such a volume would not necessarily prove anything, I would respond with some questions: If we say that a student's examination of his or her own experience is an important part of a program and we are congruent in our affirmation of that endeavor, need we compile any more than those statements as evidence that something is happening, even if that perception is projection? Do we need to analyze the comparative impact of our programs in this regard with the impact of more traditional programs? Should we, in turn, be evaluated by an outside agency if word-of-mouth comments about our programs convince prospective students that they, too, might find these alternative opportunities to their liking?

KEEPING THE FIRES BURNING

Demands on individuals staffing such programs are often so heavy that people sometimes burn out relatively easily. I personally have experienced great fatigue in attempting to maintain intensity, despite my own self-concept of and belief in human endurance as an important value. I also have counted many colleagues as victims of this demanding way of life. But my observation includes the view that one needs to number among the advantages of working in such a program the positive illustrations as well as the negative experiences. Two other colleagues and I have pleaded with our peers to place "Joyful Experience" on our faculty meeting agenda, for we know we'll hear plenty of war stories during any conference! Shortly after she joined us, a new colleague asked me one of the most useful

questions anybody asked me during the first five years of our
existence; namely, "Would you mind sharing some of the high
points as well as some of the low, in writing?" Out of that query
came an informal letter to a colleague, quoted here with only enough
editing to protect the privacy of the individuals whom I am discussing.[1] Fortunately, I decided to wait until I was in the midst of a
good experience before dictating the note, and I began by saying, "I
am enjoying a rather high point at this moment, here at R's terminar
in Navajo country in Arizona. . . ." Let me deal with the ups first:

> This is an especially happy occasion for lots of reasons, among
> which is the fact that we have had a great deal of difficulty get-
> ting R to find the appropriate number of adjuncts, peers, etc.
> In fact, a lot of hassling has been going on, as the files indicate.
> But, here in the setting of the Southwest Poet's Conference, the
> atmosphere is a pleasant one, as songs and poems dedicated to
> and by Pueblo, Apache, and Navajo persons create the mood.
> We will be holding the terminar at the close of the conference.
> It is a beautiful setting seven or eight thousand feet above sea
> level with the air perfectly clear. Today there was a poetry fes-
> tival held in the bottom of the canyon about 1½ miles from the
> college. The air was threatening, as lightning zig-zagged off
> the local mesas and the sun played hide-and-seek with
> ominous black clouds. Yet, the beauty of the setting and the
> spirit of the participants was unmistakably joyful.
>
> Getting off a jet in Zurich and being met by A . . . present-
> ing him with a cane that Maryllyn had obtained from a friend
> who was in Africa at the very time when he was experiencing a
> bout with the gout and laughing about the synchronicity . . .
> meeting two outstanding Jungians, his adjuncts, whom we had
> met the year before . . . hearing A's account of his own re-
> searches and enthusiasms and dreams . . . doing it all in the
> setting of a glorious feasting . . . talking privately with A and
> his wife about their enthusiasms over Switzerland and their
> feelings about the United States . . . a memorable two days be-
> fore we hopped a plane, somewhat tearfully, to fly off to
> Nairobi.
>
> Meeting in a Greenwich Village colonial kitchen with a

cozy atmosphere, a prepared student, a complete committee, plenty of cheese, wine, and bread, and an observing North Central team present. After a round of too much concord, we got into some critical issues involving Rock's two or three years in UGS. I think I mentioned this to you last December after the session, but I simply wanted to reinforce the imagery.

As you well know, M's presentation of Aeschylus' *Oresteia* in California was, indeed, a fantastic experience. As I reflect upon her presentation of the Greek trilogy, I only regret that I had not insisted, perhaps even *demanded,* that she video it as we had talked about it at her certification session. Although art forms have a way of being evanescent and all too fleeting, the video might have captured some of the Jungian dimensions of her approach. Also, you would have dug her emphasis upon the feminist aspects of Aeschylus' work. Those male chauvinist pigs who were writing tragedy in the fifth century!

Another memorable occasion was a double terminar in L.A. during which P and B completed their work. Again, it was in the setting of good food, some extraordinary questioning and evaluating, and general camaraderie. I do think it was in the context of celebration. B's skit, written for the occasion, was a creative highlight of that particular occasion.

E's concert at O, in which she reviewed the history of black people in music and song, was a culminating point in a very important two-year process for both E and for me. We had discussed what she might do in UGS in May 1970, before she joined the program. It had been my response that she should attempt all those things she fantasized doing. These not only included an enormous amount of reading in the black studies field, visiting some of the most prominent black historians in the country, taking a trip to Africa to rejoin herself with her own tradition and fantasy, but also moving from elementary teaching into university teaching and administration. She achieved all those objectives during her two years with us, a feat which I doubt she ever imagined doing before she joined us. In short, she fulfilled her own self-designed objectives.

The gory war stories are much more difficult to deal with if one is going to protect the privacy of individuals. Hence, I must be more

vague about the particulars; here, too, it seemed important in retrospect, to indicate parenthetically to my colleague what I thought
went wrong:

> At an early colloquium one person attempted to hold a certifi-
> cation session, and it was a genuine disaster. He offered and
> perhaps even insisted upon doing it as a demonstration before
> the colloquium participants. He and I had chosen his peers
> somewhat sight-unseen from this particular colloquium, rely-
> ing all too heavily upon paper, my judgment, and a cursory
> contact with the peers in question. Also, only one of his adjunct
> professors was present. He was defensive, tongue-tied, ill-in-
> formed, etc. You name the problem, and he had it. (Perhaps I
> have already cued some of the reasons why it failed, but it
> made me very leery of holding certification sessions during col-
> loquia. Also, it was a badly constructed committee which back-
> fired on him. It was also a traumatic experience for him, one
> requiring almost ten months from which to recover. He even-
> tually completed a piece of work which a new committee ap-
> proved, but I had a feeling down to the very end that his con-
> tinued tightness resulted from the trauma.)
>
> Another case had a very difficult ending. One of his peers
> refused to attend the terminar in New York City because he
> felt that the student should have taken several more years to do
> a more empirical kind of study. (That the peer was projecting
> his own values and skills was without question the basis for the
> difficulty and the misunderstanding. Such instances as this led
> us to the forms which must be signed prior to scheduling a ter-
> minar. Also, this was an instance of peers serving on one
> another's committee, a practice we now discourage. I'm not
> sure, however, that one can ever completely prevent a last
> minute dissent on the part of one member of a committee . . .
> especially if that member hasn't participated as much as
> he/she should have along the course of the person's work.)
>
> Another grim experience pivoted around a man's having
> his committee wiped out from under him because of profes-
> sional conflict between him and his adjunct professor. It seems
> that they were "political" rivals in their particular professional
> field. The man in question had not done a good job explaining

UGS requirements; also, he did a poor job assembling his committee. Having scheduled his certification session just prior to another one also made things tight. I thought two hours would be enough to do it, but we should have had fifty! Anyway, it required reconstructing the committee as well as written clarification of the process to eliminate the difficulty.

Another very uncomfortable situation resulted when J chose two European-educated professors for his adjuncts. Although he claimed he had thoroughly explained to them what we were trying to do, it wasn't all that clear that they understood our procedures when we actually got to the certification session. Fortunately, his peers were state-side. Although I rarely have much difficulty with *ambiguous* situations, it was the *ambivalence* of the two adjuncts that upset me.

There have been several situations where a student failed to bring his/her entire committee together which have created untold agony for me. Some of these situations, which need not be spelled out in great detail, led us to both the certification and the terminar forms which would be signed by the entire committee. In one of the very earliest situations, I was literally shocked when a student in question arrived at the certification, and only one of his peers showed up. I simply was appalled by the fact that he had not done his homework. I refused to continue the session as a certification meeting. (This was a case of freedom becoming license and too much "business as usual," two syndromes we must avoid like the plague or be called a "degree mill.")

In another case we actually held another terminar, this one long before adopting termination and certification forms as well as prior to using the signed learning contract. The terminar blew sky-high, even on video! The trauma was so great in this instance that the student left for two years before returning to complete his work. (This was a case where the person attempted to move entirely too fast. Although a colleague and I had repeatedly indicated to him that we were "unhappy with his work," he persisted in holding the session. He also made the mistake of having business cards printed in which his name was followed by "Ph.D." In fact, I had to ask him to "desist using the cards" both orally and in writing a few months following the terminar. I still feel uncomfortable when people use the letters behind their name too soon following a terminar, sometimes before the paper work is done and the diploma has been issued, even though I recognize the terminar as our brand of graduation, our ritual!)

Another terribly uncomfortable situation resulted at the close of T's terminar when one of her peers asked some incredibly double-bind sexist and racist questions which almost precluded rational answers. Unfortunately, T refused to respond at all and that only precipitated further anger and anxiety. That situation was somewhat comparable to the one which you encountered with A recently. (I suspect there is no way to avoid hidden agendas about which we as core may know little or nothing. Far from excoriating ourselves for failing to soothe the troubled waters in such instances, I suspect that we must learn that motto which I invented during the Antioch-Putney evolution; namely, "To be of use, you must take abuse!")

Another uncomfortable situation resulted when two adjuncts asked me to a command performance the night before a certification session. We had dinner to discuss their concerns. It turned out that both adjuncts were so traditional that they couldn't even *begin* to see the person's program in anything other than traditional format of empirical research and dissertation. Although it was pretty agonizing and bloody for the student, he eventually had to dismiss them and reconstruct his committee. He learned, as did I, that his own personal and professional affiliation with the two people in question did not constitute a viable rationale for asking them to serve. Although neither nepotism nor private interest were in question, there was a genuine misassessment of the persons. As core I served as mediator in the situation for as long as viable; fortunately, the student moved across the country; hence he found the shift more congenial.

As so frequently happens in reporting on pioneer endeavors, the number of battles outnumbers the number of ecstatic situations, but I concluded my memorandum to my colleague with a couple of generalizations; namely,

... that we sometimes suffer from the fact that our students do not do their homework for one reason or another in indicating to their adjuncts the nature of UGS. Maybe adjuncts can never be told what their role is; they may have to grow into it. I for one do not think that we will necessarily have any better adjunct input from a complex program of socialization than we will to attempt to get our students to be more realistic.

And finally,

I have not mentioned several very complex situations involving transfer of students from one core to another. That is usually traumatic for all concerned. I have attempted to serve as a humane mediator in such sticky cases, and it is not easy.

The latter instances could fill a volume in themselves. Name any brand of miscommunication, misconception, misunderstanding, misperception, and it would probably show up in these instances. Naturally enough, human foibles, ambitions, jealousies, human aspirations, fantasies, and value systems being what they are, "sticky cases" are bound to arise, especially since we have consistently said that students may change their committee members, including the core, if it becomes impossible to work with them. And, our progress review system, instituted in our fifth year of operation, endangers the integrity of that change potentiality. After all, a core faculty member may institute an inquiry into a student's progress! And that eventuality may occur if a core finds him or herself thrown off a student's committee. Nor does the new core in these instances necessarily have a bed of thornless roses to lie in; after all, he may be charged by his colleague with "being easy," for lacking high standards, for being of questionable morality, etc; in other words, charged with the usual fictional and nonfictional sins to which colleagues are heir where there are professional jealousies, ambiguous procedures—in short, humans! That jeopardy is potentially as great in programs such as UGS as it is in any standard academic situation. What diminishes the threat to both student and faculty, however, is the due process dimension of our progress assessment procedure and the fact that we are still small enough for face-to-face meetings among both students and faculty.

A SCENARIO

The day after the terminar in the Greenwich Village kitchen I sat down to my typewriter and tried to catch some of the affect of that meeting. In perspective this summary from my own log reflects a kind of universality in its uniqueness:

You know that it's never happened quite like this before. In fact, you know that even though it seems to have happened before that it has not. You know that you are a part of a total experience which can never be totaled by adding up its parts. That is at once the glory and the awe of it, something like watching an eidelweiss shed its dew in an alpine bog or a rose open in the morning. Yet you *know*, though you may not be willing to feel, that any analogy, any explanation, any analysis will not recapture, recover the situation. You know that it is a phenomenon never to be explained in any ultimate sense, yet you want to try. You want to try because you hope that the vision of the repetition of such an experience will somehow or other capture the imagination of another or many another. You want to try to capture it somehow, in words, in picture, in song, through some esthetic dimension because you are selfish enough to want to jog your own memory in order to live the past in reverie or compare with the present to gain a sense of movement (even going backward is movement, and not all of us believe in the great sugar daddy of progress) or even use the experience as the touching point to triangulate the future.

Such was the feeling I had there as I sat in that cozy kitchen. You could just see the glisten in the eyes of those sitting around that long table, groaning with cold cuts, cheeses, salads, crusty breads, and light wines. A leaden sky outside with an occasional slant of rain made the scene the cozier: ten people gathered together to celebrate a man's completion of one leg of his journey into his own mind, his journey into so many spaces and "only salvations" that Ulysses himself would have been envious. At one point I inquired whether or not he ever felt like Ulysses, as he stopped first at the port of the Buddhist monastery and then at the feet of a guru and eventually in the arms of an LSD therapist, I asked him, "Ulysses, do you ever feel that you have stopped at the same port twice?" And he smiled his own genteel smile, took another sip of rosé and nodded slowly.

But we were a ring of friends and he one of the links, a link across and around the parameters of that table. He called us each by our first name, asked us to describe our own "I" succinctly but existentially. And we obliged,

"I am a friend of twenty years."

"And I as his professor have become his friend, and I am no longer embarrassed to call him 'friend'."

"I, Jonathan, am his peer. My journey was like his, so I have shared in his and he in my growth."

"I am there at the other end of the copper wire, ready to take his calls, any time up to midnight."

Each of us responded to his request. Then it was *his* turn to tell each of us why he had chosen *us* to be on his formal committee.

"You, Sam, I had heard of, and I wanted to work with you and your dying cancer patients. It seemed to me that you could help me understand ways of understanding my each succeeding dying self. . ."

"And you, Hazel, reassuring me with music during my LSD trips that there were other cosmos out there somewhere if I looked for them in here. . ."

The party then got self-congratulatory, each saying how much he/she had enjoyed Rock's work, each for six straight paragraphs praising, beyond all counsel what this had meant to them.

As each poured libations of praise, I pondered to myself, "Can it be that the presence of external evaluators at this terminar is keeping them from coming to grips with some of the obvious weaknesses of Rock's work?"

So when it came my turn in the round table response, I pulled out my own papers as a kind of crutch, peered quizzically under the lights diagonally across to Rock, took a deep breath and said, "Well, all of this concord is lovely, but somebody has to be a son of a bitch here. So I guess it has to be me."

Laughter.

And I began to read from a letter which I'd written to Rock the previous Monday in Ohio, 600 cool jet miles from the Greenwich Village in which we were sitting so comfortably on that December Sunday. I raised the question about Ulysses, wondering, too, if his own startling revelations about youthful debaucheries, lost loves, and "salvations" as he shed former selves didn't need some kind of epilogue. Did he not need to recognize the paradoxes that the only endings were in new beginnings?

"If only one sentence, Rock," my voice pleading, "to let us know that you can accept the irony and paradox of the journey! And, knowing you as I do, just the merest whisper of humor to counterpoint all that dying!"

That broke it open. Not the nasty, typical Ph.D. oral exam to trip him up over logical lapses, not testy debating over moot points or the crossing of a verbal barrier. No, it was a deep searching by us all gathered there. Each his/her own person, but each synergetically related to Rock, leading him, encouraging him, making sure that he was not led down stray paths by us but spinning at his own centripetal center. All participated, even the friend of the friend who just came along because she was asked. She, too, a first-class citizen, no feeling of intrusion, no feeling of irrelevancy. And the silences, too were poignant, punctuated only by an occasional snapping of the fire or gust of wind in the grey back courtyard, half a story above that cozy cellar kitchen.

A far-off clock struck four to bring us back to essential questions. What more had to be done? Who would be satisfied with what? And the everlasting question of when? Gentle probing but precise, leading to exact answers and a round of nods from those at the table affixed with the responsibility of saying, "Yes, we are with you, Dr. Rock!"

Such was the occasion, called unfortunately a terminar, constituting the next to last step for Rock Tush and his journey into himself and through our program. It had been a long journey, begun on Lido Beach at Sarasota, Florida, where shells come boiling out of the Gulf with colorful trips up and down the beach and where he and thirty peers commenced their learning journey with intense discussions twenty-four hours a day, massage and debate on the beach in the mid-winter sun, volleyball to stay warm on brisk days. Rock's journey began there where he had an opportunity to meet persons of national stature in their disciplines who had come to share insights about scholarship, their interface with the world, their own journeys. Here, too, he shared his own views on what he was designing to do in this self-directed learning experience, not a blueprint at that time but surely a plan to hook together his youth in a wealthy family, his patrician education, his Marine Corps trek in Vietnam, and his study at the feet of Zen master and guru. In many ways the thrust to the future was a blind stab, too, full of unknowns, no curriculum structure, no required courses, no classroom attendance, no required milestones to pass. In fact, both he and his peers expressed the notion that it was downright scary. One of his counterparts presented her plan one sunny afternoon, when the sun was streaming in from the Gulf and the sound of a roaring sea gushed thru the slightly opened window, but she melted into irreconcilable tears. The future for her was, indeed, an open sea. But facing oneself alone in a boat is no comfort, even in the sight of beaches sporting a thousand seagulls.

So Rock flew north on a National jet, toyed with teaching, visited workshops from Maine to California, met his learning colleagues, both faculty and student, taught French for a living for awhile, eventually landed at a psychiatric research laboratory as a video technician, recording the journeys for both professional and terminal cancer patients. Here was a job very close to the death that he at once pursued and shunned. Here was an internship in life struggle and survival, coming through his own musically guided trips to know the paths of physical rebirth as well as the intensity and poignancy of life and death. He not only accompanied one young woman through a trip but also returned with her to California to emphathize with her final gasps—a trip to end *her* trips but to begin another of *his own*, interacting with her poetic father.

So the celebration that Sunday afternoon in December was at once a culmination and a challenge. Given the challenge of our learning set, no pause is more than the deep breath for the harder run. We eschew the notion that any stop, to collect degree or accept other honors, is anything less than a genuine commencement. If this learning approach means anything, it means an end to the notion that one obtains a degree at a particular age, works in a particular mode which can be replicated a thousand times in any part of the world. It is an effort to put meaning, life, and force into the rhetoric of individualized learning, working with unique humans, enabling them to actualize their potentiality or become self-actualized. The institution and persons who identify with that institution's purposes are committed to support the humans who want to learn. It is a commitment to lifelong learning processes, the notion that persons can tune in with us for a year or four and thereby gain the booster to spin them into new orbit. This learning approach is a commitment to process-as-product, to the weaving of human supporting networks which never have been woven before and which may last only as long as a snowflake on the end of one's nose, to the constancy of changing institutions as well as changing persons, to the view that all the talk about social revolution may be more romantic than the revolution that may occur when a single person changes his own perspective. In fact, if that person reinvents the wheel, something new is born in the universe, so long as that is a revolutionary act for him and he is not deluded into thinking it is a new social invention.

So Rock's terminar was a celebration at the end of his formal academic work, hardly a castration. As each of us left that kitchen table for our respective destinations, we knew that he was part of us. We knew, too, that he was both the weaver and the woven.

MORE SYNCOPATION

Upon another occasion, in another kitchen, this one in the Ohio countryside, I spent a spring Sunday afternoon with a UGS student and his committee. Before we began struggling to encourage this man to be himself, one of his peers read a letter she had written to him that morning *in advance of the certification* thanking him for his hospitality at the certification:

> Dearest W:
>
> Sitting here in the here and now of your family farm kitchen watching you make pancake banana bread, my

thoughts fly to being home in Florida—back to my daily routine which in no way includes writing letters—so why not now—?

It was a glorious certification—you deported yourself with outstanding poise, imagination, decorum, intelligence, sensitivity to the needs of your committee—you helped allay our anxieties about how to be good, tough but supportive committee members by telling us just what you really wanted from each. F was as bright and charming as you had advertised and I enjoyed her comments and suggestions. Roy's spur-of-the-moment haikus and grooks were appropriate as usual—no better, no worse—didn't show the strain of his hectic past weeks. I admired the way he cut through all your meanderings and kept bringing you back to the point—while at the same time shattering your train of thought whenever you began to get focused.

S was beautiful in cutting through to the essence of the essential W bringing you always back to the here and now of your work—a warm beautiful lady as befits someone you would choose to be in therapy with.

J was eloquently quiet but seemed always to know just where you were.

Now that it's all over and you've had a chance to live with the aftermath of the meeting, I'm sure you will agree with the committee's consensus that you should abandon opera singing (and cartography) as a career and stick to your original plans of training the Mt. Everest guides in Gestalt techniques of mountain climbing.

The reading of this letter at the start of the meeting nearly cracked us up, but it served the purpose of reducing anxiety and getting us down to the task for which we had gathered. It illustrates the value of peer involvement. It is also symbolic of the daring and inventiveness of humans in innovative educational situations; it's difficult to imagine a student reading such a letter at a traditional oral exam. Had I made a discrete list of such occasions that I have personally witnessed, it would number into the hundreds. It would surely include a great many character sketches, the UGS drinking song, dozens of incidents from the colloquia, and a lengthy description of Erection City (a tent village at a colloquium) where the mayor's second child was conceived. In fact, such examples are as rich in texture, variety, and imagination as any other substantial scene from the human comedy.

INTERVIEWING

Not all interviewing for admission turns out as negatively as that mentioned earlier in this chapter. And just as a UGS application has often inspired poems from my pen, sometimes an interview and its subsequent description for the Admissions Committee carries more insight than one might normally find in educational circles. I offer another example from the "Note to the Files":

>I met with H in New York on the night of December 1 between the hours of 10:15 and 1:20. It was truly an amazing meeting for the simple reason that she was invited to come down to the Village for a postterminar dinner party which Mary was holding in Steve's home. It was even more amazing in view of the fact that she brought her two-year-old child with her, since she could not get a babysitter. The setting was fantastic: a fire in the fireplace, lots of wine, several UGS students, wives, adjunct professors and wives, and other friends present. It was truly a test of a person's nerve, courage, openness, flexibility, and intelligence. This was not deliberate, for I had planned to talk with her for an hour or so in the hotel lobby and go to bed early!
>
>We started in a rather gentle way, all sitting on the floor and asking gentle questions such as why did she want to go to UGS, what was she doing now, etc. The party got pretty rough when Mary said that she felt that H was not leveling with us and had a greater probability of getting into UGS if she were honest. That opened an incredible number of avenues of thought and discussion, not only relating directly to H's own interest in anthropology, the work she was doing in the field of research, etc., but she began talking about herself as a woman and indicated that she had only recently separated from her husband.
>
>The intelligence which I had sensed and the potentiality which I had intuited in reading her application was certainly borne out in the course of our two hours of interaction.
>
>When I observed her Phi Beta Kappa key and asked why

she had chosen the largest one available rather than the medium-sized or small one, I gave her the option of "taking the fifth amendment." She chose to answer the question and indicated that this award, coming unsolicited after she had studied in five or six different colleges, was the thing that meant most to her, hence her decision.

There is no doubt in my mind that many of the objections which were raised during the admissions meeting; namely, "Couldn't she stick with a traditional program at the University of Pennsylvania?" "Couldn't her husband support her going to Pennsylvania?" etc., were pretty well resolved.

BH, who is working in a similar field, indicated that H was right in saying that there is no graduate school in the United States that would permit her to do what she wanted to do.

All the persons in the room were enthusiastic about her, not only as a person but as one who was competent and represented a lot of creative potentiality. These UGS students in question were not only BH but also Mary and Steve. Also, BJ, an adjunct professor, accompanied her in her car from upper Manhattan to the Village, having an opportunity to talk about their mutual interests in the field of parapsychology. He indicated to me that he certainly would be willing to endorse her.

I asked the persons who were at the interview to write a letter of endorsement for her and send the letter to me. Whether or not they will have an opportunity, I would like to push full speed ahead toward admitting her.

One test which I always use in talking with prospective students is the following: "Would I enjoy working with the person?" I can say unequivocally that I would enjoy working with H. She is intelligent, perceptive, has lots of organizing ability, is articulate, and I think that the Union Graduate School would enable her to weave together a great variety of interests into a creative program.

One footnote: You will note that I have scribbled longhand comments all over the back of her folder as well as the inside cover. I can probably use those notes to go into more detail during the admissions meeting if it becomes necessary.

Respectfully,

Not all interviewing is as insightful or exciting as this particular session was. Some of it is dull, routine, uninspiring. But the number of interviews like the one involving H certainly is larger than that which I have encountered in other programs where game playing often was the rule rather than the exception. Incidentally, we admitted H to the program. I served as her core faculty. In retrospect, my claims for her didn't begin to assess her full potential. And she far surpasses me in her ability to write grooks!

LETTER WRITING AS AN ART

As I have observed elsewhere, much of the correspondence that is so vital to innovative programs has been informative, supportive, and sensitive. The art of letter writing is not dead; it has not given way completely to electronic media. While few of us would challenge some of the great letter writers of the past, Thomas Jefferson, for instance, many of us do aspire to functional and humanistic artistry in communicating with one another. Over the years I have personally felt most fortunate to have had exchanges with several persons numbering in excess of a thousand letters each, over a decade or two. This may account for my lack of self-perceived need for therapy! And I have been most fortunate while serving as faculty for Antioch-Putney and UGS to have had the supporting system (dictaphone, secretarial help, administrative assistance, etc.) making it possible for me to practice what I preach as well as preach what I practice with wholehearted effort at congruency.

Although I have enjoyed lengthy and intensive communications with many of my students, nevertheless, I sometimes learn more when a person I am not working closely with writes about a particular problem. I am forced to think through a particular issue or set of problems from a different angle of vision, thought, and concern. One such instance occurred when a woman whom I met at the colloquium where the women challenged me to take up handiwork wrote to say,

> I find myself writing to you out of a need to communicate thoughts and to ask questions that are not readily understood by most people, out of a (temporary) feeling of discouragement. I don't mean to lay on you a kind of last-resort-advisor trip. It's that you have a poetic head, and these are poetic/artistic thoughts and questions.

It also bothers me—my feminist self—that I am writing to you and not to a UGS woman. Not because you are a man but because they are women. Does that make sense? I'm trying to be superhonest. I am terribly aware that it is natural for a man to be centered within himself, at least to a large degree, but that women are socialized from babyhood to be centered outside themselves. It takes years of pain and struggle for a woman to recenter within herself—to get, as Virginia Woolf said, to the "point where men begin"; and that is why there are so few women artists: the time and energy spent on this struggle can be destructively exhausting and draining. But there is more to it than that. Few people can or want to be artists, and those few seem to have different motivations, styles, anxieties, values in comparison with others, even intellectuals and social activists.

She went on to recount the experience of being turned down to teach a course because she refused to write a syllabus and did not require specific social action. While reaffirming her own faith in being "a damn good teacher," she concludes that her faith in "real education, self-education, is incompatible with educational systems." Finally, some questions: How does one survive in this society as an artist? Why can't people see the profound value of the imagination, except rhetorically? And, as for peer tyranny:

I am often charged with elitism or exclusiveness. I don't feel elite—but I do feel different. My goals, both temporary and long-range, are often not those of my friends and of people I most sincerely admire and respect. But I do not question their aims—why do they question mine?

I am obsessed with both form and content. . . . I believe with Anais Nin, that it is a matter of vision, not technique.

How do you survive?

I reread the letter several times and reflected at great length before attempting to respond. It was an important letter to me, not because she asked for my opinions but because she was asking questions about which I had particular viewpoints and had thought and read for half a lifetime. And, of course, I found myself in lots of double binds, *not* being her core, *not* being a woman, and *not* being close enough geographically to have talked face to face. My response, though a bit lengthy and dictated, seems to be an example worthy of including here because it suggests several dimensions of UGS not yet discussed. And I leave it to the reader to measure those dimensions.

I hasten to respond to your good letter asking some of the most vital questions of our day . . . and I do hear you, B_____, even though I realize we live in a deaf land. I think you know me well enough to know that I could never not respond wherever I hear the asking, regardless of the context. (My other self is saying, "Roy, be not conscious of the responding no matter what Erich Fromm says about humanness as the *capacity* to respond.")

I'm going to make a few comments, B_____, but I think I would welcome the opportunity to sit down and talk with you about some of these issues. I expect to be in C_____ sometime in April or in June at the latest. Shall we plan to have some lengthy interaction about these fundamental questions?

First off, regarding your being a damn good teacher but fired from jobs and not welcomed at G and R, I wish deeply that I didn't understand all of that damn nonsense about requiring syllabi and other such externals. Once upon a time, this bothered me a great deal, but I found in the works of Ronald Laing (especially in *The Divided Self* and *The Politics of Experience*) a kind of message which I hadn't really understood before. I have never heard anybody talk about "creative schizophrenia," and I'm not even sure that Laing uses the term. But for years I have been saying that everybody needs at least two mutually exclusive value systems, one for Monday, Wednesday, and Friday and another for Tuesday and Thursday. If they have three, the third one for the weekend, so much the better! Or, they might like to have a fourth one, one for days and one for nights! Whenever I made those comments, my friends told me that I was cynical and not terribly constructive. The longer I live, however, the clearer it is to me that it is okay to have the mutually exclusive value systems so long as one is clearly aware of where the parameters of one leave off and the other (or the many) begin. As you know, I've done a great deal of self-experimentation on the creativity frontier, especially logging in a variety of forms. If you go back to take a look at my November mood piece where I included the four haiku for my dead Vermont friend, you can probably get some sense of where that frontier is. I have increasingly seen the aesthetic dimension as a kind of bridge between tensions one feels between the practical world and that of fantasy. I wish you might be here with me at this very moment as I wander around my study, dictaphone in hand, observing robins out on the front lawn. I think it is okay for me to write a haiku as follows:

> Welcome home, robin,
> your breast is so red, you must
> have had good flying.

I think it is okay to talk to robins and to develop one's own fantasy life even at the very same time that I may be perceived as doing something quite "practical"; namely, writing to somebody such as yourself for whom I care very much. In short, I think the artist can survive in the society, survive *psychologically*, only in being pretty sensitive to these frontiers between the practical and the fantasized.

Surviving practically may be a more difficult task, but perhaps not. I can appreciate the difficulty of writing a syllabus about fantasy! It is pure bullshit! It is like the time the guy at Doubleday tried to get me to write a book on educational theory which was also phenomenological! Hence, I guess my thought would be: okay, write the goddamn syllabus for the jerky deans and otherwise, then go ahead and work on fantasy. Both of us know that bureaucracy is with us always, very much like poverty! In other words, I know that I have survived personally because I believe deeply in what I am doing at both the practical and the artistic level. If I have to create bullshit, I do it with the clearest knowledge that even those who read it know it is bullshit, but they are engaged in the minuet of irrelevancy! Far be it for me to advise that you or anybody else follow suit, but this is an honest answer to what I perceive as an honest question.

One practical thought: have you ever had any experience editing books? If not, do you think you could develop such a skill in order to earn your daily bread in a kind of free-lance context while at the same time doing your own writing?

Regarding "peer" tyranny: I share your concern, remembering Jefferson's comment to the effect that 180 tyrants are worse than one when he was criticizing legislatures! I could talk at some length, of course, about the reasons why people may charge you with elitism or wish to lay their own trip on you. I don't really think there is any way to avoid that except to listen and forget. The irony is that any effort to answer such people merely brings the charge that one is on the defensive! It helps me to recollect that Carl Jung is alleged to have said that perception is 95 percent projection! This may be a kind of game I play with myself when I get charged with doing all kinds of nasty things I didn't do, but it does help a little. Although it may be true, as you say, that I *as a man* may tend to center on myself, I find that constant interaction with people and the world (especially through poetry and haiku) helps carry me away from my worst defensive self! I fear that we have to resist to a very large degree the tendency to have too large a percentage of our time devoted to living up to somebody else's value systems and/or expectations. Maybe I'm saying that one has to be a certain kind of maverick (maverickess?) in order to maintain one's sanity and survive. I don't know whether or not you saw Russell Baker's column the other day or not regarding the mad, mad world in which we live; hence I'll enclose a copy.

The question of vision versus technique is, of course, another age-old one and a difficult one to resolve with any finality. In my judgment, one has to resolve it for oneself and let the rest of the world go hang. I could kick my rear end for having listened to a college poetry teacher tell me to "forget it" sometime in the early 1940's. I wish I had not listened and been able to deal with the question you are asking all the years between then and 1967 when I again began interacting with the world in a poetic way. If you believe that vision is more important than technique, then it seems to me that you can only follow your muse in that direction. This is a topic we can discuss when I see you.

Regarding your poem: I like it for both its imagery and its insight, B_____. I shall send it on the poetry editor of the magazine. Unfortunately, I can only recommend that it be published. I have no part of the decision making when it comes to poetry in the *Humanist*. Some years ago, Paul Kurtz, the editor, decided to hire a person for that purpose, hence taking me out of the decision-making process. I'm going to take the liberty of typing your address on the poem so that the answer can come directly back to you and thus save time. Incidentally, are you continuing to keep your poetry flowing toward magazines? Somebody once told me, "Roy, you'll never get anything published if you leave it in your desk drawer." By taking that comment seriously, I've continued to push stuff out into the world and let whatever happens happen. I do think that the artists in the world have to have some acknowledgement from the world that she/he exists. Are you getting that kind of feedback? If not, may I suggest that you take some kind of step to do so, even if it is only a matter of sharing your poems with your own circle of friends. In my judgment, your poetry has extraordinary insight, sparkle, profundity, and metaphorical depth. It is eminently worth sharing.

Had I had more time, B_____, I might have written a shorter letter. I've taken advantage of the fact that I have a support system for handling such effusions. Perhaps I should have taken to my typewriter rather than dictaphone; yet, I write this with joy and without the slightest tinge of guilt that I have to do it in a spontaneous rather than a more contemplative way.

I'll pass the good words along and hope to be seeing you in the relatively near future.

Love,

SPONTANEITY AND BEING

Rare is the person with whom I come into association—as peer, as colleague, as teacher, as friend, as whatever—who is not aware of my idiosyncrasies. I am as likely to demonstrate taping an ankle at a colloquium as I am to discuss some concept such as Alfred North Whitehead's "fallacy of misplaced concretion," as likely to share a newly written fable or poem as to meet somebody's need that I "lecture" on some topic. Discussing such idiosyncrasy in this context of "for instances" makes me seem (to myself) a bit manipulating, contriving, or histrionic; nevertheless, my initial response in most instances is pretty spontaneous. It's the intellectualizing about it which accounts for the appearance. When a student requests that I read a book, for instance, Arthur Koestler's *The Roots of Coincidence*, in order that he may discuss it with me, I really must respond. If I recognize the merit in a student log, letter, PDE, whatever, and I feel the urge to encourage, cajole, assess, then I would be something less than myself if I didn't turn immediately to my typewriter or dictaphone to communicate my perception. Or, if I am editing a book, such as *Humanizing the Workplace*, and at the eleventh hour discover an essay or an idea that a UGS student or adjunct might incorporate, I would be remiss not to do so.[2] I do not prescribe such behavior for my colleagues; I must recognize the particular style of each and hope that every program manifests a multiplicity of styles appealing to a broad spectrum of student taste. We may be able to *describe* the characteristics of a large number of faculty in extended degree programs as Edelstein, et al., do in their analysis, but we will be guilty of an enormous hoax if we don't recognize the infinite possibilities lying along a spectrum between one end of the probability curve and the other. In my judgment much of the difficulty that faculties and students face in higher education results from failure to recognize and accept that variety as well as failure to capitalize upon spontaneity.

Some of my intensest joys in the past several years have grown out of interacting with a very spontaneous man named Ulysses, a man whose journeys both in society and in the mind would surely challenge that other Ulysses whom Homer, Tennyson, Joyce, and Kazantzakis depict, a man who shared his journeys through the poetic medium with a varied and sensitive committee. I found it increasingly difficult to respond in prose to his lengthy poems. So he helped me gain confidence in my own spontaneous responses through the poem-letter form, helped me by accepting my reactions much as I accepted his. In rereading eleven such responses written over a twenty-month period, I was struck by the first few lines of my expressions (and I swear that I began each such poem-letter not really knowing how it would go or where it would end). Someday, our exchange may see the full light of day. For the moment, a few "for instances" from my end may say something about spontaneity and being:

No
mountains
snow-capped alpine
or
rounded appalachian
dams the feeling FOR
even as
feeling AGAINST . . .

● ● ●

Your words

       hot from the cannons

           and canons of experience

         and love . . .

        ● ● ●

The eagle
      bringing messages
            from western climes . . .

I read your lines
with the swiftness
of skater . . .

  ● ● ●

    You asked that we not comment
and I shall obey
    but I must ask that you listen
only because fog and jets and
    too many other buts and yets
will carry me off for sev'ral weeks . . .

And, then, I am ever aware that he is Ulysses; several letters begin,
"Dear Ulysses"; three continued like this:

    . . .ye, of many wanderings
and meanderings
going straight to the heart
of a people whose courage to be free

even in slavery
is challenge enough
to the absurd
to assure victory . . .

● ● ●

. . .of many wanderings
and returns
to Day One
never done
to catch a seagull
by the tail
the fate of all Ulysses
for in the reaching
is the caught
and catching
process product
and
product process . . .

● ● ●

Oh ye
of the wandering
archetype
to visit
such inner seas
as Agony Wave,
    Despair Cave
    Wonder Island
with or without constant
companions . . .

And the Ulysses metaphor is an apt metaphor for many humans who find themselves on some vast learning Mediterranean. So I am Ulysses, and Ulysses me. So are my colleagues, whether student or faculty. And the examples for us are those points on shoal and shore which may or may not return us to some new Ithaca.

13   Epilogue: Some Milestone Weighings

If it is true that "past is prologue," then perhaps future is epilogue. Hence, anybody even remotely related to UGS and the vision of such programs as ours must learn to laugh at adhocracies, bureaucracies, educracies, and taking oneself so seriously that one loses the impact of a fully conscious learning experience. Persons in UGS, Walden, Fielding, Nova, HPI, and those schools yet to be born, those persons—black/white, male/female, scientist/humanist—will work toward new dimensions and new configurations of self-actualization wherever they are able to retain some of the vision reflected in the UGS key concepts (Cf. chapter 1). Wherever a person catches the spirit embodied in those keys, wherever one attempts to combine theory and practice with organic integrity, wherever or whenever one tries to mix his or her life and work into a significant mixture, the vision of the external degree emerges. Whenever a person "looks for a sign," disaster lurks. By self-directing, person-centered learning, we mean the individual *directs self* (albeit with some help) along the path, along the parameters of identity and authenticity, amid the possibilities of speculation, into the valley of personal meanings. If one raises the flags of self-doubt, probably he is doomed to wallow in his own paranoia, convert the self-fulfilling prophecy into the self-defeating or self-deceiving prophecy. There is little room for that in the last quarter of the twentieth century. As somebody said so eloquently in a recent letter, better to fail in striving with an imaginative approach to a PDE than settle for a standard thesis. I would extend this hope to an entire student program, in *any* school.

We all must struggle through our own personal Slough of Despond, weighed down by the everyday clay of norms, restricted by the world's love of factuality, of literalness. But perhaps we can soar with the verbs, adverbs, and adjectives of poetry. Perhaps that's what keeps so many of us alive when the world would pronounce us dead. I know that it probably keeps me going to discover better ways of seeing, even when an occasional student writes to say, "Scratch me from your list, I never want to read another haiku you write." Yet I think I see the cardinal better as he sits on my study window sill (at 5:43 p.m., June 5) when I write

> A cardinal digs
> spiders from my study sill
> racing heavy rain.

I *know* that cardinal better than I would if I heard only his shrill whistle and were unwilling to play hide-and-seek with him. I think life is *that* pregnant with joy and human transfiguration. It may be why I find myself constantly on a kind of high plateau. It enables me to appreciate the fertilizing quality of the bullshit I find *us* taking from UGS persons who don't capture the vision. Concurrently, I'm sensitive enough in reading applications to write:

Gate Keeping?	Surprise!
Finding so small a peephole	Pick up each package
into his or her life . . .	to scan a name
no Solomon I	wond'ring
to cut and dissect	whether bright-eyed
along biases	and bushy-tailed
with pinking shears	or maimed
of the mind	by
and say "yes"	grotesque self-doubt
on this side	trapped in a child's
"no" on that	deep cave
to start them	no carer near
down a road	to roll back
I cannot see . . .	a rock. . . .

At the same time I can stick with a PDE or a position paper or a lonely plea for help long enough to mark up the margins as creatively and as patiently as I know how. And even as I write notes to UGS students, on dictaphone, in margins, in poems, I poignantly remember some of the first marginal notes I wrote to students at Bates College many years ago and ask, "Ye Socrates! I have measured out my life in careful response to human need. Has it, indeed, made any difference?" Then I remember my five-year project, a manuscript on the teacher as radical humanist, focusing on the critical dimensions and importance of evolving appreciation for paradox, irony, and humor. And I answer myself, "Yes, it makes a difference," and I set the clock early so that I can get up and put in another sixteen-hour UGS day. Then I remember another written effusion, a kind of Spoon River Revisited, reflecting upon students I have known speaking out of the graves of their changing self-concepts. They speak free verse I've invented. And I answer, "Yes, it does make a difference." And I keep on, listening at as many levels as I know how, listening to students saying, "I think I *must* do this, but I *want* to do this." And the listening improves, I think, each year. And I hear myself, too, so I walk Shamus, my kerry, each night and listen to my own responses to whatever is out there on a given night. Sometimes, it is this:

> Sweet honeysuckle
> drifts thru the bright moonlight night
> to move still lovers.

and sometimes it is this:

> Wish on falling star
> blazing light in shallow arc
> under a June moon.

And fortunately, I've shed much (50 percent? 75 percent? 90 percent?) of my puritanical heritage, *often* feeling sorrow but *rarely* feeling guilt. And I do perceive myself as learning ("becoming" if you prefer) new ways of perceiving, and I come away from some UGS certification and terminar sessions deeply grieving because UGS has made so little difference to some persons. And I survive that grief by devising morals for fables. And fables take me home, home to my beloved Maine coast where I've sat for an hour by a waterhole to watch a periwinkle move half an inch, where I wrote fables about seagulls long before Jonathan was born, where the geese cry mournfully going north to south, south to north at dawn and dusk; and it's

OK to cry under the great Milky Way and compete with the pounding waves on the nearby beach; it's OK to cry for the mortality which is this life, but also to cry for waste of petty politics, both nationally and in UGS, knowing full well that in the long haul of history such events mostly signify nothing.

And the sounds of geese and seagulls bring me back to irony, too, the irony of M. C. Escher, whose gulls and geese often emerge from the ground of the reality-testing which all of us must contemplate at times. Escher depicts the reality/illusion interlockings so well.

There are many realities:

- As in Escher, one human's tuna is another's goose.
- The good determine who the bad are.
- We'll hold the terminar at 2 P.M. at the Holiday Inn with the following persons present: . . . .
- We recognize your need for a transcript, and we shall help you write one, but no credit hours and grades, *please*.
- Your PDE stinks; your PDE soars; your program needs reorganization.
- My colleague is busy, so you'll have to wait another week until he can read your manuscript and tell me what he thinks.
- Without cash flow we die!
- Meet me at 9:25 A.M., TWA #75, and we'll talk while riding into the city.
- *Of course* I couldn't sleep thinking about your dilemma.
- I wrote the poem to celebrate you. . . .
- I am in tears as I write this: (a) because I may have drunk too much midnight sherry; (b) I care too much for the vision of this program to see it flushed down the drain with one flick of the toilet handle; (c) I am too tired to be coherent.
- During the strike we carried the files home every night to protect them from potential arson.

Which reminds me: somewhere in the middle of a certification session, I heard a student say that she was looking for the great mind that would give her an organizing principle. I conjured up a piece of doggerel for the occasion, which seems appropriate for this moment:

Search for great minds?
an empty trip
look to yourself
'neath iceberg tip.

Notes

Preface

1. There is a vast literature of such criticism consisting of books and essays by William James, Nevit Sanford, Christopher Jencks, David Riesman, Theodore Roczak, and many others.

2. In this book I frequently use Max Weber's concept, "charisma to bureaucracy," even including it in the title of one chapter (No. 5). For a full discussion of the concept, see S. N. Eisenstadt, ed., *Max Weber on Charisma and Institution Building*, Selected Papers (Chicago & London: The University of Chicago Press, 1968).

3. Members of the Union (1976): University of Alabama, New College; Antioch College; Community College of Baltimore; Bard College; UWW Berkeley; Universidad Boricua; Universidad de Campesinos Libres; Chicago State University; UWW Flaming Rainbow; Florida International Univ.; Franconia College; Friends World College; Goddard College; Governors State University; Hispanic International University; Hofstra University; Johnston College (University of Redlands); Loretto Heights College; University of Massachusetts; University of Minnesota; Morgan State College; Northeastern Illinois State University; University of the Pacific; Pitzer College; Roger Williams College; University of California; Extension San Diego; Shaw University; Skidmore College; Stephens College; Webster College; University of Wisconsin at Green Bay.

CHAPTER 1 SOME NEW DESIGNS: TO BURY THE ALBATROSS?

1. Much of this chapter was published under the title, "To Bury the Albatross?" *Journal of Research & Development in Education* 5, no. 3 (Spring 1972): 107–18.

2. Letter, Matthew Fleischman to Roy Fairfield, Jan. 21, 1975.

3. Ford Foundation *Letter*, Vol. 3, No. 7 (Nov. 1, 1972), p. 1–2.

4. *Ibid.*

5. Frank Newman, et al., *Report on Higher Education* (Washington, D.C.: U.S. Government Printing Office, 1971), p. 34.

6. Samuel B. Gould, *Diversity by Design* (San Francisco: Jossey-Bass, Inc., 1973), p. xv. Emphasis added.

7. Quoted in Benjamin DeMott, "Reforming Graduate Education," *Change* 6, no. 1 (February 1974): 26.

8. *Ibid.*

9. *Ibid.*, p. 28.

10. Memo, Nyquist to Chief Executive Officers of Higher Institutions, Sept. 24, 1971.

11. This is, of course, the classic definition of the recipient of the Ph.D. For some specific titles of Ph.D. dissertations that reflect the "more and more about less and less," see the story on Xerox's *Comprehensive Dissertation Index,* which runs to thirty-seven volumes, more than 35,000 pages, listing more than 417,000 theses (*New York Times,* Feb. 11, 1974).

12. C. Wright Mills, *The Sociological Imagination* (London: Oxford University Press, 1967, paperback), pp. 50–75.

13. Newman et al., *Report on Higher Education,* p. 38.

14. Obviously, one can obtain a brochure from any or all of these programs, graduate and undergraduate, if more details are desired. The Alverno program is well outlined in Malcolm G. Scully, "No Grades, No Credits, but 40 'Competence Units'," *Chronicle of Higher Education* (Feb. 3, 1975): 5. For another overview of nontraditional programs, see Edward C. Moore, "Some Forms of Nontraditional Higher Education," *The North Central Association Quarterly* 49, no. 3 (Winter 1975): 313–20. For a superb empirical study of sixteen extended degree programs, see L. Medsker, S. Edelstein, H. Kreplin, J. Ruyle, and J. Shea, *Extended Opportunities for a College Degree: Practice, Problems, and Potentials* (Berkeley, California: Center for Research and Development in Higher Education, University of California, 1975). For a general overview of graduate programs, see Lance Corden, "Off-Campus Graduate Schools," *Christian Science Monitor,* May 14, 1976. Corden reports 127 external degree programs.

15. HPI flier, May 1973.

16. "Bulletin of the National Ed.D. Program for Educational Leaders" (Fort Lauderdale, Fla.: Nova University, Spring, 1974), p. 16.

17. "Walden University: Institute for Advanced Studies" (Naples, Fla., 1975–76), p. 5.

18. There are many such stories in and around several institutions; see, "A Probe of Indiana's Unusual University," *San Francisco Chronicle,* August 3, 1972; Linda Charlton, "Doctorates from a Canadian College Questioned Here," *New York Times,* July 14, 1973; Linda Charlton, "Many Here Hold Doctorates of Unaccredited College," *New York Times,* July 13, 1973; *New York Daily News,* July 13, 1972; "'Docs' Eye $7M In a Psycho Biz," *New York Daily News,* July 17, 1972; "The Diploma Mills Problem," *San Francisco Chronicle,* Sept. 1, 1972; M. A. Farber, "How to Control 'Diploma Mills' Has Become a National Problem," *New York Times,* July 30, 1972; M. A. Farber, "Panel Urges State to Ban Ph.D. Programs That Fail to Meet New Criteria," *New York Times,* Feb. 6, 1973; "Diploma Mills Are Hiding Behind Many Facades," *The Sunday Bulletin* (Phila.), August 20, 1972. For a penetrating analysis of the "rip-off" potential, see George E. Arnstein, "Ph.D., Anyone?" *American Education* 10, no. 6 (July 1974): 6–11; and, "Bad Apples in Academe," *American Education* 10, no. 7 (September 1974): 10–14. Also, *Consumer Protection in Postsecondary Education,* Conference Report and Recommendations. Education Commission of the States, Report Number 53, June, 1974. Further, see "Ph.D., Anyone?" *New York Teacher's Magazine,* March 9, 1975.

19. *Psychology Today* 8, No. 5 (October 1974): 143.

20. For a discussion of the origins of the UGS program, see Judson Jerome, *Culture Out of Anarchy* (New York: Herder & Herder, 1970), pp. vii-xxii. Also, excellent for raising basic questions about experimental and experiential learning.

21. From the UGS brochure, any edition.

22. These questions and most of the text at this point are verbatim from my article, "To Bury The Albatross?" *Journal of Research & Development in Education* 5, no. 3 (Spring 1972): 112–117.

23. Benjamin F. Thompson, "Education: The Most Dangerous Game," in Roy P. Fairfield, ed., *Humanistic Frontiers in American Education* (Buffalo, N.Y.: Prometheus Books, 1974), pp. 312–14.

24. With appropriate thanks to T.S. Eliot and Prufrock.

25. Unpublished UGS working paper circulated widely among UGS participants.

26. Two other position papers, "Where is Antioch?" and "What is Antioch?" written in 1968 and 1970, are included in the Appendix (G) since they also catch some of the vision of this kind of education. Although written in an effort to catch the spirit of a changing Antioch, one expanding from a few centers to a nationwide network, they also reflect the leading edge of an era which would come to accept the external degree as a viable kind of learning enterprise.

27. Jonathan Kozol, *Death at an Early Age* (Boston: Houghton-Mifflin, 1967); Nat Hentoff, *Our Children Are Dying* (New York: Viking, 1966); Ivan Illich, *Deschooling Society* (New York: Harper & Row, 1971).

28. With thanks, of course, to Paul Tillich.

CHAPTER 2   RHETORIC TO RISK

1. It seems hardly necessary to include a bibliography, but perhaps a few books will be suggestive: Thorstein Veblen, *The Higher Learning in America* (New York: B. W. Heubsch, 1918); John Dewey, *Democracy & Education* (New York: MacMillan, 1916); Abraham Maslow, *Toward A Psychology of Being* (Princeton: Van Nostrand, 1962); Carl Rogers, *Freedom to Learn* (Columbus, O: Charles E. Merrill, 1969); Sidney M. Jourard, *The Transparent Self* (Princeton: D. Van Nostrand, 1964).

2. Quotes from UGS applications, well edited to protect anonymity.

3. Cf. the work being done in "bone-head English," not only where there is open access to higher education, as in New York City, but also in such prestigious places as the University of California at Berkeley, where nearly 50 percent flunked the basic English exam. Also see Marlene Griffith, "Thoughts on Teaching Writing," *College Composition and Communication* 25, (December 1974), pp. 368–73.

4. Roy P. Fairfield, "An Individualist Manifesto," *Phi Delta Kappan* 45, no. 5 (February 1964): 230–35.

5. UGS Application Form, March, 1974.

6. Quote from UGS application, well edited to protect anonymity.

7. *Ibid.*

8. The politics of survival have made it almost imperative that doctors award doctorates; most UGS student committees have at least three doctorates present (two

adjuncts and the core); sometimes UGS students begin on a committee as students and wind up as graduates; hence some committees are comprised entirely of doctorates. We do, however, recognize that it is next to impossible to find persons in some fields with doctor's degrees, but we insist that the persons who are chosen are persons who have made a considerable contribution to their field or fields.

9. I am indebted to Martin Erickson, a UGS adjunct, for these helpful suggestions. He has shared them frequently at colloquia.

10. Practices vary from institution to institution in paying adjunct professors. Most pay adjuncts or field faculty a flat fee per person per year.

11. See Arthur W. Chickering, *Education and Identity* (San Francisco: Jossey-Bass, 1969).

12. Cf. Roy P. Fairfield et al., "Changing Careers at Midstream," *The Humanist* 24 no. 3 (May/June 1974): 14–23.

13. This is a variation, of course, of Paul Tillich's title, *The Courage to Be* (New Haven, Conn.: Yale University Press, 1952).

14. Tony Jones, "Lines to Power: Where They Are and What To Do with Them," *Harper's* (March 1974), p. 3.

15. Joseph Arbuckle, November 8, 1974, during his terminar.

16. May Sarton, *Journal of a Solitude* (New York: Norton, 1973), p. 39.

CHAPTER 3 THE USES AND ABUSES OF FACULTY

1. This document, edited only slightly for stylistic clarity and to eliminate anachronisms and irrelevancies, is unpublished. I find it interesting that Clark Moustakis came to a similar conclusion about taking a lashing; see *Loneliness & Love* (Englewood Cliffs, N.J.: Prentice-Hall, 1972), p. 121. Goodwin Watson, a widely known psychologist, was a UGS faculty from 1970 to 1976; Betty Poole was administrative coordinator from 1970 to 1976.

2. *Alleged* to have been held by Jung!

3. Once pushed to define the requirements for a great writer, Ernest Hemingway said that he must have "a fool-proof crap detector." Cited by Neil Postman and Charles Weingartner in *Teaching as a Subversive Activity* (New York: Delacorte, 1969), p. 3.

4. The credo was embodied in a document called "Saratoga Raceway," the major point being:

> We urge that UGS affirm its commitment to diversity in the student body, and to qualification for learning free of the clichés of pedigree and a prepackaged program. Further, we seek a student body sensitive to the spirit and purpose of UGS.

> We affirm that UGS must be person-centered in every sense, and that Union graduates should be committed to the fundamental question of human existence, with all its attendant problems. The UGS graduate should be one who is continually evolving a better self and a better world.

This remained the major credo for nearly three years, and it was implemented with a *positive* (affirmative) approach to increasing minority and female "representation" among students and core. In April 1974 an Affirmative Action statement was adopted, which was, ironically enough, perceived by many students, both male and female, both ethnic and Caucasian, as being *negative*! It seemed to them that UGS ought not let itself be pushed by such bureaucratic and impersonal forces!

5. See Appendix G.

6. An obvious paraphrase of the title of Barry Stevens's book, *Don't Push the River* (Lafayette, California: Real People Press, 1970).

7. Thomas Jefferson College. Cf. David Hilligoss's Project Demonstrating Excellence, Unpublished, p. 10.

8. Robert Pirsig in *Zen and the Art of Motorcycle Maintenance* (New York: Morrow, 1974), p. 35, discusses the question of "that strange separation of what man is from what man does" and suggests that we may get "some clues as to what the hell has gone wrong in this twentieth century" if we can figure this out.

9. Englewood Cliffs, N.J.: Prentice Hall, 1971; Buffalo, N.Y.: Prometheus Books, 1975.

CHAPTER 4 WRITING: SPONTANEITY AND GROWTH

1. Robert Pirsig, *Zen and the Art of Motorcycle Maintenance* (New York: Morrow, 1974), p. 84.

2. The developmental theories of B. F. Skinner and Jean Piaget are well known, but fewer persons may know the ethical patterns that Lawrence Kolberg, of Harvard, has developed. For a concise statement, see "A Cognitive-Developmental Approach to Moral Education," *The Humanist* 32, no. 6 (November/December 1972): 13–66.

3. Johanna Halbeisen has given her permission for using this material. Letter to Roy Fairfield, February 23, 1975. Since she cannot locate some of the passages which she used, these have been removed from the text to avoid potential copyright problems. The first three paragraphs were used in Gary MacDonald, ed., *Five Experimental Colleges* (New York: Harper & Row, 1973), p. 69.

4. Sarton, *Journal of a Solitude*, p. 77.

5. I am indebted to many UGS persons for some of these insights, but especially to Gene Grossman for talking through this particular configuration.

6. See Gregory Bateson, *Steps to an Ecology of Mind* (New York: Ballantine, 1972), for interesting insights on the nature of individual and mass learning experiences.

7. For some reflections of my view of manual work, see my "The Dignity of Hands," *The Humanist* 32, no. 3 (May/June 1972): 36–77; also, "To Saw a Board," *The Humanist* 35, no. 1 (January/February 1975): 37–39.

8. William T. Going, ed., *99 Fables by William March* (Baton Rouge: University of Louisiana Press, 1960).

CHAPTER 5 "CHARISMA TO BUREAUCRACY": INEVITABLE?

1. *Harpers*, Vol. 240, No. 1441 (June 1970), p 18.

2. I've never felt that enough has been written on the *positive* side of the dissent issue. My own views may be tasted in the chapter of a book, "The Student Dissenter as Learner Teacher," in *Crises on Campus*, ed. by Russel B. Nye, Ray B. Browne, and Michael T. Marsden (Bowling Green, Ohio: Bowling Green University Press, 1971) pp. 34–54, in an essay-review, "Ten Books on College and University Dissent," *So-*

cial Education 34, no. 1 (January 1970): 109 ff.

3. In addition to Judson Jerome, the original Union Committee included Evelyn Bates (Goddard), Denis Cowan (Shimer), Jim Rice (Stephens), Carl Selinger (Bard) and John Elmendorf (New College), the last serving as chairperson. From Memo, Sam Baskin to the Committee, November 29, 1968.

4. See Douglas McGregor, *The Human Side of Enterprise* (New York: McGraw-Hill, 1960).

5. C. Northcote Parkinson, *Parkinson's Law* (Boston: Houghton Mifflin, 1957), p. 60.

6. Friedrich W. Nietzsche, *Skirmishes in a War with the Age;* cited in John Bartlett's *Familiar Quotations* (Boston: Little, Brown, 1941), p. 1081.

7. Gary Wills, "Working Within the System Won't Change Anything," *The Center Magazine* 4, no. 4 (July/August 1972): 36.

8. Roy P. Fairfield, ed., *The Federalist Papers* (Garden City, N.Y.: Doubleday, 1961), p. 17 (*Federalist No. 10*).

9. Pirsig, *Zen and the Art of Motorcycle Maintenance* (New York: Morrow, 1974), p. 121.

10. *Ibid.*, p. 102.

11. For some instructive insights, see Lewis Thomas, *The Lives of a Cell* (New York: Viking, 1974); and *The Graphic Work of M. C. Escher* (London: McDonald & Company, 1967), Plate 11.

12. At press time there are five (5) UGS units; the original one, mainly discussed here; the Innovation in Elementary & Secondary Education program, with slightly different colloquium and residency requirements and primarily attracting school personnel; the Regional Learning Center, part of a "five dimensional" program for minorities, Baltimore; the Goodwin Watson Institute for Research and Development, for those desiring to do research with distinguished mentors; and, UGS/West, virtually a replicate of the original program, save for geographical attraction and some minor variations on colloquia requirements. This is as good a place as any to mention two formal affiliations that have had regional implications; namely, UGS affiliations with the Institute for Policy Studies (IPS), Washington, D.C., and the Center for Studies of the Person (CSP) in La Jolla, California. IPS is a kind of think tank in whose "fellows" research and discuss governmental policy-making from a radical perspective; UGS persons in that program follow a mentor model, handle residency in the context of IPS requirements, substitute a public seminar for certification, develop learning contracts and the fulfillment thereof in conjunction with one of the IPS fellows and a core faculty member. UGS students in the CSP program utilize CSP members to work through their internships; otherwise, their program is essentially the same as for other UGS students. As a matter of historical fact, nearly one hundred organizations, educational, corporate, etc. approached UGS during the first few years of our existence with a view to developing affiliations; both governing board and core faculty encouraged experimenting but warned about letting such affiliations become the tail wagging the dog—no doubt an important survival policy.

13. It is a process reminiscent of Jean Jacques Rousseau's "volunté generale" as spelled out in the *Social Contract;* also the consensual approach depends considerably upon the evolution of trust relationships among the participants and some real con-

cern for the future of the institution.

14. See "Report of a Visit to UECU with Particular Reference to the Union Graduate School, Yellow Springs, Ohio" (North Central Accreditation team to the NCA Board, late winter, 1974), p. 47; also, see Appendix C.

15. As Betty Pool might attest, both orally and in collected evidence, one could cite volumes of memos, position papers, etc. to document the generalizations in this brief section on administrative trends.

16. For consultants we've had such nationally known persons as Carl Rogers, Robert Theobald, David Riesman, Elizabeth Sewell (who also served for three years as a consulting core), May Sarton, Eugene Maeroff, Sidney Jourard, David McClellan, Thomas Hanna, Arthur Combs, Charles Weingartner, John Vasconcellas, Alvin Eurich, etc.

17. From a position paper shared with my colleagues during September, 1973.

18. See another position paper, "Decision-Making in UGS."

19. Technically, a UGS graduate cannot serve as an adjunct until five years have elapsed following his or her graduation.

20. Betty Pool not only submitted a questionnaire regarding her own performance but also, in conjunction with her own Ph.D. work in UGS, developed an analytic instrument for gaining insights regarding graduate reactions to their experience; part of the latter is included in Appendix D.

21. We employed three persons with lots of experience in experimental education, three persons whom we knew would be critically constructive rather than destructively critical: Dr. Esther Rauschenbush, formerly professor and president of Sarah Lawrence College; Dr. Milton Schwebel, dean of the Graduate School of Education, Rutgers University; Dr. Harold Hodgkinson, research educator, Center for Research and Development, University of California at Berkeley.

22. March 17, 1974.

CHAPTER 6 EXCELLENCE: HANGUP OR OPPORTUNITY?

1. Some of the quality issues discussed in this chapter have been scrutinized by Cooperative Assessment of Experiential Learning (CAEL), founded in 1974. For information about their work, write to Educational Testing Service, Princeton, N.J., 08540. For concerns of the Council of Graduate Schools in the United States, see their publication, "External Degrees—Foreign and Domestic," *Communicator* 8, no. 8 (April-May, 1976), pp. 1–4. For the concerns of a regional graduate school association, see three essays by James A. Norton, Roy P. Fairfield, and Lloyd E. Berry, all entitled "Territorial Rights in Graduate Education,'" *Proceedings of the Thirty-Second Annual Meeting of the Midwestern Association of Graduate Schools* (Chicago, 1976), pp. 7–27.

2. One could apply for Veteran's Administration benefits after two years of existence even if unaccredited. UGS did just that.

3. A book with wide significance for *all* aspects of education, not merely teaching: Neil Postman and Charles Weingartner, *Teaching as a Subversive Activity* (New York: Delacorte, 1969).

4. Cf. Book I of the *Republic*.

5. Leo McLaughlin, Speech, Northfield Colloquium, July, 1973.

6. *University Without Walls, First Report* (Yellow Springs, Ohio: UECU, 1972), p. 35.

7. Roy P. Fairfield, "Teacher Education: What Design?" Yellow Springs, Antioch College *Reports* no. 8, (January 1967); cf. Appendix A.

8. NCA, "Guidelines for Institutions Offering Advanced Degree Programs," *The North Central Association Quarterly* 45, no. 4 (Spring 1971): 338–39.

9. Unpublished document by Goodwin Watson.

10. Aage Nielsen, *Lust for Learning* (Skyum Bjerge, pr. Snedsted: New Experimental College Press, 1968), p. 276.

11. Our "Status Study Report . . .," a quasi-public document submitted to North Central Association in 1974, reflects many of the points made here, of course, in greater detail.

12. We've attempted to reflect total process by means of a filing system enabling an evaluator/observer to follow a student's process through the program, from admissions to terminar, step by step; also, our program summary calls for a narrative "summary" of each student's program, also demanding evaluation of each step. Each student's privacy, however, is protected in those instances where the student wishes it to be.

13. To "go interim" means to take a leave of absence for a nominal fee in order to maintain one's status as a student.

14. At the outset of the program a student faced $2,000 per year tuition costs for an indefinite number of years! Before the end of our second year, we adopted a $3,500 package for those who held tenure for twenty-one to forty-eight months, prorated at $500 per calendar quarter between the minimum time (four quarters) and the seven. At the same time that a person accepted the package, he or she agreed to a four-year statute of limitations. This plan, though having both academic and financial advantages from a student viewpoint was fraught with budgetary dangers when a large number of students paid up long before they finished; naturally we "owed" them services (especially core faculty assistance) which were costly. In 1974 we developed a sliding-scale tuition; first year: $2,400; second: $2,400; third: $600; fourth: $600; and in 1976, we returned to a flat tuition of $2800 per year.

CHAPTER 7 PROCESS AS CRITERIA: DESIGNING NEW ACCREDITATION MODES

1. Patricia A. Thrash, "Nontraditional Institutions and Programs: A Challenge for the Accreditation Process," *The North Central Association Quarterly* 49, no. 3 (Winter 1975): 321–29.

2. Matthew W. Finkin, "Federal Reliance on Voluntary Accreditation: The Power to Recognize as the Power to Regulate," *Journal of Law-Education* 2, no. 3 (July 1973): 339, 342.

3. Thrash, "Nontraditional Institutions and Programs," 321–22.

4. *Ibid.*, p. 322.

5. The NCA team consisted of Dr. Paul Silverman, chairman of the Biology Department at the University of New Mexico; Dr. Paul McStallworth, professor of History, Wright State University; Dr. Ben Davis, dean of the School of Education at the University of Wisconsin, Milwaukee, chairperson; and, Dr. Patricia Thrash, associate

executive director of the NCA, served as the NCA administrative liaison.

6. For UGS consultants, see note 21 for Chapter 5.

7. See Chapter 6, note 12 for statement on the student's portfolio.

8. Letter, Norman Burns to Samuel Baskin, April 5, 1974.

9. Thrash, "Nontraditional Institutions and Programs," p. 327.

10. Ben Davis, Betty J. Pool and Roy Fairfield, "Process as Criteria: Designing New Accreditation Means," unpublished, pp. 11–12.

CHAPTER 8 FACULTY LOAD: MEASURABLE OR MYSTERIOUS?

1. One can then, of course, compare one's own viewpoint on a self-anchoring scale with the perceptions students have on a similar scale or on one designed to cross-check one's own value structures.

2. From Robert Maynard Hutchins's & Joseph P. Lyford's cassette on the philosophy of Dr. Alexander Zuckerkandl, available through the Center for the Study of Democratic Institutions, Santa Barbara, California.

3. Dividing a college job is a reality for a Minnesota couple; cf. *New York Times*, May 25, 1974. Two graduate students, about to receive their doctorates, applied for a UGS core faculty job. And in another instance a UGS graduate and his wife, both doctorates, created a powerful explosion in a university department by agreeing to split a position! Subsequently, they did split such a job at a different institution.

CHAPTER 9 WHO/WHAT RESIDES IN RESIDENCY?

1. Most of this article originally appeared with this title in *Phi Delta Kappan* 56, no. 6 (February 1975): 409–11.

CHAPTER 10 CREATIVE SOLVENCY?

1. The first half of this article originally appeared, though in a less-polished form, in *Interface Journal* 1, no. 1 (Winter 1974–75):11–12.

2. From a position paper by Rose Pinckney, November 1974.

3. Letter to the Editor, *Change* 5, no. 10 (Winter 1973–74):6–7.

4. David Gray, "Radical *Input* . . . A Venture in the Sociology of Knowledge" (Union Graduate School, January, 1973), unpublished.

5. Benjamin DeMott, "Reforming Graduate Education," *Change* 6, no. 1 (February 1974):28.

6. Stewart Edelstein, Hannah Kreplin, Leland Medsker, Janet Ruyle, and John Shea, *Extended Opportunities for a College Degree* (Berkeley, California: Center for Research and Development in Higher Education, 1974), pp. 59–64.

7. See reference to CAEL group at ETS in Princeton; also occurring, however, as at Walden when determining the eligibility of prospective students; cf. Walden catalogue.

8. See Edelstein et al., *Extended Opportunities for a College Degree.*

9. Sometimes the impossible is the only thing worth doing. See Robert Theobald, *An Alternative Future for America* (Chicago: Swallow, 1970).

10. I say this even *with* the awareness of a vast number of analyses of power

structures in this country by John Kenneth Galbraith, David Riesman, James Mc-Gregor Burns, Erich Fromm, Richard Rovere, C. Wright Mills, etc.

CHAPTER 11 PROBLEMS, PARADOXES, PROCESSES AND PROGNOSTICATIONS

1. Robert Pirsig, *Zen and the Art of Motorcycle Maintenance* (New York: Morrow, 1974).

2. Edelstein et al., *Extended Opportunities for a College Degree.*

CHAPTER 12 SOME "FOR INSTANCES"

1. Memo to Phyllis Walden, July 11, 1974.

2. This happened in my book, *Humanizing the Workplace* (Buffalo, N.Y.: Prometheus Books, 1974); see Jack Russell's chapter, pp. 151–55.

As this goes to press perhaps it's as good time and place as any to mention a few sources not previously cited. Compiling lists of nontraditional programs: John Bear, Littleriver, California; Jennifer Eis & Don Ward, *Taking Off* (Center for Alternatives In/To Higher Education, 1118 S. Harrison Road, East Lansing, Michigan, 1975); Empire State College, *Innovative Graduate Programs Directory* (Saratoga Springs, N.Y., 1976). Always helpful: keeping one's eye on the Jossey-Bass lists of publications which include such relevant books as Samuel Messick et al., *Individuality In Learning* (1976) and Morris T. Keeton et al., *Experiential Learning* (1976). A provocative and fascinating volume: McGregor Smith et al., (faculty and student) *On Your Own—But Not Alone* (Miami-Dade Community College Foundation/Life Lab Fund, 1976). Publications by regional accrediting and graduate school associations are also insightful. And, if willing to share, institutions doing innovation file interesting reports to regional accrediting associations. No doubt somebody "out there" is doing a comprehensive bibliography which will be of value to future researchers.

Appendices

Appendix A: Teacher Education: What Design?

By Dr. Roy P. Fairfield

Particularly since the appearance in 1953 of Arthur Bestor's Educational Wastelend, *every year has been open season for criticism of teacher education in America. Not only have professional journals been loaded with rifle shot, but general periodicals have used buckshot liberally, some of it fired at random across the educational landscape. Both laymen and professional educators have entered the hunt with gusto, notably, Admiral Hyman G. Rickover, James Bryant Conant, Myron Lieberman, James D. Koerner, and Paul Goodman. But many questions remain: How many educators have they hit? How many educators feel hit? What and who have been killed? maimed? What has been changed? What remains? What responses have resulted from such verbal battles?*

Historians may require decades to present a comprehensive view of these challenge-response relationships, but it is certain that some reforms have resulted. Master of Arts in Teaching programs have gained wider currency. The concept of the internship, so long employed in other professions, is now accepted as an integral part of the teacher education scene. Professional specialists in the liberal arts have left their offices to enter public school rooms to develop new curricular materials and processes. Antioch's recent entry into graduate teacher education is a relevant part of the challenge-response pattern. In many ways Antioch gained a running start. Not only had the faculty tried out many ideas at the undergraduate level, but, also of import, Antioch absorbed an extant graduate program: The Putney Graduate School of Education, Putney, Vermont.

This report, the eighth in a series of reports on new program de-

---

SOURCE: Antioch College Reports, Office of Program Development and Research in Education, Antioch College, Yellow Springs, Ohio, 45387 (January 1967). Reprinted with permission.

velopments and research at Antioch, describes the origins and development of the program in social sciences for prospective secondary school teachers, leading to the Master of Arts in Teaching degree. The author, Dr. Roy P. Fairfield, is director of the Antioch-Putney Graduate School.

BACKGROUND

Founded in 1950 and directed by Morris Mitchell for more than a decade, the Putney Graduate School stressed direct confrontation of and involvement in some of the critical issues and protest movements of our time. Hence, it was characterized by study trips to Harlem, southern Appalachia, Mexico, and other continents. Such trips were alternated with seminars and independent study that gave students an opportunity to reflect, read, and write about their observations. The school remained small and operated from a 38-acre estate overlooking the Connecticut River valley. Dr. Mitchell encouraged his students to see, feel, and hear about cooperatives and experimental schools in New England and the South.

Asked to assume responsibility for this program, Antioch studied the feasibility of extending its work-study curriculum into graduate education. Eventually it was clear that Antioch was willing to risk some funds to develop a program that was (a) experimental, (b) individualized, and (c) aimed to develop secondary teachers sensitized to work in four critical areas: civil rights, poverty, emerging nations, and the non-Western world. Moreover, as one typical report (September 1, 1963) suggests, "Most of all it means a program of maximized interpersonal relationships, vast variety of experiences from which to choose, and a study program geared to the needs and concerns of each participant."

Projecting the Antioch work-study program into the graduate arena, the planners conceived a program in which the students would have full access to the resources of Antioch's main campus during one quarter, savor the more intimate living accommodations and close student-faculty associations at the twenty-three-room Putney estate during two quarters, and do student teaching during a fourth quarter.

It was expected that some experienced teachers would join the program; thus, internships with the Experiment in International Living nearby at Putney might constitute a significant educational experience in lieu of student teaching. It was hoped, too, that poverty and civil rights problems might be seen in a global context.

Precise details of curriculum were left to the Antioch-Putney faculty, but it was generally agreed that a student should not only earn an M.A.T. degree but also gain enough professional education and social science credits to obtain a teacher's certificate, preferably in the state of his choice.

THE FIRST YEAR'S DEVELOPMENTS

Since the Putney property did not change hands until June 1964, the pilot group of students was recruited late and consisted of only ten students, who represented a cross section of American colleges and universities. Beginning at Yellow Springs in September 1964, the students audited courses, did independent study in their weakest academic areas, and met weekly for a class in learning theory with Antioch Professor Benjamin Thompson (chairman of the Antioch-Putney faculty advisory committee)—a class now nicknamed "From Rote to Zen." They also met frequently at the author's home for discussion with Antioch social science professors: to evaluate a political scientist's proposal for writing a book, to discuss two studies in the sociology of learning, and to consider the question: "What can a school psychologist do for the teacher?" In this setting they met educators from Liberia and India and a lawyer relating the social sciences to law school curriculums. Meanwhile, the Antioch-Putney students took part as full-fledged members of the Antioch community, attending controversial meetings with George Lincoln Rockwell and Mae Mallory, accompanying their instructor to nearby Central State University to hear James Farmer and John Howard Griffin.

Such common endeavor was, of course, supplemented by wide reading and field trips consistent with individual interest. Each student was urged to write reaction reports, keep logs, engage in tutorials with professors, and develop other means of evaluating growth.

Assembling in Vermont after New Year's Day 1965, both students and faculty members plunged into a sixteen-hours-a-day routine of seminars, field trips, and independent reading. They also engaged in the housekeeping required by community living. In addition to preparing them for student teaching through seminars on educational problems and methods, we held sessions on poverty and civil rights. In keeping with the Antioch faculty's directive that the Antioch-Putney program be maximally individualized, we encouraged students repeatedly to engage in dialogue with the faculty, whether on field trips to Vermont schools, on a visit to Harlem, or in the back dooryard. In January we watched President Johnson give his State of the Union address, then sat up half the night discussing it. We worked in small groups of two and three to discuss Huxley's *Brave New World*, to weigh the Supreme Court's recent approach to civil liberties cases, to discuss an article on "The Negro and Humanism." And even as Berkeley students clamored that winter of 1964-65 for more contact with their professors, we engaged in continuing discussion about both academic and administrative matters. Students contributed significantly to program planning, purchasing library books, and recruiting.

Eight members of the pilot group did student teaching in southeastern Vermont. Of the four holding teaching certificates, two (Peace Corps returnees) chose to take internships with the Experiment in International Living and the Job Corps during the student teaching quarter.

The final stretch, back on the Putney campus, was equally full. After a two-week trip to southern Appalachia, the students settled down to complete major projects on topics ranging from automation to Turkish education. They also did intensive reading and writing in the philosophy of education and the economics of emerging nations. All work that summer was of the order of independent study. In their degree-terminating oral interviews (examinations), they faced a member of the Putney faculty, one from Yellow Springs, the superintendent of the Brattleboro Public Schools, and a historian from Ohio's Central State University.

The reentry of these students into the educational world was as diverse as their backgrounds and interests: Four took teaching posts in the public schools of Indiana, Michigan, Washington, D.C., and New Jersey. One entered a private school in Vermont. Another joined the Tanzania Peace Corps. The Peace Corps Volunteer from Turkey returned to Istanbul to teach at Robert College. The Job Corps intern went back to the Job Corps. One graduate began work on a Ph.D. at the University of Wisconsin. The tenth of that first group of students joined an educational foundation.

THE SECOND YEAR

During our first year, we planned to increase the number of program tracks from one to three. We did this by negotiating with the District of Columbia Public Schools to place our students in their classrooms as interns.

The arrangement: twelve students worked during the 1965-66 academic year in four core city schools, teaching a three-quarter load. In short, they filled nine full-time teaching slots, had full responsibility for conducting their classes, were paid three-fourths of a beginning teacher's salary, and lived as close to school as feasible.

During the year, they worked closely with Professor Francis Silvernail on teaching methods, educational philosophy, and urban school-community problems. Professor Silvernail also arranged with public and private agencies in the city of Washington for visits, seminars, and other types of field trips. For instance, they met with the commissioner of education and school officials as well as officials of the Office of Economic Opportunity, National Education Association, and American Federation of Labor. All told, they held sixty-five seminar meetings during the year.

Then, of course, we encouraged the interns to use the District as a laboratory in following their own educational interests. There was little need to conduct field trips to study poverty and civil rights problems, since their schools were immersed in such problems. Several interns studied the Washington home rule battle at close range. Others attended community meetings on poverty problems and visited student homes. One used his affiliation with Americans for Democratic Action to sensitize some of Washington's opinion makers about the conditions of the Washington Public Schools.

Most of the interns kept logs. One log—detailing a daily encounter with reluctant learners, unmotivated colleagues, and a murder in his apartment building—etched the raw educational crisis more vividly than Bel Kaufman's *Up the Down Staircase.* Upon two occasions our students invited their students to seminars to discuss educational problems, resulting in surprising learning experiences for both groups.

The intern track, superb as it may be educationally and financially, did upset the neat organizational symmetry of the original Antioch-Putney model. Originally we intended to enroll two groups, missing one another geographically as do the undergraduates, in a Yellow Springs-Putney-Student Teaching-Putney sequence. But now we have both a regular track, which the pilot group followed, and an urban intern track. Also, Washington school officials insist that an intern acquire some teaching experience before entering a classroom; hence, if entering students have not done student teaching or taught in the Peace Corps, they enter a special program at Yellow Springs the summer before interning. The schedule is further complicated when Peace Corps returnees are unable to join us until late August. The neat schedule has been replaced by the following:

Term	June Interns	August Interns
June-August	Beginning at Yellow Springs	. . . .
August-June	Interning in Washington Public Schools	or Baltimore
June-August	Finishing at Putney	At Putney
September-December	. . . .	Finishing at Yellow Springs

The summer program at Yellow Springs is designed to prepare students for the urban internships through student teaching experience, observation of video tapes of teachers in urban classrooms, and consideration of ghetto problems. Otherwise, the programs at both Yellow Springs and Putney follow the essential patterns of the pilot group.

FURTHER CONCERNS

During 1966-67, we have twenty-two interns in Washington, five in Baltimore. Also, we are responsible for directing the academic work of twenty members of the National Teacher Corps in an in-service training program in Washington. Fortunately, we obtained from the

U.S. Office of Education eight Prospective Teacher Fellowships for the urban interns, enabling us to reduce the teaching load of all interns from three-quarters to about one-half.

Although our interns still spend most of their daylight hours in their particular schools, the lighter load enables them to work on objectives that beginning teachers with six classes cannot do, namely, plan better, study their students' respective motivations, assist particular students, observe colleagues who use different teaching methods, and attend seminars in educational methods, philosophy of education, and urban life in America.

We hope that both interns and those in the regular track will find more time, too, for individual projects and reflection. The Putney quarter affords an opportunity for reflection in a "retreat" setting; it also provides further opportunity for reading and discussion in social science areas in which students know, especially after the teaching practicum, that they are weak.

Meanwhile, in the fall of 1966 twenty students at Putney continued to experiment with a new process of curriculum construction. The first group to begin at Putney, its members are experiencing their quarters in the sequence of Putney-Student Teaching-Putney-Yellow Springs. More important than the sequence is that this group ran its own community life and planned almost all of its "courses."

During the first week, a four-man planning committee took an inventory of interests and needs. Toward the end of the week the committee held seven-minute sessions in each of ten areas where students expressed an interest, each session being directed to those indicating an intention of working in a given area as well as to faculty and peers. The result: eight groups, of from two to ten, met weekly all fall. Students were primarily responsible for the presentations at each seminar, with outside speakers occasionally enlisted to share their knowledge and experience. A faculty member served as a resource person at each seminar.

The planning committee also assisted in choosing speakers, planning field trips and film showings, and so on. Since membership on Putney committees rotated, each student shared in responsibility for planning.

It is safe to say, following the original directive, that we are maximizing individual learning experiences. In fact, the student must discover ways in which he can use the Antioch-Putney faculty.

It is the faculty's task at all our centers to guarantee that there will .
not be one program for all students but as many programs as there
are students.

TOWARD EVALUATION

As we have increased the number of students from ten to thirty-two
to forty-eight (1966-67), the full-time faculty has increased from
three to five, with a growing number of supplemental faculty from
the main campus and the Washington community. From the outset
we have used consultants in different fields. At no time have there
been more than twenty-five students based at any one place.

We maintain our original objectives: We expect our students to
understand and gain competence in employing the methods of the
several social sciences; we expect them to develop teaching ability
through experience; and we expect them to appreciate problems of
poverty and interrelationships between poverty and civil rights issues
(both domestic and international), not only from reading, but also
from discussion and field trips. We hope that our graduates will em-
pathize with other peoples and cultures, and develop a sense of international citizenship and its implications.

Among our ambitious list of objectives is also the anticipation
that our students will develop their self-concepts, since we believe a
teacher ought to now who *he* is if he intends to help his students
identify who *they* are. Furthermore, we believe that an educator
ought to develop the courage to act upon his insights.

Thus far, we have chosen a variety of methods for evaluating the
realization of these objectives. Since we have no grades and no formal examinations in the traditional sense, other "instruments" of
evaluation are necessary. In addition to lengthy conferences held at
the program's outset and periodically during the student's tenure
(often with the aid of tape recorder and portable TV), day-to-day
dialogue between faculty and students serves as one cornerstone in
the evaluative foundation.

Then, too, as intimated above, the student is encouraged to
keep a log of his experiences—not a mere "Dear Diary," but a "global" journal for recording impressions; criticism of books, movies,
and lectures; or the writing of a poem after a silent walk in the woods
(an exercise facetiously called Silence 501). The log becomes part of
the Accumulative File, a private record for student and faculty use

only, a file in which he deposits more formal written papers (book reviews, research projects) for "final" evaluation.

During the closing quarter of his tenure, a student submits a major project (we have studiously avoided the term "thesis") on a topic of his own choosing, preferably one on which he has worked, with faculty guidance, all year. Topics have ranged from "The Alliance for Progress" and "The Kashmir Problem" to a study of the power structure in a tiny Vermont town. One woman compiled a *Handbook for Using Folk Songs* for American history teachers trying to reach the disadvantaged through music.

The major project serves not only as a creative instrument, to help the student weigh his own analytic and synthesizing powers, but also as a springboard for discussion during the terminating "oral interview" (conducted by at least one member of the Antioch-Putney faculty, one from the main campus, and one "outsider").

During his teaching experience, the student is visited by a faculty member who, with the aid of notes or video equipment or both, discusses ways of improving teaching and learning processes.

In three years students from one overseas nation (Kenya), sixty-eight colleges and universities, and more than thirty states have participated in the program. The special features of the program all tend to encourage creativity in those who dare to be free.

The program has been short on diagnostic evaluative devices and long on learning *processes.* Although it was originally thought that Graduate Record Examinations might be used as reference points for both student and institutional evaluation, this has not yet been feasible. We have, however, used the Minnesota Teacher Attitude Inventory at all locations and will expand use of such instruments from time to time. An all-day written evaluation was used with the first two classes.

In any event, evolution has certainly resulted from continuing discussion of the program, periodic innovations in it, and constant self-evaluation, by students and faculty alike.

RETROSPECT, PROSPECTS, AND DREAMS

Whether our students have come from "name" schools such as Dartmouth, Harvard, or Berkeley, state universities such as Ohio State or Wisconsin, or denominational colleges such as Maryville or St. Francis, we have encouraged them to carve out their problems and questions, then seek means by which to attack them. We have also expected them to gain competency in social science disciplines as well as understanding of interdisciplinary attitudes and methods. We have encouraged the student to overextend himself, to reach into fields he may not have dared to explore as an undergraduate because of unfortunate high school experiences or fears of poor college grades.

When students have held a teaching certificate or been willing to study an extra quarter, we have given "credit" for quarters spent studying with an Experiment in International Living group in India, at the Great Lakes Colleges Association center in Bogota, Colombia, and at St. Dunstan's University on Prince Edward Island.

Twenty-six Peace Corps returnees, representing service in seventeen countries, have participated in the program, and they have been liberally "quizzed" at all of our locations. It is significant that more than half of our 1966-67 students have lived overseas, where they have experienced the culture of another country at substantial intensity.

The program is not yet fully developed. Recruiting, except among Peace Corps Volunteers, has been arduous, as might be expected for a new program. Shoestring financing and the necessity of upgrading the Vermont plant have created their share of faculty and administrative gray hairs. Expansion from a one-track to a three-track system has required unforeseen administrative flexibility and pioneering. Inadequate scholarship funds and uncertainty in funding from the National Defense Education Act have made competition with more established M.A.T. programs somewhat of a nightmare, and the financing of some students' programs has required more ingenuity than that of recent spacewalks. With the stress on openness and new learning theory, all faculty members have had to learn new tricks.

Our dreams include the inaugural of better evaluative devices and processes, the extension of the program overseas for a quarter or two (or three), improvement of the internship to make more impact upon urban problems, and development of unique curriculum materials for the most difficult urban and poverty terrains in America. We hope that Antioch-Putney graduates will be ready for the "new social studies" that are just making their way into education.

In an era of fantastic change, we hope that our graduates, accustomed to living in several locations, fresh from the adventure of self-discovery and the discovery of self, and familiar with the processes of linking theory and action, will be capable of giving birth to freedom in their classrooms. Never has there been such need for more relevant effort.

Appendix B: Table of Organization — UGS

Board of Union for Experimenting Colleges & Universities

Executive Council

President

Coordinator

UGS NATIONAL
POLICY BOARD

Rotating Core Faculty Member
Chairman IPS-UGS Committee
UECU President ex officio
Administrative Coordinator*
Coordinator*
    8 Student Members
    5 Board Members or
    Designates
    2 Empty Chairs, open to any
    UGS person desiring expres-
    sion (nonvoting)

Attends Union Board Meetings
Member Affiliate Coordinating
    Committees
Member Student Committee as
    Core Faculty
Member Core Faculty Meetings
Member *Ad Hoc* Administrative
    Committees (Admissions,
    Finances, etc.)
Member NPB
Member NPB Task Force Groups

*Column 2 reflects the coordinators' functional relationship to other
UGS groups.

Appendix C: Summary of Strengths and Concerns

Strengths

1. The UECU Board, and the UGS National Policy Board and administration, are all competent and committed. The NPB functions particularly well as the UGS policy-making body.
2. The adjunct faculty list is impressive. The core faculty are committed.
3. The students are a mature, responsible, self-directed, highly motivated group with diverse interests and backgrounds.
4. Students, faculty, administration, and staff all participate fully and responsibly in decision making.
5. Admissions procedures are thoughtful and intense.
6. The colloquia are exciting experiences in which students and faculty engage one another in a variety of ways. Students learn from one another, and plan many colloquium activities. Intensive, meaningful cross-disciplinary interactions are regular occurrences.
7. Thoughtful, regular, and meaningful communications are maintained with students throughout the educational process.
8. Certification sessions are potentially a source of excellent interchange, feedback, and guidance.
9. The terminar is a unique and useful part of the educational program, providing a springboard for future learning.
10. The program and process are flexible, humanistic, and personalized. While UGS is receptive to unusual Ph.D. studies,

---

Source: North Central Accreditation Report - January, 1974

it maintains high standards, and the intellectual caliber of the educational activities is impressive.

CONCERNS

1. There is need to reexamine the role definition of Coordinator and Administrative Coordinator, and to upgrade the latter position. Administrative roles are confused.
2. The UECU President does not devote enough attention to UGS.
3. There is a lack of long-range planning.
4. More and better qualified core faculty are needed. Selection criteria and processes for new faculty are unclear, and there is insufficient attention to new faculty orientation. Many new faculty do not have sufficient experience at the doctoral level.
5. More should be learned from the successes and failures of the colloquia in planning future colloquia.
6. Too little attention is given to ensuring that the internship provides students with more than "business as usual."
7. Faculty needs to improve procedures for counseling out students who are not benefiting from the program.
8. UGS is weak in evaluation.
9. Decision-making procedures and implementation need improvement.

Appendix D: Union Graduate School Questionnaire

**Part I Changes in Life
Situation: (Circle One)**

December, 1974

1. How has the UGS experience affected your life in general?

not at all	somewhat	considerably	very considerably
.02%	18%	51%	29%

2. Was the experience:

blah	average	favorable	very favorable
.03%	.03%	39%	55%

3. For you, what was the most significant aspect of graduating from UGS?
   (some marked more than one)

Psychological	Personal Growth	Economic Gain	Prestige
25%	76%	.06%	13%

4. Why did you choose UGS?
   (some marked more than one)

a. dislike traditional programs	=	23.00%
b. residence requirements	=	0.08
c. innovative program	=	31.00
d. felt self-directed	=	0.40
e. all of the above	=	39.00
f. none of the above	=	0.30

SOURCE: Compiled by Betty Jo Pool, Administrator Coordinator of UGS; data based on a 72% response from 162 graduates, December, 1974. By permission, Betty Jo Pool.

5. How do you generally characterize your occupation?
(some marked more than one)

education (teaching)	=	42.00%
administration	=	0.30
business	=	0.50
professional services	=	43.00
other	=	11.00

6. Have you been able to make a *desired* change in occupation since graduating from UGS?

yes = 42%   no = 17%   did not want to = 41%

7. Have you received a promotion since graduating from UGS?

yes = 37%   no = 22%   not applicable = 41%

PART II: Perceptions of UGS and its Processes

	Agree	Disagree	No Response
1. Self-directed study is in fact a workable concept.	99.9%	– %	0.1%
2. Self-directed study works, but only for certain persons.	86.0	7.0	7.0
3. In general, the UGS process is very effective.	83.0	8.0	9.0
4. Three hundred students is the optimal size for a self-directed program such as UGS.	42.0	25.0	33.0
5. UGS should be regionalized.	39.0	42.0	19.0
6. Affirmative Action, as a general concept, is very workable.	57.0	24.0	19.0
7. The UGS Affirmative Action Plan has been working very well.	16.0	27.0	57.0
8. As a mechanism for student input the present governance structure, National Policy Board, etc. is working well.	27.0	37.0	36.0

9. The UGS faculty is, in general, well qualified. 77.0 15.0 8.0
10. The Adjunct Professor Model works well. 81.0 10.0 9.0
11. Adjunct Professors should be paid directly—a set fee—by the Graduate School. 52.0 40.0 8.0
12. Adjunct Professor fees should be negotiated by the student. 49.0 45.0 6.0
13. UGS graduates are discriminated against in the job market compared to graduates of "traditional" programs. 19.0 47.0 34.0
14. Nontraditional education is the "wave of the future." 51.0 31.0 18.0
15. As/if UGS expands—growth should be in the direction of new, specialized programs. 39.0 34.0 27.0
16. Ten years from now the Union Graduate School will be one of the strongest Graduate Schools in the country. 44.0 31.0 25.0

PART III: Statistical Updating*

We can make the following statements about the UGS program based upon students' and graduates' responses.

Question	Percent
1. Most UGS students attended a traditional undergraduate college.	76
2. Morale was higher as a UGS student than as an undergraduate.	76
3. UGS educational processes are communicated very well.	72
4. The UGS process is very effective.	91

---

*In 1976, as part of the self-study analysis for full accreditation, more than 850 UGS students were polled with a complex questionnaire; 587 replies reflected the above generalizations in the percentages indicated. Used with permission.

5. Self-directed study works.   99

6. Students experienced the UGS program design as being flexi-
    ble.   95

7. The UGS faculty is well qualified.   81

8. Core faculty are available as needed.   90

9. The adjunct professor model works well.   87

10. UGS succeeds in being interdisciplinary.   78

11. UGS does well what it claims to do.   99

12. UGS efforts to combine theory and practice succeed.   94

13. Most students would enroll in UGS again if they had it to do
    over again.   97

14. Most students would recommend with confidence or en
    thusiasm a respected associate to UGS.   95

15. Students and graduates overall attitude toward UGS at the
    moment is good or very good.   95

16. Most UGS students and graduates regard UGS academic
    standards as being at least above average.   76

Appendix E: The Project Demonstrating Excellence*

What a PDE is and is not: Our brochure states that the PDE

> is not limited to what traditionally termed "dissertation" conjures up. It may be a book, a unified collection of articles or essays, a research undertaking, a project of significant social change, a body of poetry, paintings, musical compositions, dances, films or other art forms.

Most importantly there must be a *product*. As much as we encourage human growth, that growth alone, no matter how measured, is not enough to constitute a PDE. The product must be a publicly verifiable piece of work even though the immediate "public" constitutes only a student's committee. In addition, the project must relate intrinsically to the other major components of a student's program, i.e., the Learning Strategy or Study Program and the Internship. Normally, it constitutes the culmination of one's program, logically, chronologically and organically.

In practice the limits of acceptability with respect to both subject matter and mode of expression are very wide. The actual process of determining what is and what is not acceptable rests with the individual student's committee. The Core Faculty, as the link between UGS and the committee, is in a strategic position; what he/she communicates to the committee as to the limits of acceptability, biases, and committee processes can be crucial. Not only must he/she properly convey the School's intentions with respect to the Project, but it is frequently necessary to demonstrate to the other four mem-

SOURCE: This statement was authored by Goodwin Watson, Elizabeth Sewell, Norris Clement, and Roy Fairfield.

bers of the committee that *their* biases are real and may be conditioned by their own (possibly traditional) notions of what a Ph.D. is and is not.

TOWARDS STANDARDS OF EXCELLENCE

It is obvious, of course, that for every mode of expression (whether book, social change project, poem, dance, etc.) there are many criteria for determining excellence. One person's insight may be another's blindness. What's "in" today is often "out" tomorrow. But this does not necessarily mean that there are no standards, that anything goes at any time. The absence of standards can be equally as destructive as too rigid ones. Therefore, two plus two *is* four—unless the basic rules are changed. Some kind of logic is just as important as relevance to the human condition. On the other end of the continuum, however, if we are to keep the limits wide and the processes of evaluation open, we must avoid such narrow prescriptions as the application of classical and/or neoclassical absolutes, whether we are working in an art field or sociology.

Keeping in mind then that while there are no absolute standards, the following guidelines may prove helpful.

A. *For Scientific Research Reports*

Standards for Research Reports should be essentially similar to those for scientific research investigation in other Ph.D. programs. The usual concerns for hypotheses worth testing; reliability and validity of measures; for adequate controls; for appropriate statistical tests; and for good suggestions for subsequent research are applicable.

B. *For Philosophic and Theoretical Contributions*

The writer must demonstrate familiarity with what his/her predecessors have written in his/her and other closely related fields, but must go clearly beyond previous publications. He/she must present a concept or system of concepts which he/she believes to be demonstrably superior (simpler? more applicable and productive?) to what others have written.

C. *Biographies, Case Studies and other Historical Inquiries*

Standards of excellence in this field are similar to those in other graduate schools. Better studies build upon all that has previously been written, but also enter new territory.

They may do so, for example, by taking subjects who (or which) have been important but relatively neglected. New territory may also refer to a fresh viewpoint, exploring relationships not well developed in earlier studies. Source materials must be properly documented and critically appraised. Primary sources should be used when available. Individuals and events must be interpreted in context, with awareness of the multiplicity of factors (biological, economic, social, psychological, etc.) which have been influential. A self-examination does not constitute a satisfactory project of this type. A superior project has implications for understanding not only the past but also the present and the emerging future.

D. *Reports of Creative Action Projects*

Excellence in creative action projects is evidenced by competent diagnosis of a social situation requiring action; by ingenious invention of procedures for meeting the need; by measures of effectiveness in actually changing the situation; and by critical thinking in evaluating what was done so that others can learn from the writer's experiences, both his/her successes and failures. It is seldom, if ever, satisfactory simply to recommend new social structures or actions of intervention. These must be tried out in actual operation, at least so far as completed pilot project. A handbook on social action or organizational development should have been tested in appropriate field situations.

E. *Artistic/Creative Projects: Fiction, Drama, Poetry, Films, Music*

1. The subject matter must not be trivial, must demonstrate seriousness of purpose (which is perfectly compatible with humor and perhaps inseparable from it), and a sense of depth.

2. It must explore something new, not "a rage for novelty" as Samuel Taylor Coleridge calls it, nor striving after originality at any cost, nor a passion to be avant-garde, but something in the work should surprise one with a shock of discovery and insight.

3. It should bear clearly the overall stamp of whoever made it. The reader should not feel, "I could have

done this." Also not too reminiscent of any other artist, past or present, however great or fashionable.

4. Craftsmanship should be perceptible in the style and in the organization. Structures and rhythms at the small level (sentences and stanzas for instance) should strike the reader as having been attended to and shaped by the writer even if only half-consciously. Structures and rhythm in the overall work should be apparent also in the sense of continuity and completeness; the magic of sudden reminiscence where an earlier detail, unexplained then, fits later in the story, or the lovely way in which a poem may circle back on itself, the end repeating the beginning, leaving the mind and body with a sense of profound satisfaction.

5. If particular forms or traditional structures are used, e.g. a sonnet, a symphony, they should be able to stand up, as far as is reasonable, to comparison with the work of other artists who are accounted good.

6. The work should have a public as well as a private dimension. It must not be so individual as to be comprehensible only to the writer or a coterie of like minds. It should be capable of addressing itself to, also, as is often necessary, educating a public.

F. *Other Projects*

Many, perhaps most UGS students' projects, will not fit neatly into the above categories. In such cases multiple guidelines must be consulted and/or new guidelines constructed. In cases where many media are used to report projects from categories A through D above, e.g., video reporting of a social action project, it may be necessary to complement the video tapes with written reports in order to present data not appropriately reported on video. What is crucial here is that the necessary information is communicated; however, there is no need to restrict oneself to one particular medium. One should choose that medium most appropriate to the information to be conveyed and use that medium as effectively as possible.

Appendix F: Some Representative Projects Demonstrating Excellence*

Walter Abilla	A Guide for Public Health Service in Tropical Africa
Joseph Abramajtys	Interdependent Lives: A Model for Prison Education
Joseph Arbuckle	A Portrait of a Change Agent Learning His Craft
David Oyugi Aseto	Heterodox Political Economics of Nation-Building in Africa with Special Reference to Kenya
Stevanne Auerbach-Fink	A Report on Child Care Consumers in San Francisco: A Study of Parental Expectations for Child Care Services from Cross-Cultural Perspective
James T. Brown	The Systems Approach to Resource Management in Higher Education
Joanne Chickering	The Story of Six Women's Struggle to Be: Six Years in the Lives of Six Women Who Re-entered School and Work After Motherhood

---

*As we point out so frequently to "external" observers of the UGS process, projects do not necessarily stand alone; they must be seen in the *total context* of a student's program. Titles were chosen that best described both project and program.

Norman Don — Cortical Activity Changes during a Psychotherapeutic Procedure: A Model for Changes of States of Awareness

Mary Elmendorf — The Mayan Woman and Change

Lonnetta M. Gaines — Building a Pan-African Pre-School

Alan Gartner — The Professional Preparation of Doctors, Lawyers, Social Workers and Teachers: A Cross-Sectoral Study of Efforts to Integrate Theory and Practice

Mark Gelber — University without Walls at Skidmore College: The New Education in Process

Richard Graham — Self-Determined Education

Spencer Grin — World Education . . . An Emerging Concept

Richard Hailer — Toward a Cultural Democracy

Charles Hitchcock — Psychiatric Attitudes toward Homosexuality

Gustav Jackson — The Conceptual Foundations of the Geo-Physical Sciences

Richard Johnson — A Project for Joint Action: A Case History of a Community-Initiated Training Program to Evaluate and Improve Local Public Schools

Leander Jones — Which Way Out? Communications in Prison

John Konikoff — Biological and Medical Implications of Weak Electrical Fields

H. Stephen Larsen — Myth and Consciousness

Peter Lazes — People get HEP—Health Education Project

Virginia Lester — The Relationship of College Goals to College Functioning: A Comparative Study of Six Institutions on a Continuum

Richard Leuba	The Application of an Educational Philosophy to Some Elements of Engineering Education
James Lewis	Developing an Effective Performance Appraisal Program for Educators through the Participatory Decision-Making Process
Joyce Livak	A Student's Process Guide to Contemporary Nutrition Using the Humanistic Approach to Humanizing Nutrition . . . with Teacher's Supplement
Ruth Lovald	The Legal Rights of Children in Vermont
Joseph Lucero	English for Survival: Guidelines for Establishing English as a Second Language Program
Minerva Marquis	Production of Aeschylus' *Oresteia*
Donald Mathews	Humanistic Marketing
Jane Hamilton Merritt	*Beyond the Bittersweet; Lahu Wildfire; Boonmee & the Lucky White Elephant* (a journal and two novels about Southeast Asia)
Arnold Mindell	Synchronicity: An Investigation of the Unitary Background Patterning Synchronous Phenomena
Kermit Nash	Black Success in Predominantly White Institutions
Dolores Pacileo	Botanical Art
Robert Paige	Career Education: Awareness, K thru 3
Antonja Pantoja	A Plan for the Development of a University That Could Help Puerto Ricans Acquire a Liberating Education: Universidad Boricua

Marilyn Persons	An In-depth Analysis of the Development and Evaluation of a Peer Counseling Training Program
George Pruitt	Blueprint for Leadership: The American College Presidency
Margery Robinson	Lessons Man Can Learn from Animals
Francine Shaw	New Ways to Teach Creative Writing and Literature
Fred Shulman	Reflections of Society . . . Ocean-Hill Brownsville Revisited
Eleanor Smith	History of the Black Man in Narrative & Song (concert & script)
Joe Smith	Colleges in an Urban Environment: A Study of the Relationships Between Higher Education and the City
Lorraine Smithberg	Studying the Child as a Person: Teaching as an Interaction Process
Don Swanson	Castles in the Sands: Perspectives on Latin American Development
Sigmund Van Raan	The Street School, Bronx, N.Y.—A Three-Dimensional Approach of Remedial Education, Therapy, and Family Involvement
Glory Van Scott	Education of the Multi-Gifted Child (Education-Theater Arts)
Sol Ward	The Ecological Determinant in Land Use Planning
Gaye Williams	On Reparenting
John Wood	The Joy of Being Fired
June Wyatt	Cultural and Educational Development in a British Columbia Indian Community

James Zarnowiecki   The School District Ombudsman: A
                                     Resource Book of Organiza-
                                     tion and Source Material for
                                     Boards of Education

Appendix G

WHERE IS ANTIOCH?

Where is Antioch ... Antioch-Putney? ... Antioch-Columbia?

In Yellow Springs? at Putney? "over there" in Phillie? or out in San Francisco? or "down there" in D.C.? or in Maryland? Where?

Or maybe, When is Antioch ... Antioch-Putney? ... Antioch-Columbia? How? Why?

Can there be either-ors if we would destroy that last parochialism of easily visible place clearly spaced in time? or space time? or what Whitehead once called the fallacy of simple location? Also, how retain that 360-degree angle of vision, on every plane of space-time-psyche if abstracted from the processes of Antioch? Antioch-Putney? or Antioch-Columbia?

Antioch

Is:

- students in a seminar in Putney, Yellow Springs, Columbia (Md.), Philadelphia, D.C., or in Bogota, Tubingen, London, or Guanajuato
- students on a co-op job in Brattleboro, Berkeley, or Boynton Beach
- a faculty member reading a log or a term paper or a prospectus for independent study in a 707 over the Rockies or Omaha... in a hotel lobby in Chicago ... or waiting for a train in Grand Central, in an office in Putney or Dakar ... or going to a dentist in Columbus, an optometrist in Boston, or an internist in L.A.
- a student and a teacher sitting under the big birch in Vermont, on a park bench beside the White House, visiting a school in Harlem, talking by a winter's fire in the Glen

- or a student-teacher, in Yellow Springs, Bennington, or Germantown
- two students sharing a room and the agonies of self-discovery during an internship, or ten students recounting experiences to a teacher in a cellar bar in the District (zip code 20009), or others sharing openness in a professor's study or living room or backdoor yard, talking, talking, talking
- or a student . . . or a teacher . . . or the president, talking-walking, walking-talking, reflecting on the pregnancy of silence
- and even teacher-student-friends and friend-teacher-students, arguing vehemently over the tactics and strategy of decision-making, in marathon sessions which make the eyelids heavy and the arteries dilate . . . arguing the gaps between self-expectations and realization, dream formulations, the eternal chasms between ideal and achievement, hypothesis and conclusion, the chasms within the ravines and gaps within the crises of confidence and communication
- carving out projects, proposals, and plans for working in a thousand settings, from Tucson to Franconia Notch to Lagos, from Lagos to Calcutta, the Marianas, or Appalachian and Hawaiian Beachheads . . . projects as extensions of flesh and blood and nerves and the heady speculations of Marshall McLuhan, or what seems like the inevitable marriage of TV and the computer: computervision
- or talking with alumni in Chicago or Miami or New York, or visiting them in Cameroon, Senegal, or Bangkok

Where is Antioch? When is it? How is it? It is when, it is where, and it is how you look at the it . . . the identity of heart-mind-nerve in a process whose implications run through the fingertips, in lightning-flash hot-lines between Putney and Stockholm, Cleveland and Guanajuato, in thunder confrontations with Mississippi sheriffs, Cincinnati judges, and Washington jailers.

Just as New York is not America, neither is Yellow Springs Antioch. Our cosmic village encourages the perceptions and feelings of paradox, irony, and tragedy; challenges the parody and pathos of those parochialisms which paralyze men's humanness. Comedy, yes! tears, yes . . . if perspectified . . . And for any particle in the amalgam to call atom "Adam" is to risk the fallacy of simple location in space-time-psyche and hence breed self-defeating and even self-deceiving prophesies! The whole system lights up during each brainstorm.

Where is Antioch? Antioch-Putney? Antioch-Columbia? Maybe where anybody is asking, "Where, when, who, how, and even ought there be an Antioch?" (1968, 1970)

What Is Antioch?

Antioch College is a fortuitous concatenation of cacophanies, as though Beethoven's *Ninth Symphony* and Prokofiev's *Love for Three Oranges* were being played simultaneously in a room filled with Van Gogh, Dali, and Klee. Antioch College is the surging power of human creativity unleashed on the worldscape as though unleashing were birth and renewal. Antioch is *process and people over* program and plant. Antioch is what its constituents wish to make it because Antioch is people rather than place. Antioch is an experiential laboratory on the frontier of evolving potentiality.

Ours is a commitment which grows out of the conviction that *humans can become,* that societies can become, that energies spent tutoring a ghetto child or picketing a General Motors factory *can make a difference* in shaping a livable future. We know, too, that past is prologue; and, if we look back, we look back to the future. We live in the knowledge that the only security is in the realization that there is none . . . at least in the static sense, that security is a function of adaptation, that stable institutions are dynamic and able to grow. And we know that process is reality. Hence, whether we are engaged in advocating a strategy for learning or a social strategy for ending the Vietnam War . . . whether we are talking about a new Antioch Constitution or even talking about talking about it, we know we must involve persons and roles of all kinds in that process. This means that ours must be a pluralism, with both its joys and horrors, and that the very notion of "our" is both message and massage. For we see the individual's rights, hopes, imagination as both process and community. This includes all roles in the institutional processes: faculty, students, administration, alumni, friends, for Antioch is a *network of connectors,* knowledges, feelings, tied together with telephone wires, computer codes, mailings, the silent languages of tolerance and gesture as well as the common languages of the disciplines, the commitment to advocating social change, the education (drawing out) of persons of both low and high income groups, the development of alternative learning strategies which address themselves to objectives as diverse as building a bridge or removing an appendix to conceiving of "organic populism" or writing a poem.

Ours is a caring for those who care about knowledge, feeling, and the freeing of human imagination from any bondage. Ours is the daring to dare, Ours is the valuing of deriving values. Ours is a diversity of people, ideas, organizational structures, individual and community needs, human thrusts. Ours is a program of processes stressing self-direction, processes which verify themselves when persons involved, whether freshmen in a First Year Plan or graduate students interning in an urban ghetto, evolve criteria for evaluating those processes, evolve them not in a vacuum but in the stream of work-study experiences, evolve them not for their own or an esthetic's sake but for their human worth ... even if that worth applies to a quorum of one. Ours is an educational process where action research is more probable than none or the traditional. Ours is a "city on a hill," too, for no process from budgeting to person-employing is a closed process; no committee is a closed committee. And in that openness we believe there is health. And in that health we believe there is a model worthy of emulation.

In short, we have faith in mobility, adaptability, diversity, pluralism, model construction and model testing, human role as continually evolving process. We believe in the continuous reconstruction of institution and personality. At Antioch students become teachers and teachers remain as students, and it is our hope that any party in the learning process develops a keen sense of perceiving self in the role he is living rather than playing a role of which he is unaware. There is sharp focus on seeing, feeling, hearing, touching and tasting, *as well as* knowing, in an infinite number of dimensions.

Ours is the monsoon curriculum rather than the ticky-tack; it has power and pattern but enough unpredictability and beauty in the hands and minds of student-faculty-administrator to be both boon and bane for person and landscape. We are both threat and threatened by "silent majorities," for nobody loves a monsoon ... unless he lives at the groundings of his existence and sees both a grain of rice and a haiku in the blade of grass nourished by the rain.

Green copper towers
rise over winter landscapes:
Antioch College. (1970)